EX LIBRIS

Cecile Weaver

Raising
Children in
a Difficult
Time

Dr. BENJAMIN SPOCK

Raising Children in a Difficult Time

A Philosophy of Parental

Leadership and High Ideals

W·W·Norton & Company, Inc., New York

First Edition

Published simultaneously in Canada by George J. McLeod Limited, Toronto

Library of Congress Cataloging in Publication Data

Spock, Benjamin McLane, 1903–
    Raising children in a difficult time.

    1. Children—Management. 2. Parent and child.
I. Title.
HQ769.S683 1974   649'.1   73-21848
    ISBN 0-393-01106-2

This book was designed by Andrea Clark.
Typefaces used are Gael and Americana Bold.
Manufacturing was done by Haddon Craftsmen.

Printed in the United States of America

1 2 3 4 5 6 7 8 9 0

I dedicate the book to these children
and to you parents who do the hard work and
suffer the frustrations and anxieties,
without audible thanks.

Contents

III   Teaching Beliefs and Ideals

IV   Control of Children

V   Children Who Could Benefit from Psychotherapy

XI The Changing Family

Preface

The Need for Firm Parental Leadership,
and Cooperative Children: The
Statement of an Antipermissive Author

I've always believed and written: that parents should stick by
their ethical convictions, and feel no hesitation in showing
them to their children; that they should ask their children for
cooperation and respect; that children who are held up to
high ideals and considerate behavior are not only a lot pleas-
anter to live with, but they are happier themselves. To put
it frankly, I'm as much irritated as anyone by children who
are chronically rude, unhelpful, and always demanding more
for themselves. How did I ever get the reputation among
some people of being an advocate of excessive permissiveness? That accusation was not made during the first twenty-
two years after *Baby and Child Care* was published. It came
first from public figures—Spiro Agnew was the most vocal—
who supported the Vietnam War which I opposed and who
wanted to believe that my theories of child care were somehow responsible for the opposition of so many young people.
The accusation was accepted mainly by people who had
never read *Baby and Child Care*. A typical letter to me read,

"Thank God I never used your horrible book! That's why my children have turned out well." My critics didn't stop to think that most of the young people who grew up quite conservatively and never protested against anything were also raised with the help of my book.

In the first edition of *Baby and Child Care*, published in 1946, I did oppose the extreme rigidity in infant feeding that prevailed then: Babies were to be fed only on the dot of every four hours, no matter how miserably they cried. I was for working gradually toward regularity with a recognition that individual babies vary in their readiness. Even at that time, I warned against the confusion that might come from going abruptly from extreme rigidity to the so-called self-demand infant feeding schedule, which was just beginning to be talked about. Because the swing away from rigidity did come with extreme suddenness and perplexed many parents, I put more emphasis in the second edition (published in 1957) on the need for firm parental leadership in general, and emphasized that children who are raised to be considerate are also happier. Half the monthly magazine articles I have written since 1955, have touched on the same points.

Some people believe that there are only two ways to raise children: with overpermissiveness, which produces brats, or with sternness and punishment, which makes good citizens. Neither of these extremes works well, I'm convinced from knowing thousands of American families and from observing child rearing in other countries, too. Children grow up behaving well and responsibly primarily because they love the parents who have loved them. They want to please their parents (most of the time) and be like them.

But, for this system to work well, the parents must have ideals of one kind or another. They have to know what they expect of their children and communicate this to them clearly.

This can be done without oppressiveness or frequent

scolding. But it does involve a lot of hard parental work—watching, explaining, guiding, reminding, encouraging, disapproving, stopping, and occasionally becoming very serious indeed, with or without punishment. What I've been stating here are my general principles. But what parents most often ask for is discussion of specific situations and problems. That is what this book is about. The difficulties in raising children are greater today than ever before, I feel. Partly this is because customs which used to last for generations, have been changing with unprecedented rapidity—sexual behavior and drug use are prime examples. But, also, many of our most revered values are being challenged. The dream of continual material progress for the nation is being shattered by our sudden awareness of pollution and the depletion of resources. Young people themselves have been questioning our faith in individual advancement through rugged competition, asking whether we might not have a more just society and happier people if we made an ideal of living simply instead of ostentatiously, of living by brotherly love instead of by rivalry. Such questions, which surely have a bearing on child rearing, are discussed in this book.

Some of the topics in this book were first discussed in my column in *Redbook* magazine. These earlier discussions have been revised, brought up to date, and incorporated in new material, to present a rounded statement of how we can raise children capable of making a life and a world better than those we have today.

I'm grateful to Georgia Griggs, Amy Levin, Sheila Poulos, Mary Shuford, Lois Woodyatt for indispensable help.

Raising Children in a Difficult Time

Chapter I

Can Family Life
Be Easier, Happier?

:: 1 ::

The Family Isn't Finished Yet

Wherever I go on speaking trips (most commonly to universities), and in the publications I read, I am made aware of the mounting criticism of marriage and the family in America.

We have one of the highest divorce rates in the world. But perhaps more serious is the amount of tension and hostility in many of the families in which the parents are still living together. Our high levels of delinquency, crime, alcoholism, drug abuse, mental illness, and suicide partly reflect the unsatisfactory state of our family life.

Numerous critics, particularly the young people and the anthropologists and sociologists, put much of the blame on the isolation of today's nuclear family (consisting only of father, mother, and children). In previous generations grandparents, aunts, uncles, and cousins lived nearby and participated in the care of the young. They constituted the so-called extended family, which provided mutual support and love for the various members and diluted the tensions between parents and children.

The solidarity of the extended family has been broken mainly by the unprecedented mobility of today's living, the fact that young couples are ready to go anywhere in the nation—or the world—to follow the careers of their choice. And the same mobility—because of changing job assignments, changing homes, or changing employment—keeps many young couples from growing roots in any neighborhood. This isolation from the community further concentrates dependence—and antagonisms—within the nuclear family.

I think there are other potent generators of family tension. The authority of religion, which used to give people a strong sense of direction and duty, has been progressively weakened. There has been unparalleled prosperity in the thirty years since the end of World War II; and unusual prosperity is, I believe, always somewhat demoralizing to human societies. It substitutes a preoccupation with money and things for a reliance on loving relationships and other spiritual gratifications. More specifically, it accentuates the greedy and rivalrous aspects of human nature.

Critics of the family and of marriage have proposed a variety of alternatives: couples and individuals living together in communes in order to approximate the wider circle of the extended family; easier termination of marriages, with less need to admit failure in doing so; man and woman living together without marriage, on the assumption that marriage often is not a blessing but a prison that in itself makes some persons impatient to be free.

The critics recognize the fact that women in our society are much more dependent on marriage than men because they have less earning power and less independence in other respects. Men are favored for admission to professional schools. Men get the better jobs and are paid more to perform them.

Women start out with occupational handicaps, and when

they become mothers they may fall further behind because they are less able to accumulate job experience and seniority. If they are separated from their husbands, they have the responsibility for the care of any children. So if women are to be as free as men to get out of strained marriages or worn-out affairs, they must gain educational and job equality, and there must be first-rate day-care centers for their children.

When a national magazine *(Look)* devoted an entire issue to the future of the family, and a number of well-known people made predictions, three were particularly challenging to me.

Alvin Toffler, author of the book *Future Shock*, envisioned a much more mobile family based on temporary rather than permanent relationships.

Actress and author Shirley MacLaine gave her opinion that the autocratic family, which produces repressed personalities, is obsolete, and so is the ideal of monogamy. She expressed doubt that a love relationship usually lasts more than two to five years and saw no sensible reason why a marriage should last longer.

Erich Segal, author of the novel *Love Story*, foresaw an ever-lessening differentiation between masculine and feminine—all the emphasis going instead to what is human. As a result, he felt, romance would be replaced by love, "because to me romance implies . . . something of an illusory nature, and with illusion comes the ultimate disillusion—and dissolution—of so many marriages."

I agree that there are sad deficiencies in many American families and marriages, and that new thinking and experimenting are called for. But I don't see the traditional family as so easily dispensed with.

Some of the scorn on the part of young people is motivated as much by the emotions normal to their biological stage of development as by the actual deficiencies of the families they see around them. Most young people would never leave home if they didn't become intensely impatient with the way their parents live—no matter how pleasant or harmonious it really was. Otherwise they would prefer to live with their parents forever, enjoying the economic and emotional security. So they overlook the strengths and gratifications in their parents' relationship and exaggerate in their minds the tensions, antagonisms, absurdities, and banalities.

I can remember so well, in late-night discussions at college, saying that I would rather die than descend to the appallingly humdrum level of my parents' existence; they would sit in silence all evening, reading their newspapers and books. A few years later, after my hard day's work in pediatric practice and Jane's at home and in committee work, we didn't think there was anything dull about relaxing in the evening.

Men and women have always daydreamed of transient sexual affairs with charming, nondemanding partners, affairs followed by no responsibilities and no reproaches. There is no harm in having such fantasies as long as it is realized that they don't jibe with the more compelling need of most mature people for an ongoing, meaningful love relationship, a relationship that actually welcomes responsibilities, a relationship that usually is threatened by infidelities.

How does a human being come by his desire for such a lasting relationship?

Marriage was not invented and imposed on mankind in prehistoric times by some kill-joy tribal priest or other authority. It has always been part of the human pattern (with variations in different societies) because of the biological needs of our species and the way children mature psychologically. Childhood in our species lasts fifteen to twenty years. Parents have to be devoted to each other and to their offspring in order to give their children the security, the training and the material things they will need for all those years.

Children sense deeply how important it is to them to have both a father and a mother, and to have them get along with each other. Any talk of divorce fills them with alarm and protest. If their parents separate, they beg them to get together again. This early awareness later becomes, when the children have grown to be parents, an element in their sense of responsibility for providing domestic security for their children.

Children, especially in the three-to-six-year-old period, mature emotionally and intellectually by overidealizing their parents and by aspiring to grow up to be like them. They glamorize their parents' marriage, exaggerating its virtues and minimizing its defects. The boy at this age particularly admires his father and patterns himself after him. His mother becomes his romantic ideal. At the age of four he'll say with great sincerity that he's going to marry her. The girl tries to become just like her mother and falls in love with her father. Each child yearns secretly to have a baby in partnership with the parent he loves romantically.

Most people by the time they are adults want to marry not primarily because of sexual hunger, for that can be satisfied easily in casual relationships, but because they have been yearning since childhood to carry out the grown-up aspects of marriage that they admired in their parents. (Children imitate these aspects in their manner and words when they play house.)

And the primary reason (among several) that people desire children is that ever since infancy they have wanted to love and cherish babies of their own, the way they were loved and cherished themselves. (Children show this in the delight they take in caring for their dolls.) A majority of people, by the time they come to the last part of their lives, realize that their greatest satisfaction comes from having produced fine children and grandchildren, and their greatest joy comes from visiting them.

So early childhood is looking forward to adulthood, with basic expectations set; and adulthood at its core is living out childhood fantasies. Psychiatric experience shows again and again the truth of this statement, both in the people who have serene lives and the people who have turbulent lives.

When adolescents or youths fall suddenly and violently in love, we believe, it is a recurrence of the same kind of over-idealized romantic love that they felt for their parent (there is often some similarity in personality or appearance between their parent and their beloved). They see their beloved as supremely beautiful, charming, accomplished—almost flawless.

If young people are also capable of a generous, tender love, and if further acquaintance shows that there is a genuine compatibility between them and their loves, then this tender generosity becomes the strongest and most important component of the relationship.

Nevertheless, the element of overidealized romantic infatuation persists to a degree in the most successful marriages. It continues to lend intensity, and excitement and magic to the relationship. Each partner continues to over-value the other, to exaggerate the other's good qualities; this, of course, helps the other to develop them further. Each partner keeps trying to be worthier of the other's love.

I agree with Erich Segal that there is an illusory element in romantic love, but I don't agree that this illusion necessarily leads to disillusion. It all depends on the strength of each person's ideals and the desire of the other to live up to them.

One way to glimpse the effectiveness of idealization and illusion is to look at the opposite—the process of disillusion. When two married people who once thought each other nearly perfect come to a hostile marital breakup, each wants to see the other as all bad. Furthermore, what their friends can usually see is that each is provoking the other—by exaggerated accusations, by taunts, by mean acts—to retaliate with even worse behavior. Then they can rush to their friends to tell the despicable details and prove what a scoundrel the other really is.

Of course, all idealization is not healthy. If an individual is so very unrealistic or so emotionally disturbed that he always idealizes the wrong people, those whose characters bear no relationship to his expectations, he is bound to be disillusioned again and again.

The constructive idealization that I'm speaking about is the one that exceeds by only a moderate amount the level of excellence at which the other person already is functioning and which in turn spurs her or him on to accomplish greater things.

What many of the previously married critics of marriage and the family seem to imply is that they once had expected to have a glorious marriage bestowed on them, as if it were a gift from life or God, and then were disappointed with what they got. But all people who have had a good marriage know that they and their spouses had to work hard to make it good —and still have to. And work in this sense doesn't mean just toiling in the kitchen or in the office. It means being sensitive to our spouses, listening, trying to understand their feelings, wondering in a dispute whether they might be right and we might be wrong. It means generosity of spirit.

I'm not suggesting that marriage should be all give and no take. There has to be a balance, of course, between providing and receiving and a balance between the spouses. But I do think that, as in other occupations, what you contribute gives greater satisfaction than what you receive. To put it another way, you gain happiness most often not from seeking it hungrily but as a by-product of having done something well or of giving happiness.

Though some individuals, afraid of the blighting effect of marriage, may prefer a succession of love affairs throughout life, a majority of us who are married would only have to visualize the rest of our lives without marriage (or the prospect of marriage) to realize that we would feel quite at loose ends and forlorn.

A minority can go comfortably through life without children and grandchildren. But a majority of us, if we stop to picture a life without offspring to need us when they are young or for us to turn to for renewal of family ties when we are older, would unhesitatingly choose to take a chance on all the trials of family life.

I'd predict, in fact, that in a considerable majority of the cases in which a man and woman have no ongoing commitment to each other or to their children and who are giving each other no continuing emotional support, the children will suffer from emotional neglect and will have impaired personalities the rest of their lives. The best of foster care will not make up for this deficiency. If a couple is not willing to strive for a permanent relationship for their children's sake (whether or not they can achieve it), they shouldn't have children.

In my view one of the promising trends is that more young people in their twenties who are serious enough about each other to want to live together but are not sure enough to be ready to marry feel free to live together openly. This gives them a better opportunity to find out whether they are really compatible and lessens the possibility that physical sexual attraction is the main thing that is drawing them together.

I'm not speaking here of teenagers who are not yet in any position to marry, nor of casual or promiscuous relationships. I'm not suggesting, either, that all young people should live together before marriage. Most parents are not yet ready for any such unconventional arrangement. Probably a majority of young people will continue to want to make up their minds about marriage without openly living together first.

In the future the young people who are afraid of marriage, or who never seem to find just the right person, are not going to feel the pressure from relatives and from society to marry anyway, for convention's sake, as they have in previous generations and I think that's all to the good. As a result, there will be fewer marriages, and more people who are living together without marriage and without children.

The new emphasis on limiting the growth of population will probably make it easy for those couples who have no great desire for children to decide to get along without any. This will be an advantage all around, for children who are not deeply loved usually do not turn out well.

One of the most helpful things that our society could do to improve family life, I think, would be to organize interesting activities for mothers and fathers in neighborhood meeting places that would relieve the isolation of child care in the early years. I'm thinking, for example, of classes in painting, sculpture, literature, writing, and languages, of clubs devoted to stamp collecting or to producing plays. There could be a nursery where babies were watched, nursery groups for preschool children, activity clubs for school-age children, so that the children could be occupied with constructive activities at the same time that their parents were. Such classes and activities for parents could be organized at public libraries, health centers, church houses, shopping centers, universities, and community colleges.

Great efforts should be made to divide our huge, impersonal metropolises, which make everyone feel ineffectual and neglected, into small communities where people can know one another and can govern themselves as far as possible. They would control their own police, schools, health services, real-estate zoning, recreational facilities.

More fundamentally, the quality of marriage and family life could be improved, I believe, by a major revision of our American philosophy and priorities along the lines that so many young people advocate: a simpler style of living in terms of the size and style of our houses; fewer, smaller automobiles (more travel by bicycle and on foot); much less in the way of gadgets and possessions of all kinds; simpler, cheaper clothes (blue jeans for people of all ages?); much less striving for money, position and power. Instead, an emphasis on service to fellow men, in the spirit of brotherly love.

:: 2 ::
Pleasure in Parenthood

We think of parenthood mostly in terms of the obligations and the problems that go with it. When my children were small I always forgot to think of the pleasures until I was away on a trip and realized how much I missed them, or until the children were grown and lived at a distance, either in college or in homes of their own. This made me sorry and a little bit ashamed each time, but it didn't seem to change my behavior the next time I was with them.

The main reason is that most of us feel we always have to be keeping after our children—about their eating, their boots, their clothing and running noses, their chores, their manners. Or about the dangers of fire, of being run over, of poisoning, of falling out of a tree or an upstairs window.

Grandparents have often asked me why they couldn't have enjoyed their own children the way they are now enjoying their grandchildren. I thought this over for many years and finally decided that there is no magic way for parents to get around their constant preoccupation with their children's behavior and safety. That's what parents were made for, although, to be sure, the amount of fussing varies greatly from family to family.

Grandparents, on the other hand, feel close enough by blood to their grandchildren to take pride in their accomplishments and delight in their charms; but most grandparents—not all—manage to escape that anxious sense of responsibility they themselves had as parents.

So I don't believe I can point out ways for parents to take a lot more pleasure in their children, but I'll try to help just a little.

First, it's important to remember that all the worrying and fussing does no good, and even sets you back some. The main factor that makes children's characters turn out sound is their deep desire to grow up to be like the parents they admire and love. Most of that work is done by the children themselves. But the more they are nagged, the less is their eagerness to copy and to please. Of course, I'm not recommending that you let children misbehave or get into trouble —only that you try to avoid the automatic and often unnecessary watching, warning, directing, forbidding, and chiding. I learned in pediatrics practice that the effects of parental preoccupation and worry can frequently be seen in the contrast between first and second babies in the first year or two of life. Many mothers have told me that they had yearned to have a cuddly baby. But their first child usually foiled them by twisting away impatiently when hugged. Their second child was much more embraceable. "Why the difference?" they would ask.

Of course, this contrast doesn't hold in all families, by any means. But I think that many first babies feel crowded by all the attention they get—especially by the worrisome attention, but also by the eager, proud attention. Why is she hiccuping? Does her stuffy nose mean that she has a cold? Why isn't she sitting up yet like our nephew? Is this thumb-sucking a sign of insecurity? Why doesn't she go to sleep? And then, "Don't put that in your mouth!" "Make patty-cake for Aunt Mabel." "Say Daddy."

With a second child parents make allowances for individual differences. They take it for granted that there are many quirks in every baby, quirks that can't be adequately explained but that have no particular significance. They've learned that a baby is tough and durable despite her smallness. Most important, they've learned from their first baby that they themselves are adequate as parents and usually manage to do the right thing. So they can trust themselves and act in a more relaxed manner with the second.

I believe that babies and young children know instinctively that they must have some freedom to make their tiny decisions—to choose their own activities, to play with a toy in just the way they want to, to turn down a food today that they liked yesterday and will like tomorrow. They sense that they must not allow their parents to control them too much, physically or psychologically. If parents direct them too exactly in how to use a crayon or put on a sock, if they try to snuggle them too long, if they want to clean their ear or peer in their mouth for more than two seconds, they feel a strong impulse to fight their way free.

Second or third children, usually given more freedom to go their own way, are less ready to suspect that people are trying to dominate them. So when they feel they'd like some loving or when their mother feels she'd like loving them, they can enjoy a hug for five or ten seconds or sit in their mother's lap for a whole minute before sliding off to go about their business.

Now for some positive suggestions. A great pleasure for parents comes from reliving the delights of their own childhood by identifying with their child (lets say it's a girl) through every new experience. When you pat a dog for your eighteen month old, you can see her shrinking back with caution, reaching out to touch with fascination, smiling in response to the dog's friendliness, and feeling proud of her own courage—all at the same time. The first time a three year old sees a steam shovel working, you realize that it takes her a long time to absorb all the impressions: the noise, the jolting of its motions, the enormousness of the bite of earth and the huge hunks of rock that it takes, the sudden vomiting of the shovelful into the waiting truck that shakes as it is loaded, the fact that an ordinary-looking man can control such vast power with levers. A child will talk about her first sight of a working steam shovel for hours afterward, with eyes sparkling; and a parent can share in the wonderment.

Excursions to zoos, museums, circuses, woods, streams, and beaches are intensely stimulating. Yet there are several problems. Too much may be attempted for small children; then they have to be urged or prodded or yanked along to see more sights before their curiosity is half-satisfied with the previous ones. This creates unnecessary impatience in the parents, balkiness or fatigue in the children. Let them set their own pace and let the other sights wait till another occasion. Sometimes it's possible to take children of different ages separately so that one isn't always dashing ahead and the other lagging behind.

There's always the temptation, in public places where there are various mild dangers, for the parent to take on a constantly warning attitude. Better to stick close to small children instead of trying to control them with shouts from a distance.

It isn't necessary to go on elaborate excursions to delight children and enjoy their reactions. Watching a worm or a bug in the backyard can give both of you pleasure for half an hour.

Don't forget about reading aloud. Children of all ages and all sorts are fascinated by stories. The libraries are bulging with children's books. All you have to do is get in the habit of reading aloud. One reason this is an ideal way to have fun with children is that you drop other obligations for the time being and give the children full attention. Let them set the pace in the reading. Let them ask questions, hear one page over again if they wish or hear the whole book a second time. This is the way for them to get what they want from the story and for you to get in harmony with them.

To work at hobbies with children—carpentry, sewing, bead stringing, model-building, gardening, fishing, picture painting, cookie-making—can be friendship-building and soul-satisfying. But I know from my own experience as a father that it often can be frustrating instead—for both generations—if the parent sets the standards too high or is too controlling or too critical.

I ruined the fun of model trains for both my sons by buying equipment that was way beyond their stage of development, making track plans that were much too complicated and always directing the work. You have to be able to let the child take the lead in a cooperative project. Even if you and the child have separate projects in the same hobby, you have to be tactful about not making yours so elaborate that it puts the child's to shame.

Working together at home chores of even the most humdrum kind can be mutually enjoyable for parents and children. A child feels proud to be able to work alongside an adult, and the parent is apt to feel comradely at such times. But adults have to remember that children can pay attention to business only for limited periods of time, are not very efficient and tend to go off on imaginative side projects of their own after a while. So a parent has to be ready to suggest that the child has done enough when enthusiasm begins to run out. Of course, you can and should expect more as a child grows older.

Last but not least is conversation itself, one of the fundamental ways in which human beings enjoy each other. Conversation can be just as delightful between parent and child as between two people of the same age. Of course, the reason it is not fun oftener is that the parent so frequently uses the verbal channel for directing or correcting and the child uses it for begging or complaining. So both acquire the habit of turning a deaf ear.

The way to have an agreeable, meaty conversation—even with other adults—is to put yourself in tune with them by listening attentively and sympathetically, with your eyes meeting theirs and your facial expression mirroring their mood, whether that mood is humorous, indignant, or awed. Then when it's your turn to speak you take off from their remarks, showing that you respond to them in thought and feeling. So a conversation is woven by two sympathetic souls working with the same threads.

There has to be a feeling of wanting to share something on the part of the first speaker and a real response on the part of the other. A conversation between a parent and a child can't start with a prying or probing question from the parent such as "What did you do in school today?" This never brings the smallest nugget of significant information.

If it is the child who speaks first, the parent has to resist any tendency to seem critical or bored. For if the child says, "Charlie hit me in school today" and the parent answers, "Are you sure you didn't do something to him first?" that will be the end of the conversation. So will it be if the parents' tone of voice suggests that they really aren't paying any attention at all.

One of the most delightful aspects of children, I think, is the originality of the things they say, especially during the preschool years. Their remarks, their ways of interpreting things, are usually fresher, more vivid even than those of great philosophers and writers. Yet lots of parents never think of paying attention to these gems of perceptiveness, and even correct their children for using unconventional language. Most children will begin to be more conventional around six to eight years of age, and will soon enough be speaking in the platitudes and clichés of adulthood like the rest of us.

I recently read an article by two parents who described

one of their ways of communicating with their children, a way that never would have occurred to me and probably wouldn't to most parents. They watch some of their children's television programs with them, especially on Saturday mornings.

The parents said they found several values in this unusual occupation. They could keep track of what their children watched and veto the brutal programs. They found it easy to fall into natural, uncritical conversation about programs and related topics. The children took the occasion to ask many questions about matters that confused them and the parents enjoyed being able to enlighten them.

They found their children's comments surprisingly sophisticated and amusing—especially their cynicism about commercials. The parents were amazed to find that they even enjoyed some of the programs. But best of all to the parents was the discovery that this was a pleasant, easy way for the whole family to be friends.

:: 3 ::

Raising Children by Instinct
Instead of by Theories

There are several deeply imbedded emotional mechanisms in mothers and fathers, of which they are usually unaware, that help them to do a good job in raising their children.

By far the most important is the automatic way in which they snap into action in a thousand child-management crises every day without having to stop to ask themselves what the approved theory is, or even what they themselves consciously believe is the right method. They act promptly on the basis of what they absorbed back in their own childhood.

When you catch your child being mean to a younger one, or telling a lie, or scratching the dining-room table with a toy, you don't have to stop to think for an instant. You express disapproval in an emphatic way that makes a lasting impression on the child.

This is how parents have always raised their children—throughout the world and throughout history. Otherwise child rearing would be a matter of endless indecision that would exhaust the parents emotionally and produce spoiled children who were forever arguing and balking.

Here's a small, amusing example of how early in life a girl learns from her mother to be the same kind of parent. I once watched a bossy four-and-a-half-year-old girl giving instruction in doll bathing to a mousy three year old. Her tone was patronizing and pompous as she kept repeating, "See how I do it, dear?" Finally she said, "Now you try, dear." The three year old stepped forward and hesitantly did her best. The four and a half year old soon interrupted—in a much more condescending and pseudopatient manner, "No, dear, not like that, dear. Now, watch me more carefully." This child by the age of four and a half had already learned—obviously from her mother—a certain attitude toward children and child rearing that surely will characterize her management of her own offspring twenty years later. Her tone of voice will be the same then too.

Even professional people such as psychologists and psychiatrists, who have acquired from their training and experience a lot of new concepts about how they are going to raise their children, often are surprised to find the old-fashioned ideas they learned from their parents—about the naughtiness of touching the genitals, for instance—popping out of their own mouths. Even if they keep themselves from expressing disapproval to the child, they still feel an inward anxiety about this behavior that they thought they had outgrown long ago. I don't want to get into the theoretical question of whether calmness or anxiety is better in managing this particular situation. I'm saying only that these automatic reactions take care of most issues of the day and are usually reliable.

I think, for example, that the reason so many parents have been painfully uncertain about how much and what kind of television they should let their children watch—parents who are quite confident in laying down rules in other areas of child management—is that there was no television when these parents were children; they never learned at a basic level from their parents what attitudes or regulations to adopt.

Another way in which parents unconsciously and success-fully guide their children is through identification with them. Of course parents know that children mature by identifica-tion with their parents—the boy imagining how it would feel to be just like his father, pretending to do everything he has seen him do, copying his mannerisms; the girl identifying mainly with her mother. This is how children develop their physical and social skills, their desire to marry and have chil-dren of their own someday, their altruism and idealism—especially during the three-to-six-year-old period.

But all through the childhood and particularly the infancy of their children parents also are identifying with them. I can still remember the expression on my mother's face as she spoon-fed solid foods into my brother and youngest sister when they were babies. She would stick her own lower lip way down and out and then up, as if she herself were care-fully taking in the drippy spoonload. Without realizing it, she was putting herself in a mood to understand how the infant felt and how he or she might best be fed.

When a parent talks baby talk during a child's first and second years, keeping to very simplified grammar and vocabulary, using Daddy, Mommy, and Johnny, instead of the personal pronouns that are so confusing in the earliest years, the parent has succeeded in getting in tune with the child's immaturity and is intuitively using the language the child will be most likely to understand.

When an infant boy makes a sound something like mama and his mother delightedly repeats this again and again, she senses that this echoing of his sounds and her obvious delight in his achievement will focus his attention on the word and encourage him to repeat it.

The sensitive school teacher who is introducing reading and arithmetic to first graders intuitively thinks and feels like a six year old in order to present the material in an understandable way and to think what aspects of it may be confusing.

Even when dealing with adolescents, tactful parents are automatically putting themselves in their children's shoes as they answer questions, make requests, grant or withhold permission for privileges, and give advice. Otherwise they would run into a lot more angry rebellion than they experience now.

In the child-rearing study we've carried out for the past decade at Western Reserve University Medical School, with the support of the Grant Foundation, one of our staff members, Mary Bergen, first noted and then studied in detail the way in which most mothers—even inexperienced ones—intuitively anticipate their infant's or child's next stage of emotional development. In particular she studied the stages that bring about the child's progressive separation from the mother and that are apt to be painful to her—such as weaning from breast or bottle in the first year and demands for independence in the second year. Most parents prepare themselves by gradual steps in the backs of their minds for such separation; then they can help their children over these humps. Perhaps even more significant, Mary Bergen and other staff members found evidence that most parents sense at the unconscious level potential tensions, deficiencies, hostilities, deep within themselves (usually of mild degree) that have been left over from their own childhoods and that might interfere with the smooth upbringing of their child (for example, by overprotecting or by overstimulating), and they take steps, without being conscious of this, to protect the child from trauma from such influences or to prepare the child specially to withstand them.

These various automatic processes in parents take care of a great part of the rearing of children. What this means is that conscientious parents don't have to worry as much as they characteristically do about their own adequacy or the correctness of the methods they are using. They can spend more time enjoying themselves and their children.

Chapter II

Fostering Good
Attitudes in Children

:: 4 ::

The Beginnings of Character

When I was an undergraduate, my future wife, Jane, explained to me that psychologists believe a child's character is pretty well formed by three years of age. I immediately answered, "That is ridiculous"—not because I knew anything about it but because I didn't like the implication that a person couldn't keep changing as much as he wanted to.

Jane had worked for a while as a volunteer part-time assistant to a psychologist in a child-guidance clinic. She also had taken a child psychology course in college. As a result, she was way ahead of me in child-development theory. The only concepts I had were my own personal prejudices. The psychology course I took in college seemed to be mostly about neurons and reflexes and how rats learn—one of the dullest courses I ever took.

Fairly often I receive a letter from a mother who feels anguished because her child of two years has a feeding or toilet-training problem, or is too dependent or too demanding, and she assumes she has ruined him for good.

When is character formed, and can anything be done about it later? I don't think we know all the exact answers yet, but we have some fairly good generalizations.

In the first place, I'm one of those who believe that inborn temperament makes quite a difference. By temperament I don't mean the specific social traits—good and bad—that people in past ages have often ascribed to heredity, such as courage, dishonesty, thrift, or alcoholism. (When they were bad characteristics mothers blamed them on the father's family, and vice versa.) By inborn temperament I mean energetic or quiet, aggressive or gentle, emotionally labile or level, heedless or sensitive, relaxed or tense, bold or cautious, determined or compliant. To be sure, every one of these tendencies can be accentuated by life experiences too.

Parents can see these temperamental differences most clearly when they are presented with nonidentical twins. In fact, it is hard for them to talk about anything else at times, so dramatically different are the ways in which these twins may react to challenges, to danger, to people.

We are relatively in the dark about developments in character in the first four or five months of life. In fact, for the first three months babies give the impression of not having any clear idea of what is going on around them. Their glance wanders about quite vaguely, as if they were saying, "Where am I? What is this existence?" They seem to recognize and gaze at their mothers more than other people from two months on, so they are learning something. By three months they are much more focused in the way they scrutinize people. They now appear to enjoy all people indiscriminately, not seeming to care yet whether visitors are old friends or strangers. (This tolerance for strangers changes drastically later.)

The period from five months to a year or a year and a half is perhaps the most significant of all in setting peoples' fundamental attitudes toward life—not the specifics of their later outlook or ambitions but the underlying tone of their feelings about other people and themselves. This is the age when they begin to feel like separate individuals and to insist on a tiny bit of independence—wanting to hold their own bottles and not be cuddled too long. More important, from our point of view, they form their first real attachment—to the parents, or the parent who is taking the major part of the care. Not only is it the most crucial relationship they'll ever have, but also this is its most influential stage. If the closest parent should abruptly go away and leave them with an unfamiliar person, they will be visibly depressed until the parent re- turns. It is the parent who now will introduce them to the world of people, to the world of things and—you might say —to themselves. If the parent is a very warm person, they will come to expect the same quality in other people later. The lovingness of the parent will foster love in themselves. And the fact that they thus become friendly people them- selves and anticipate friendliness in others is the surest com- bination for evoking what friendliness there is in all the peo- ple with whom they will be dealing for the rest of their lives.

If, on the other hand, their parent is cold and suspicious (as a result of an unhappy upbringing), they will develop in that direction themselves. They will expect the rest of the world to be cold and, therefore, will find mainly its cold aspects.

In regard to their concepts of themselves, babies are led at this stage to an assumption that they are basically either appealing or unattractive, good or unworthy. This is when they tend to become optimists or pessimists.

The parent is also introducing babies to the world of inanimate things—or failing to do so, showing them what fun can be gained from putting a batch of spoons in a saucepan, looking at pictures in a book, dancing to the music of the phonograph. When the parent teaches them in this positive spirit, it gives them a sense not only that things are to be enjoyed but also that they will be able to manipulate them successfully. Or if the parent has the opposite attitude, it may teach them that most objects are to be suspiciously avoided because playing with them involves some kind of danger or parental wrath. If babies have had very little relationship with their parent or a substitute, case histories show us, they may not develop a normal interest in things. In other words, babies have to have related well to a person first in order to go on to relate well to things and ideas.

In the period between about one and three years children acquire a very definite sense of themselves as separate people, with emphatic wishes of their own. However, their increasing sense of their separateness also makes them become more conscious of their actual dependence on their parent; and though they want to try going farther away for longer periods, they have to keep running back to be sure the parent is there.

Babies don't just assert their rights; they overassert them. They say no to their parents' requests not only when they really don't want to do something, but also when they're actually willing, just to make the point that their wishes must be considered. (It is true at other stages of development, too, that when it is time for a physical or emotional readiness to appear, the child practices it endlessly, compulsively, in his or her determination to master it.)

The insistence on their individuality and their rights is one of the factors that make so many one year olds become arbitrary in their food likes and dislikes; they may turn adamantly against dishes they took fairly willingly before. (It's easy enough to substitute other foods for those that are unpopular.) Children who may have accepted matter-of-factly being put on the toilet in the last part of the first year now often balk at sitting down, or they may get the idea of holding the movement in until they are safely off the seat.

The topic of toilet training reminds me that this is the

stage when the children can be interested naturally in the ideas of cleanliness and orderliness, and take pride in accomplishing them. They enjoy, too, the sense of being able to cooperate with their parents in general. If, on the other hand, children are in an antagonistic mood, as when they are resentful about having been frustrated or about a new baby, soiling may seem the most appropriate way to express it.

At moments of specially sharp frustration they now feel the full force of their aggressiveness. First they dare let it out only against themselves, in the form of temper tantrums; but with a little encouragement they can turn it against others— parents and brothers and sisters—and be surprisingly barbaric about it.

What all this adds up to is that the one to three year olds feel a number of conflicting pulls: independence versus dependence, cleanliness versus soiling, cooperativeness versus balkiness, affectionateness versus antagonism. How individual children will come out on each of these scales and what kind of personality makeups they'll have at the end of this period will depend on the interaction of such factors as the compliance or assertiveness of their inborn temperament, how warm a relationship has developed between them and their parent, and how the two of them manage to resolve the routines during this somewhat strained period.

I'll give you some oversimplified examples of how personalities may occasionally become slightly lopsided by three years of age. If parents are intensely dominating and their child is compliant by temperament, he or she may be made too submissive, at least on the surface. If they are hostile and tactless but leave their child loopholes for fighting back, he or she may become exaggeratedly hostile. (Of course, the most valuable combination for managing children without cramping their style consists of clear-cut firmness, friendliness, and tact. Needless to say, no parent has the serenity to keep this balance all the time.)

If parents are grim-natured and make a dead-serious matter out of cleanliness and other kinds of propriety, their child, if naturally docile, may end up overly clean and scrupulous. A much commoner problem today, especially in parents who are college graduates and have read what the supposed experts say, is a hesitancy in going about training that drags it out for many months, during which time the child subtly foils and teases them and they become increasingly frustrated. This type of half-hearted but prolonged tug of war over toilet training and over other kinds of social conformity sometimes produces the persistently messy and balky character. (The parents' cue is to start toileting by eighteen months, using whatever readiness is there, to be cheerfully positive though tactful, and once started, to keep it up. This often takes a lot of persistence, but it pays off.)

If excessively anxious parents hover over children, implying that the world is full of dangers and that the parents' constant watchfulness is essential to the preservation of the children's lives, and if the children are impressionable, they may end up rather dependent. On the other hand, there are a few vigorous young souls who are so irritated by overprotection that they are forever escaping from their parents' supervision and hurling themselves into one danger after another. (Theoretically the parent should protect or warn children in regard to serious dangers but let them find out how to avoid the minor ones by themselves, also let them learn gradually how to take care of themselves independently as they develop the desire. This is easier to say than to carry out, especially with the first child, about whom the parent naturally is more anxious.)

In most cases, fortunately, children by three years of age end up reasonably good friends with their mother and father —for a major part of the average day, despite frequent tiffs. They have a fairly civilized balance in their characters. They are apt to have a bit of dependency in one particular situation or another, but they've got enough independence to keep on enlarging their horizons. They are predominantly clean and cooperative, though they'll continue to have their bad days. They can be scrappy with their peers when it's necessary to protect their rights, but most of the time they find that it's more fun to get along agreeably than to wrangle.

I started this chapter by posing the question whether there's much truth in the view ascribed to various psychologists that a child's character will be fairly well formed by three years of age. Perhaps you'll think, from all the aspects of personality I've mentioned, that I believe it is all quite crystallized by then. There are a couple of important reasons why I wouldn't go nearly that far. What I've described are certain personality tendencies which may—and in most cases are—likely to persist. But they also can be greatly modified in later childhood and adulthood if the environment or the pressures change. But there are also a lot more characteristics that won't be formed until later stages of childhood—for instance, the whole matter of individuals' specific attitudes toward people of their own and the opposite sex, which will largely determine what general kinds of lifework they will consider and what sort of marriages they will make. I'll sketch these in another place.

:: 5 ::

Lovingness—The Most Valuable Trait

If I could make only one wish for children, I'd wish them the quality of lovingness. It would be a deep and generous lovingness, not just a superficial sociability. This would imply by definition that there was a minimum of hostility in their characters.

Loving people make others feel good, and they are usually happy people themselves. They are able to form strong, long-lasting friendships.

Their careers are apt to be stable and gratifying. Their relationships on the job—with superiors, equals, and subordinates—are based substantially on mutual liking and respect. This, in addition to what their technical abilities provide, make them of greater value to their firms. It tends to prevent disruptive rivalries between them and those working with them.

For a good marriage, generous lovingness is the most crucial ingredient by far; as a positive bond I'd say it is as vital as sexual gratification, sometimes more so. Every day it fosters dozens of acts of spontaneous thoughtfulness and helpfulness that, coming from either partner, make the other want to respond in kind.

A marriage based primarily on an outgoing love is likely to be stable and happy because there is plenty of love in the partners for each other and for the children also. (When parents' love for their spouses is largely possessive, they may feel threatened if they think their spouses love the children too much.) In fact, loving parents' love for their children strengthens the ties between the parents.

The most magical thing about lovingness is that the more of it people give, the more they receive from others. Unfriendly individuals who think that very few people are worthy of their trust get confirmation of their belief all day long, because their sour manner immediately rubs everyone the wrong way and evokes their antagonism. People who show trust and warmth evoke whatever is friendly in others; even the curmudgeon has, deep inside, a yearning to be loved that will respond—though perhaps only awkwardly— to friendliness.

How do you bring up a child to be loving and lovable? (These two characteristics are interrelated, of course. Parents love children because they're lovable, and their love is what teaches children to love. If children become unlovable, the process is reversed.) All babies are born with a capacity to love, which then must be developed. As young as six weeks of age, they smile when their parents coo to them. At three months they squirm with delight when anybody speaks to them, no matter what this person's appearance or character is.

All babies, including the homely ones, are appealing in their early months. Their smallness and helplessness and big-eyed look seem designed to make them irresistible to the doting impulse in adults—even stuffy adults. Another great charm they have at this age is that they aren't opinionated or willful.

As babies grow older there are several factors that influence their lovableness and lovingness. At the start we ought to make allowances, at least theoretically, for inborn differences of temperament. I believe that these differences exist, though they are hard to prove. One kind of child is naturally active and outgoing. This child's love for people will be of an open, bear-hug type. Another child may be innately shy and sensitive, with a lovingness to correspond. So we are not talking about identical capacities to begin with.

And now as I talk about characteristics that can be fostered by parental management, I don't want you to think I'm saying that if you manipulate your child just right, you can produce exactly the kind and degree of lovingness—or anything else—you want. You can modify his characteristics to a degree. If you try too hard, you may only make him obstinate.

I want to discuss first the influence of the parents' own lovingness. Generally speaking, this is the most influential factor, and it begins to operate by the time babies are six months old. For then they are gaining their first definite impression of what people are like. If their parents are glowing with affection, this will develop the children's lovingness to the full; and it will start them out assuming that all the people of the world are basically friendly also.

It's good for parents to demonstrate physical affection too. There's been a tradition in the Anglo-Saxon segments of our American society to subdue this aspect of affection, especially between father and son. (I was brought up that way.) But I think this is a mistake.

One limitation on physical affection should be mentioned: By the time children are three years old their affection for their parents, particularly for the parent of the opposite sex, takes on a sexual element. They would sometimes like to go on caressing progressively as lovers do. It's the parents job to keep episodes of physical affection within sensible limits.*

Parents who feel that they were skimped on in some aspect of affection in their own childhood—not enough assurances in words, physical demonstrativeness, or gifts and possessions—are sometimes tempted, in order to be sure that they don't make the same mistake with their own children, to go to the opposite extreme. Better, they feel, to be speaking of their love or hugging their children or giving them another present too often than too seldom.

In one sense there is no such thing as too much love. But parental overemphasis doesn't really express an overabundance of love, but an anxiety about whether there is enough showing. Such anxious demonstrativeness doesn't satisfy or reassure children; they sense that it springs from uneasiness, and this makes them uneasy. It's the relaxed, spontaneous evidence of love that gets across best to children and fosters their lovingness.

---

*Some parents may think of tickling a baby as a form of affection. It's exciting for the parents and it makes babies laugh hysterically. But you can see that babies, at the same time, find it just too much. Yet they are too small to protect themselves. I think tickling is unfair to babies.

In helping children to grow up loving, the negative part —keeping hostilities at a minimum—is almost as important as the positive. At one year of age this means avoiding unnecessary conflicts, for instance, about not touching forbidden things. Removing most of the breakables from babies' reach and distracting them from the remaining forbidden things are helpful techniques here. But these are only partial aids, because children do have to learn to accept prohibitions. They should be taught a few at a time.

When parents put off this sort of training indefinitely because they dread conflict, it only mutes the conflict and prolongs it. For children of one year know (or soon learn) what they are not meant to touch. But they also know when a parent is afraid to be definite. So they feel challenged to test the limits, to keep on misbehaving, until the parent takes a firm stand at last. All this jockeying engenders pugnacious behavior and guilt in children and suppressed anger in parents. So it erodes love on both sides.

A somewhat similar example of subdued, chronic conflict may occur in toilet training. In the first edition of *Baby and Child Care* I wrote that once in a while an unusually tactless and bossy parent can make a child of a year and a half so rebellious about training that the fight may go on for months and the child's personality may be made lastingly obstinate. I advised that when rebellion occurs, the parent can desist for a month and then resume training more gently.

This well-meant advice had the unfortunate effect of making a lot of parents who weren't tactless or bossy so apprehensive about conflict that they hardly dared start toilet training at all. As soon as they did and the child showed the least reluctance, the parents quickly stopped their efforts. And then when they tried again, however tactfully and gently, the child promptly balked again.

In this on-again, off-again way, success in training can be delayed a whole year; the child is constantly tempted—by the parent's hesitancy—to resist. The parent inevitably is irritated, though always trying to conceal it. The child senses and reacts to the irritation with more antagonism. At the same time the child grows guilty underneath about his or her noncooperation.

Parents' experiences of this kind made me conclude long ago that when children are at the appropriate age to learn such things as not to touch certain objects or how to use the toilet, there is nothing to be gained—in fact there is a lot to be lost—in postponing the teaching for fear of conflict.

For just as soon as children have caught on to what is expected of them, and also to the realization that they can easily take advantage of their parent's hesitancy by refusing to cooperate, the conflict actually has started—whether it is out in the open or covered up. And it will continue, perhaps for many months, until the parent gets wise enough or mad enough to say to a son, in effect, "It's time for us to stop teasing each other. You are a big boy. Big boys and men use the toilet. Start being a big boy now."

It is amazing and revealing how often a child of two and a half or three, after a year of balking, will cooperate promptly when the parent gets up the courage to become a firm leader.

But it shouldn't be necessary for parents to get angry or for a whole year to be wasted. The point of this part of the discussion is that nature counts on parents to have the sense and the assurance to lead. If parents will lead, at the appropriate stage of development the child will follow. And most important, parents don't have to be overbearing or angry or even cross. They can be masterful in a cheerful, relaxed, affectionate, encouraging manner—provided they take the initiative from the beginning. What turns parents sour is being foiled and frustrated by a mere whippersnapper.

There are a few other tricks in being masterful with young children. Don't ask them if they want to do something that they have to do anyway, like coming in for a meal; they're too apt to say no and then you have to argue or force. Don't tell them they must do something, like eating their turnips, that you probably won't be able to make them do; you are only digging a trap for yourself. Don't keep saying "No! No!" from a distance to a one year old, for you are offering him a choice of whether to submit or to defy. Instead, remove the child from the forbidden object or area, reinforcing the lesson with "No! No!"

It may seem to you like a strange way to discuss lovingness —to put so much focus on the avoidance of conflict. But the fact is that in most families the problem is not insufficient love but the eroding of some of that love—in the parent and in the child—through unnecessary conflict.

In previous centuries that erosion of love was most often caused by parents' overbearing ways and their refusal to consider the feelings and individuality of their children; but today it is caused more often by parents' being too fearful of imposing their leadership.

In this discussion I've made it sound as if I thought it was possible by masterfulness to avoid all conflict. Of course this isn't possible. With the best of management there are bound to be minor spats every day. I'm only suggesting how to avoid the extended tugs of war.

I want to include one other aspect of the fostering of an outgoing love: the special problem of the first or only child. A majority of first children turn out to be as warmhearted as later children in the family. In fact, an unusually large proportion of them go into the so-called helping professions— medicine, nursing, social work, teaching, the ministry. But a minority get turned in on themselves as a result of all the attention and fussing and worrying and bossing that they are sometimes subjected to.

Parents who have grown up with high aspirations for themselves naturally will have high aspirations for their children. First children bring all these concerns into focus. They act as a lightning rod. All that the parents have achieved in the way of accomplishments or good personality traits, they want their first children to achieve too. In all that they strove for and didn't achieve, they hope that their first children will be more successful. Any mistakes they've made cause them to worry that their first children may make the same ones.

By contrast, these conscientious parents are much more ready to take it easy with their second children. To be sure, they worry about them when there is something real to worry about; they correct them when they're definitely out of line; they give them affectionate attention when they look receptive. But they don't make mountains out of molehills and they don't hover or fuss or interfere when their children are happily and harmlessly going about their own pursuits.

So second children grow up more independent in their actions and feelings. They don't miss attention when they aren't getting it. They aren't worrying what people think about them. When they do want a little attention or loving, they turn easily to some member of the family or to a friend. When they see someone who might be fun, they're not inhibited by self-consciousness from approaching him.

To come back to the first child, let's say a girl, who has been fussed at a lot, she's often somewhat on the defensive with people—both familiar and unfamiliar people. She's afraid of being managed by them, afraid of being smothered by them. Yet paradoxically she has a great need for favorable attention. It's not that such a first child doesn't have as much lovingness and need for love inside her. It's that she is awkward in showing her affection and asking for it, so that she may put other people off—and then she may be disappointed again and again.

Of course it's easy to say to beginning parents, "Relax with your first-born. Let her be herself." But that's not much more helpful than telling a person to relax the first time he rides a horse or drives a car.

It is definitely helpful, though, to make the effort to take a first child to where other young children are playing as soon as she can walk, so that she can learn the fun of being in company, of giving and taking, before she reaches the age of self-consciousness. And a good nursery school that takes children at the age of three is particularly valuable for any first child, if it is available. If not, the parents can continue to take their child to visit others and to make neighborhood children welcome in their own yard and house.

Don't take any of this analysis and advice so earnestly that it diminishes by one degree the spontaneous enjoyment that you and your children have in each other's company. For having a good time together is the essence of lovingness and the best means of increasing it.

:: 6 ::

The Joy of Giving

If we could bring up our children with more consideration for others, with a greater impulse to serve, I think that in the long run this might help to solve some of our more serious problems in America—interpersonal, intergroup, and international. I am thinking particularly of our high divorce rate, our racial hatred, and the growing disapproval of us in other parts of the world.

There are at least a couple of different kinds, or levels, of generosity. The most fundamental and significant one depends on a loving, outgoing spirit. The another one is taught and is more superficial, but it is still important.

The fundamental kind of generosity begins to be formed —or omitted—in infancy. Babies are equipped with a built-in responsiveness to love that shows, by two months of age, in their delighted smiles when they are greeted. If they regu-

larly receive affection, they develop a corresponding affectionateness of their own. In a primitive way you can see this
when, by one year of age, children try to feed their mother
just as they have been fed, or hand their toys to a visitor who
is friendly.

This early generosity remains rather crude and limited
for the first three years, however. Children of one or two
have little inclination to share with other children. And even
in their relationships with their parents their love is more
dependent than generous. They still have quite fierce negative feelings when frustrated.

All during this phase of very mixed feelings most parents,
who are both loving and good leaders, are strengthening the
warm side of the child's nature, through the friendly, appreciative quality of their attitude and taming the negative.
They do both these things intuitively, without having to
think about them consciously.

Even in the first three years I think that parents can take
conscious, active steps to foster cooperativeness in a child. At
the very least, they shouldn't let themselves be imposed on
or abused. They shouldn't let a one year old deliberately
break things or strew food or possessions around just for the
sake of making a mess. When a child hands them an object
as a gift, they can show appreciation of this generosity. A
parent can encourage a child of two to go through the motions of helping to pick up playthings even if this involves
only one or two objects out of the dozen strewn around. A
parent can occasionally ask a boy to help by carrying some
object to the next room or by bringing a diaper if he has a
new baby sister. When he sometimes starts to be mean to the
baby the parent can promptly help him to convert this into
compassion by saying, "We mustn't be mean to the baby. We
must love her and kiss her like this." Such talk may sound
hypocritical to an honest parent. But this is just how human
sympathy is generated—by turning meanness upside down
and mixing it with affection.

After the age of about three, children who have had a good start become more predominantly, more consistently, more universally affectionate, all by themselves. Partly this comes from having gotten the negative feelings under control. Partly, I think, it's that there is just naturally more glow, more outgoing warmth at this age. Partly it comes from the childish beginnings of sexual feelings. Partly it is a matter of the child's being able to empathize with, identify with others. We see this many-sided love in the adoration that children at this age show for their parents and their striving to be just like them. We see it in the speed with which they become attached to friendly outsiders—even doctors who have to hurt them—and throw their arms around them. We see it in the joy with which they play with other children, cooperate with them, share possessions with them.

From the age of three years onward the child's spontaneous affectionateness can relatively easily be molded into a conscious and habitual considerateness. (I mean this can be done more readily now than at any other age short of adulthood.) A boy should be expected to be polite, in the sense of saying please, thank you, hello. He should do his full share of picking up his things, with a little supervision. He should be encouraged to become his parents' helper in a small way— even if this doesn't really help much—in dusting, carpet-sweeping, setting the table, drying the dishes, bringing the baby's bottle, "watching" the baby. Somewhere between three and four years he can give the baby a bottle. A boy of three or more can be asked to run errands for his parent in the house, carry a bundle if he goes shopping, open the door if his parents' hands are full. Children by three can make greeting cards for birthdays and holidays, tree decorations for Christmas, simple gifts.

The reason I make such a point of having three year olds contribute to the welfare of the family is not only that they are quite capable of small contributions and are proud to make them but also that so few parents in America think of asking them, or even know that they have the ability. Two things made me aware of this. When I once invited mothers of twins to write me what they had learned from their experience, and two hundred replied, several who had only a three year old to help them out with newborn twins said, "You'd be surprised how much valuable help you can get from a three year old." Also, a group of three year olds who had grown up in a German concentration camp, apparently without much mothering, and who were brought to the nursery directed by Anna Freud in London showed surprising altruism. They not only watched out for one another and helped one another in general, but when a boy saw that another was lacking a spoon or food, he would unhesitatingly give him his, though he was left with none himself.

Parents who say, "It's easier to do it myself," or, "Let them have a good time, they're only young once" have the wrong slant, I think. It's as important for children to grow up generous and cooperative as it is for them to grow up healthy. Besides, it is fun to help. Children who are expected to be considerate are happier children.

In the six-to-twelve-year-old period there are many ways in which children can be helpful and cordial—making their own beds and keeping their rooms clean; putting their playthings and equipment away; hanging up their clothes; putting the clean laundry in the bureau drawers. They should help with meal preparations, dishwashing, lawn care, cleaning the cellar and garage, washing the car.

Whether children receive an allowance as their right or in exchange for certain chores is not crucial. But I think it is important that they do at least some of their jobs as a contribution to the family, not for pay. And parents should feel free to ask children occasionally to do extra jobs that aren't too time-consuming, without having to pay for them. (A two- or three-hour job is different.) If they ask, "How much do I get?" I'd say, "This is to help all of us," or words to that effect.

Manners in this age period should be more elaborate than just please or thank you. Children should be taught to be cordial in their greetings, spontaneously thoughtful in helping parents or strangers. Greeting cards and gifts can be more painstakingly made. It is good for children of this age to occasionally become involved, as a school or Sunday-school group, for instance, in altruistic projects such as Trick or Treat for UNICEF or making some kind of contribution to a local cause.

Adolescents can take a lot more responsibility for jobs around the home, including baby sitting when the parents are out, even assisting the parents sometimes in the supervision of the younger children, e.g., on getting up, going to bed, at mealtime. (With the amount of homework children have in high school these days, and the need for some recreation, it's not reasonable, I feel, to ask them to take on a lot of the care of younger children or major responsibility in food preparation.)

It is particularly in the high-school years, when young people's idealism is being stirred, that they should have opportunities in school to study the miseries of the underdeveloped countries, the inequities in the United States, the unsolved problems right in their own communities.

The fact that this whole article is focused on ways to foster generosity may give you the impression that I think a parent should be demanding helpfulness from his child all day every day. That would be more likely to backfire. For whenever a particular theme is overemphasized in the rearing of children—overemphasized in the sense that a parent is talking about it all the time or using an insistent or strident tone—this is apt to bore or irritate the children, particularly in adolescence. It makes them antagonistic instead of receptive to the point of view.

I'll go a step further and suggest that even if a parent asks for cooperation and consideration only occasionally but always asks for it in a reproachful or nagging tone, the response will be a reluctant one that won't please anybody. This brings us back to the essential truth about genuine kindliness—that it's a reaction to having been treated kindly. This doesn't mean, however, that a parent can't bring up a generous child unless the parent is totally loving, always smiling. That's not possible for anyone. In fact, a parent has to be firm—or even stern, occasionally—to make children behave well enough so that the parent can love them and be kindly to them the rest of the time.

If the underlying feeling is much the most vital aspect, then why do we have to bother at all about surface manners and about asking children to be helpful every day? One way of answering this is to say that there is enough meanness, selfishness, heedlessness, and thoughtlessness in even the choicest human beings to make them at times unsatisfactory citizens or family members unless their outward behavior has been disciplined and smoothed throughout childhood by careful parents. For instance, I've watched quite a few children grow up whose parents were truly loving, generous people, but also too permissive and indulgent to ask for much consideration from them. Such children will develop reasonably sound characters, good consciences. They will become law-abiding citizens and devoted parents in their turn. But they can still be—as children and adults—unappealing or uncooperative or even irritating people. Perhaps they tread on the toes of others without noticing it, speak rudely to shopkeepers, quarrel freely with their spouses, hold strong prejudices, or fail to participate in community projects. They make little effort, that is, to understand others, be considerate of them, go out of their way to help them.

In many other parts of the world and at other periods in history, children have been brought up with a strong sense that their lives are to be devoted to some group or ideal that's much more important than they are as individuals. In Sparta in ancient times, in Israel and the Soviet Union in the last couple of generations, children have been raised to serve their country. In the Middle Ages in Europe and in early New England, children felt that they were on the earth primarily to carry out God's purposes. In many societies it has been made very clear to children at all stages of growing up that their major responsibility is to advance the welfare of the extended family; this includes being always respectful to and cooperative with the elders, taking up whatever occupation suits the elders, even marrying the person the elders choose.

Our American philosophy is remarkably different, particularly in the twentieth century. The parents' main ambition is to bring up children who will be successful and happy at whatever they themselves choose. Usually no strings are attached. The young people often feel that their only responsibilities are to accept a good education, to make sensible choices, and then to forge ahead—not for the sake of others or their country but for the benefit of themselves and the new families they found.

This philosophy of each for himself worked fairly well during the rugged past, when the frontier was being pushed back and the country was being developed. But I think it is not adequate for the solving of some of the most urgent problems of today.

We have one of the world's highest divorce rates. This is harmful to the adults involved. (Their second marriages break up as easily as their first, and their third even more so.) Divorce is upsetting to their children. This instability of marriage may increase as more and more children grow up half expecting failure in their own marriages.

We have a bitter problem of racial discrimination and hatred that threatens to become progressively more disruptive to the country. It is caused not by real differences between the races but by unreasoning fear and arrogance.

As a nation we have recently incurred the animosity of other peoples around the world because of what they consider the heedlessness and ruthlessness with which we have been interfering militarily in the affairs of such countries as Vietnam and the Dominican Republic. Ever since World War II we have been arousing resentment because of the financial, industrial, and even political domination we have exerted over other nations. In addition we can count on being disliked as the richest country in a world where starvation is mounting, until we can do more to reverse that trend.

All these problems have been created by a variety of forces. To bring up the next generation of American children with more considerateness and desire to serve will not guarantee the solution of any of them. But I think it would help with all of them. Besides, it would make American people happier as individuals. For human beings are by nature happier when serving others.

:: 7 ::

Friendliness

It's possible for children to grow up to be socially well adjusted without ever having had much chance for friendships with other children, but I wouldn't recommend this as the best way.

I've known quite a few children who had no play experience—except with their accommodating parents—until they were three, four, or five years old. But in their first experiences with children their own age they were frightened, or at least put off, by the way the other children behaved— coming up to them abruptly, not bothering to smile or say anything polite, perhaps grabbing a toy to try it out, often turning noisy and rough in play. Children encountered for the first time can seem as strange and dangerous to inexperienced children as gorillas would to grownups.

I'll always remember a girl of sixteen, an only child, who'd been raised on a remote estate in Switzerland and who, instead of going to school, had been taught by tutors. When she and her family came to New York, they moved into a hotel on busy Madison Avenue, and she began to attend an average noisy school. Within a few days she was weeping with nervous fatigue. She made an adjustment to the sound and confusion after a while. More slowly she made friends with a couple of the quietest girls who were in her class.

How fast children without much experience can get over the strangeness of other children and go on to the pleasures of companionship will depend on what kind of relationship they have had with their parents. If it has been one of enjoyable give-and-take, they will eventually find the way to establish the same kind of relationship with contemporaries. But if their parents have kept them in the center of the stage or have kowtowed to them and spoiled them, it will take them a long time to find out how to have fun with others on a democratic, mutual basis.

Generally it's easier for children to learn friendliness in the earliest years. If they get the knack at the start, when they are least self-conscious and learn the fun of mutual exchange, then they increase their skill and self-confidence with each subsequent acquaintance.

But if they make a slow or poor start and feel rebuffed, they come to anticipate unfriendliness. As they are subsequently thrown into contact with others, they have a chip on their shoulders—or at least a scowl on their faces—which provokes the very unfriendliness they fear. Each social failure subtracts from their self-assurance and increases their bristliness.

Learning friendliness does not really mean learning a set

of rules from one's parents like "Be polite to your friends," "Share your toys," "Do what your visitor wants to do, not what you want to do," though parents often do have to give such reminders.

Friendliness is basically a love of other people, an enjoyment of them and a spontaneous desire to please them. It comes most fundamentally from the fact that we are social beings, ready to love company if things go right in our development.

The development of our sociability has to be given a good head start by our having parents who are delighted with us in infancy, who smile at us, hug us, talk baby talk to us. Then, after the age of one or two, the warmth engendered in us by our parents turns increasingly outward to other people—adults and children.

At one year, you will notice, a baby observes a stranger for quite a few minutes at first. Then if the stranger has shown quiet friendliness—by smiling, not by rushing up to him and talking a blue streak—the child gradually will approach the stranger, perhaps hold out a toy, not to relinquish, but to serve as a sign of friendship.

At two years a child enjoys playing alongside another child and perhaps doing the same things; but this is parallel play, so-called, not cooperative play. By about three years, loving children begin to find the fun of playing together—acting as husband and wife or bus driver and passenger. One pulls the wagon and the other rides, and they take turns. Of course, a parent or teacher has to make suggestions from time to time, but the readiness for cooperative play is in the child.

By the age of six or eight, children are able and prefer to be away from adults for most of their sociable play, so that they can prove to themselves their ability to function independently and in a grown-up way.

But this is also the age when they tend to be clannish and

intolerant. In trying to find their own standards they naturally flock with those who have been brought up with similar
outlooks and tastes, and they look down critically on those
who are not just like them. Because of this intolerance, the
child who seems different or the child who has never learned
to submerge herself or himself easily in a group is apt to find
the period between six and twelve rather painful.

Adolescents are not much more tolerant either. Most of
them are almost slavish in their conformity to their own
group styles and customs and scornful of nonconformers.
There is such a need at this age for intense emotional attachments, however—both with those of the same sex and with
those of the opposite sex—that the child who is not expertly
sociable or who has an unusual personality or unusual tastes
tries particularly hard to find, to win, and to hold the friendship of one or two kindred souls.

There are several ways, I think, in which infants and small
children can be delayed in the development of their friendliness. They may not get the ideal balance in the various kinds
of attention their parents give them or they may not get a
good balance between adult and child companionship.

One example—and a rare one—is when the parents simply aren't very outgoing. They don't hug, they don't smile,
they don't talk to the baby. This is not because they aren't
devoted to him; they've just been brought up to be reserved
and solemn. But a baby needs an obvious show of affection,
and I don't mean boisterous attention or tickling that makes
her or him hysterical.

Another general type of imbalance that's rather common
with first babies occurs when the parents fuss over them a
great deal in one way or another. Then they become too
self-centered, at the expense of their outgoingness. For instance, the parents may hover in an anxious spirit, worrying
constantly that the babies will hurt themselves. ("No, no!
Don't climb on the chair. You may fall down." "Don't put the

stick in your mouth. It's dirty and will make you sick.") Even babies detect parental concern and adopt some of it themselves. They're always thinking of their bodies or their safety instead of how to have fun with others.

Or their parents may boss them every minute. ("Mustn't touch." "Don't hold your spoon that way." "Hurry up and eat your meal." "Say ta ta.") This bossing is apt to be a reflection of the fact that the parents themselves were prodded and corrected all through their own childhood. They developed a fundamental assumption that all children are naturally naughty and can be civilized only by constant nagging. This impairs the children's enjoyment of their parents and makes them somewhat antagonistic to them. As the children grow a little older they develop the same bristly feelings toward others.

In other cases the parents' pride in their first-born, which is very natural, takes the form of showing them off constantly whenever there is any company around. ("Do pat-a-cake for Aunt Nelly." "Where is your nose?" "Tell Charlie your name." "Dance for Mr. Summers.") So the children come to think of people not in terms of their being fun to do things with but as an applauding audience. When they become old enough to be with other children, they don't go forward to engage them in play but wait passively for their adulation. When it's not forthcoming their feelings are hurt.

Or parents are so aware of their first children and so delighted to pass the time of day with them that they always give the first greeting, always speak cordially no matter how grumpy the children are, always make up new games to play with them. The children are royalty; the parents are their servants. The children never have a chance to take the initiative or feel the need to be charming. There is nothing to stimulate and develop their outgoingness.

Of course, I'm not saying that parents shouldn't warn their small daughter of dangers that are really imminent or

correct her when she's out of line or show her off occasionally. They'd be strange parents if they didn't do all these
things sometimes. It's the constant fussing that I'm advising
against.

And I'm certainly not suggesting that parents be cool or
distant. The warmer, the better. I'm only suggesting that
they go about their own business three-quarters of the time
and leave the initiative to the child. Of course, they occasionally should take the initiative.

Second children who are one or two or three years old are
more apt to be left to their own occupations much of the
time. But when, being human, they want company, they
toddle over to their parent. The children make the first
greeting and have the real gratification of evoking a response. When they want to be read to, they fetch the book
and ask. When they want their sister or brother to play with
them, they suggest it. If they selfishly try to keep all toys to
themselves and alienate a playmate, they sense the loss and
offer to share in order to lure their friend back. All these
initiatives come under the heading of learning how to make
and keep friends.

From the time your daughter is an infant until she
reaches school age, and especially when she first begins to
walk, it's a good idea to take her, several times each week,
to where other children play—to a playground or to a
friend's back yard.

Don't interfere right away when she gets pushed or hit or
temporarily robbed of a toy. Don't sympathize too easily
with her hurt feelings, for this gives her the idea that she has
been grievously injured or wronged. Let her find out that a
little roughness is not fatal. Let her learn all by herself how
to meet push with push or how to hang on to a toy when
another child is trying to grab it. In other words, she gets her
basic feelings about the meaning of aggressiveness of other
children from her parents. If her parents consider it danger-

ous or cruel, she is frightened by it. If they take it casually, she learns to do the same.

Of course, you can't let your child be seriously injured or regularly intimidated by an unusually aggressive playmate. If the problem arises only occasionally, you can casually move in between bully and victim, which ordinarily will stop the attack. If it happens constantly, you'll have to take your child somewhere else to play, at least for a few months.

If your child is always the aggressor, you'll need some counseling from a family social agency or a child-guidance clinic.

By the time children are three years old, they should be able to profit from a good nursery school or day-care center. There they will learn to develop their bodily skills, their creativity and their intellectual awareness as well as their sociability. The experience of school is particularly valuable for first children, only children, children who live far from other children and children whose parents find them frustrating to be with constantly. (In the last case the teachers should be able to help the parents find a more comfortable relationship.)

If you have a back yard, you can install equipment in it —a swing, a seesaw, a sandbox—so that children will congregate there. If they need more luring, serve juice and crackers at midmorning and midafternoon.

If your child is of school age and is still bashful or timid or unpopular, you can bribe other children to give him or her special consideration, to a degree, by inviting them, one at a time, to meals or to go on special excursions—on a picnic, to a zoo or museum, to visit a farm, a dairy, a factory. You can't make an obnoxious child popular with bribes. But you can ensure that your child's good qualities will be given fair consideration.

For a few parents the problem seems to be not how to attract other children to their child but how to break up a friendship that seems undesirable. There is, for instance, the friend who has offensive manners or who is always in trouble with the neighbors or who lies or steals or persistently seduces others into sex play despite firm requests to stop. If the problem is one of morals that seriously worry the parents, they will have to interfere. But if it's only a matter of the parents' tastes and preferences, I think they should be very hesitant about even revealing their dislike.

If one child craves the company of another, this need has some real significance whether or not the parents can figure it out or approve. They should respect it for the time being and observe the effect of the relationship on each of the pair. If it seems to have no bad effect on their own child, they should be tolerant. Perhaps he or she will outgrow the friendship. (Some of the most intense relationships are short-lived.) If they believe their own child is being affected unfavorably, I'd suggest that they consult the school principal or teacher or a family social agency to get a more detached and professional opinion before interfering.

Friendship is not simply one of the pleasures of life, like ice cream or swimming. It's an absolutely indispensible ingredient of existence for ninety-nine out of one hundred people, whether they are skillful or clumsy in seeking it. Friendship is as important as food, health, shelter, sex. So it's sensible to cultivate the capacity in your child at the age when it is easily acquired.

:: 8 ::
Creativity and Imagination

It's good, I think, for children to develop a rich imagination. This will give them pleasure all their lives—in being able to lose themselves in books, plays, travel, and daydreams. On the practical side, people who have imagination can go further in most occupations. This is particularly true, of course, of those in the highly creative professions, such as novelists, poets, dramatists, painters, fashion designers. But it's also true in advertising, science, medicine, manufacturing.

To put it the other way around, the person who is strictly literal-minded has a limited usefulness to the world and a limited capacity for joy.

At the opposite end of the scale are the people who live so much or so deeply in fantasy that they don't relate well to live people or know how to get along in the real world. Some of these are extraordinarily creative individuals, and the world benefits from their uneven development. But others turn out to be just unhappy, without any corresponding productivity. So as a parent I would prefer to aim for a moderate degree of imaginativeness in my child.

In the second year of life even such simple play activities as putting one block on top of another, looking at picture books, tending dolls, pushing toy cars around on the floor, help to develop imagination. Between two and five years children's play will become progressively more complex if they have anything at all to work with.

Some parents assume that the more expensive and elaborate the toy, the better it is for children. This is not often true. It is the simple playthings and play materials that give the widest scope to children's creativity. Children between one

50

and two years old will be inventive and fascinated for a couple of hours loading pots, pans, and spoons into a cardboard carton and taking them out again. They can vary the play by pushing or dragging the carton all over the house like deliverymen. After the age of two or three cartons are even more full of possibilities for them. They can be beds, planes, trucks, buses, houses, boats, garages, stoves, washing machines. Building blocks can be used to set the stage for a different drama every day for years. Miniature cars, trains, and planes can be worked into the plot too.

Dolls, dolls' furniture and equipment, and dolls' clothes are stimulating to both girls and boys. So are hand puppets.

Adult clothes cast off by parents or clothes bought at a thrift shop are exhilarating to children.

Finger paints, water-color paints, and plasticine clay for modeling stimulate creativity of another kind. Experience in nursery schools has shown that these materials interest all children and don't require a great deal of adult supervision. It's worth the expense to buy the liquid water-color paints that come in jars, brushes that are at least half an inch wide, an easel, and a large easel-size block of paper. The usual children's paint sets that contain hard, dry tablets of paint and a tiny brush are discouraging to work with.

Then there are all the patterns and shapes that can be created with a sheaf of papers of various colors, a pair of scissors, and a jar of rubber cement.

It's impossible, I think, to exaggerate the importance of reading aloud to children from the age of two until they can read enjoyably to themselves—which doesn't come until several years after they have begun the process of learning to read. Stories that are quite simple can be fascinating to young children, so don't look for books that would intrigue you. Consult a librarian or bookseller who deals in children's books if you haven't had experience. There is a great wealth of books these days for children.

It's not necessary to get into stories that are scary or violent in order to interest and stimulate children, and I think it is better to avoid them altogether. It's wise to read slowly to young children and allow them time to ask questions. In other words, they need the opportunity to digest each part of the story and to bend it to their own needs.

A child with a fear of dogs will want to keep hearing and discussing the part of a story that tells how a certain dog loves children and wouldn't think of hurting them. A child living through a stage of wanting to be a fireman—perhaps partly because of anxiety about fires or a temptation to set fires— wants to absorb every detail of a fireman story. Children feel the need to expand their knowledge of any subject that interests them at all and to master the emotions stirred by it.

One of the valuable by-products of reading regularly to young children is the craving they develop to learn to read for themselves. We adults who have already learned this skill readily assume that the desire is present in every child. But it isn't. Teachers of deprived children who've never been read to may have to cope with a total absence of motivation at first, which makes the job difficult and slow.

What about the effect of television on the development of the imagination? Parents who grew up in pretelevision days and who were great readers of classical literature have been suspicious of television. They feel that the stories and commercials are mostly trash and that having a story presented visually in full detail induces passivity in the viewers and relieves them of any necessity to use their own imaginations.

Educators do not generally agree with this judgment. They believe that the over-all effect of television has been to foster children's imagination, intelligence, and curiosity, especially children from families that provide only an average or less-than-average amount of intellectual and cultural stimulation. In particular, the experts point to the way in which children go to libraries to read about topics that have been featured on television.

It is probable that comic books, which similarly have been abhorred by sensitive parents, also have been valuable in fostering children's imagination and intelligence.

But I want to say quickly that I don't mean I'd recommend large doses of just any kind of television and comics. I believe programs of violence and brutality are harmful to children, especially young children, and should be forbidden. I also believe children shouldn't be allowed to sit in front of even good television fare all day and all evening. They should be shooed out of the house—or at least away from the set—for a major part of their leisure (nonschool) hours in order to exercise their imaginations actively and creatively in play, to practice and enjoy sociability with their friends, and to give their bodies some exercise.

An occasional mother (less often a father) has lived so much and so enjoyably in her imagination that it comes quite naturally to her to begin leading her child deep into the world of fantasy by the time she or he is two or three years old. All day long the pair of them may pretend they are two other people or two nonhuman creatures living somewhere else.

This is very easily done because young children love to pretend and because a story is just as real and exciting to them as reality. And one of the greatest joys of being a parent is to introduce your child to the experiences that have meant most to you. Then you relive your childhood excitement vicariously, through the child. But when parents, with their richer imagination, are always creating a delightful fantasy world, the child's capacity for pleasure in the real world and for enjoying play with other children may be impaired. Of course, I'm not saying that parents shouldn't ever take the lead in fantasy—only that they shouldn't push it too far.

Then there are the children who, without encouragement from parents, create an imaginary companion who seems ever-present and more real than the ordinary people around them. (This is quantitatively different from the com-

mon situation of the small child who occasionally mentions
—in a frankly make-believe spirit—an unreal friend.) The
basic causes for this kind of situation may be subtle and hard
to determine. But certain factors can be fairly clear. When
the imaginary companion is always doing the naughty things
that the real children would like to do but rarely if ever do,
it suggests that the children have somehow come to believe
that they would lose entirely their parents' love and their
own self-respect if they carried out or even admitted these
forbidden impulses.

It would be wise in these cases for the parents to think
over their moralizing and disapproval, to see if it has been too
severe. In any case, I think they should tell such children
from time to time in a sympathetic, affectionate manner that
they sometimes want to be naughty—as all children do, occasionally—and that the parents love them just the same,
though of course the parents try to help them to be mostly
good. This is to ease these children's sense of guilt and let
them see themselves a bit more realistically.

When a child's imaginary companion is simply someone
to have a good time with, she or he may need more opportunities to play with other real children or some help in
learning how to get along with them.

I think it's sensible for the parents of children who constantly refer to an imaginary companion to steer a middle
course, not acting as if they believed in the reality of the
companion, but on the other hand not ridiculing or arguing
with their children. To act as if they believed, to play the
children's game, will further weaken their somewhat shaky
sense of reality and lead them away from a real solution to
whatever their underlying problems are. To ridicule or
argue pushes children away from their parents and intensifies their need for solace through imagination. The middle
course is for the parents to listen in an amused but sympathetic manner, as if to show their appreciation of the chil-

dren's storytelling ability. But now and then they can indicate in a casual way that they realize the companion is imaginary. (For example, "You are a very good storyteller." Or, "I know of another boy who invented a friend, just as you have, because he was lonely." Or, "This other child kept saying that his make-believe friend did naughty things. But I think this child wanted to do some of those things himself.")

This is an appropriate time, while we're discussing imaginary companions, to think about how rudimentary small children's grasp of reality is. It is difficult for inexperienced parents to realize that children sense very little difference between something that they have imagined and something that has actually happened. Small children can't tell the difference at first between a dream and waking life. It isn't very clear to them that a movie or television program is only a performance on a screen or on a tube. To put it another way, young children's feelings are almost totally dominant. What they enjoy, what they want, what they fear, are apt to seem most real. Their awareness of reality may be dim by comparison.

One of the most important everyday jobs that parents have to take on as a matter of course is to teach their children —gradually over the months and years—to distinguish between fantasy and fact. Otherwise children remain immature in some respects. ("That's not a mean kitty—that's a friendly kitty. He likes you." "That's Georgie's bicycle, and he wants to take it home now. He'll let you play with it again another time.")

The job of helping a child to understand reality is one that lasts right up to maturity. One way in which most adolescents differ from adults is that they are so strongly dominated by certain needs—to be accepted by their peers, to be loved by someone of the opposite sex, to appear experienced and worldly—that they impatiently brush aside the realities that threaten to get in the way of their dreams. Then it's the parents' job to remind them—tactfully, sympathetically—of the value of certain conventions, the value of being cautious at times, the value of not showing one's hand too soon.

But some individuals don't ever reach maturity in the sense of being able to face reality: the individuals, for instance, who never think the troubles they get into are their fault—they can always find somebody else to blame; the ones who dream of getting rich quickly, and who as a result are always ready to be taken in by sharpsters and hucksters; the ones who hide their own hostility from themselves by ascribing to other people all the antagonism that disrupts their own relationships with them.

Of course all of us, as children and as adults, use these evasions of the truth at times. No one can face all the realities all the time. But it's the parents' responsibility to keep a child from developing a consistent pattern of evasion by helping him learn to cope with life honestly.

So there are two balances to aim for: to encourage your children to develop enough pleasurable imagination to enrich their real life, but not so much that they prefer to live mainly in a fantasy world; at the same time to encourage them to learn, all through childhood, to be more and more realistic in recognizing their own motives, their responsibilities and their imperfections.

:: 9 ::

Conformist or Rebel?

In these days when there is so much discussion of youthful independence and protest, parents may be anxious, or at least curious, to know how these feelings of dissent develop. Parents may also want to know whether they can influence their child's future attitudes—in the direction of conformity or nonconformity, conservatism or radicalism.

I used to think on general principles—and perhaps from personal experience—that it was the youths who were held down by very strict parents during childhood who rebelled and became the radicals or the Bohemians. But studies of the young people who were leaders of the civil rights and anti-war movements show that this is not true in most cases.

The radical leaders generally were reared by parents who were relaxed in their discipline and who were politically liberal themselves. (This doesn't mean that all the children of liberal parents turn out to be radicals—only a few do; most of the rest probably become moderate liberals, and a small number even end up conservative.)

There is, of course, rebelliousness in strictly raised children too. They may become difficult or even defiant in adolescence. But later most of them come around to a conservative philosophy of life. They say, "I realize now what my parents were trying to accomplish, and I agree with their methods." (They mean they are satisfied with the way they turned out.)

There are plenty of exceptions to the general observation that liberal parents produce liberal and radical youths and that conservatives reproduce their own kind. Of course, there are many sides to conformity and to independence, and various mixtures are possible. A person can be conservative in his style of life and radical in his political views (as I am). A parent can be decidedly nonconformist in his religious views or personal appearance and yet be quite authoritarian in the raising of his child. There are inborn differences of temperament that head one child in the direction of amiable conformity and that prompt another child to fight with his parents all the way.

Different stages of development foster different attitudes. Almost all babies are cheerful conformists during their first year, in the sense that they take life as it comes and don't argue unless their parents are excessively interfering and dominating. But from one to three years of age they swing in the opposite direction. Then they are ready to object to almost anything—the foods they accepted before, their toilet training, the clothes their parents lay out for them in the morning.

Parents who are tactful find ways to present matters so that young children think they're making the decisions and thus remain generally cooperative. But when parents are unsure of their authority and always make demands in an overbearing manner, various outcomes are possible.

If parents really are determined, they may intimidate a gentle child into becoming a meek conformist. But if the child is of a more obstinate makeup or if, as is often the case nowadays, the parents vacillate—first directing the child too much and then, when the child irritably objects, dropping their requests—the results may be the opposite. This combination of parental prodding and backing away is likely to make for a particularly balky personality. Throughout life such an individual may argue with everyone and have a tendency to say no on all occasions. Politically she or he may end up anywhere on the spectrum, from an obstinate conservative to an obstinate radical.

In the three-to-six-year-old period children turn more

positively toward their parents. Boys realize that they will grow up to be men, and this makes them strive to do things the way their fathers do. Girls admiringly pattern themselves after their mothers. At this age children don't know the difference between radical and conservative.

But a daughter surely senses it if her mother plays a relatively docile role, and the girl will be inclined—to one degree or another—to take on the same manner. And if her mother is spunky and independent the daughter will then lean in that direction. If a father is plodding and exaggeratedly self-controlled, his son to some degree will take on that character. But if his father is determinedly eccentric or rebellious against authority, this will influence the boy too.

None of the foregoing examples means that any child turns into an exact replica of his parent. Inborn temperament, the closeness and the particular relationship between each child and each parent, all play a part in determining eventual character. But it is when the child is between three and six years of age that a parent's attitudes and manner have their strongest influence.

In the six-to-twelve-year-old period children again try to achieve some degree of inner independence from their parents by objecting to their parents' rules and by taking their peers as their models.

But it is in adolescence and youth that children have to labor much more strenuously than ever to complete the process of emancipation. They think that what they are resisting is their parents' determination to continue to control them and possess them. There may be some basis for this belief, but a much stronger force is the adolescents' own dependence on their parents. This has been their strongest tie throughout childhood, and it is extremely difficult to outgrow. (I remember a sixteen-year-old girl who complained to me constantly that her parents treated her like a little girl and denied her the freedom appropriate for her age. But her bitterest complaint was that when she came home from high school for lunch she sometimes found that her mother, on going out, had forgotten to prepare a sandwich for her and to pour her a glass of milk.)

An adolescent can't admit that part of her is clinging to childhood and dependence. She has to keep scrutinizing her parents' behavior for evidence of possessiveness or lack of confidence in her. Because she wants and needs to be freed from a slavish adherence to their standards and ideals (so that she can select her own), she is on the alert for signs of hypocrisy in her parents. If she can convince herself that they are not adhering to the standards they proclaim, then she is freed of the obligation to live by them.

So in order to grow up, all adolescents must rebel to one degree or another, in one way or another. (It is interesting that at this same time of life they tend to conform totally to the standards of their particular friends; when throwing off one dependence they must grasp another.)

What form rebellion takes in adolescence, how far it goes and whether it will subside soon or go on for years will depend on a number of factors—temperament, child-parent relationship, educational level. There is no way to predict the outcome.

Among groups that do not worry much about standards, education, or careers, the teen-ager may simply leave home permanently during an angry quarrel with parents; and that relieves a good part of his or her rebelliousness.

At the opposite extreme are the youths brought up in very polite families, with high educational and behavioral standards, who have to remain financially—and therefore psychologically—dependent on their parents well into adulthood. They may well control the impulse to storm out of their homes or to curse their parents or even to wear weird clothes. So their rebellion may have to take some subtle unconscious form of expression, like an inability to study or to turn in school papers.

Then there are all the in-between types of teen-agers who stay at home—more or less—and rebelliously irritate their parents with their hairdos or clothes or music or friendships or behavior with the opposite sex.

Often it is the young people from the tightest-knit families who fuss and fume the most and behave most eccentrically, because they have to struggle harder to overcome their dependence. And for the same reason their period of protest may last much longer.

Another factor about youthful rebellion that has impressed me, especially when I counsel families, is the degree to which it depends on the parents' self-assurance. If the parents know what they believe, have no embarrassment about expressing it and yet have no need to overcontrol their children (you might say that they respect themselves and their children), then youths have relatively little trouble in achieving independence without making their parents and themselves miserable.

But if the parents are afraid of irritating their children or are guilty that they haven't done a perfect job of raising them, their submissive attitude tempts their children to berate them in private and to embarrass them in the community. The more the parents accept this punishment (on the assumption that their children's behavior is all their fault), the guiltier the children feel unconsciously; they sense that young people should not get away with this abuse of well-intentioned parents; but the guiltier they feel, the worse they behave, in trying unconsciously to provoke their parents into curbing them.

Another aspect of the parents' self-assurance that affects the child's behavior is whether they have confidence that they can adequately control their children, which means confidence in themselves and in their children. If they have this confidence, their children will be inclined to respect them. But if the parents are always suspecting their children of the worst or jumping on them unnecessarily, the children will be difficult and badly behaved.

If all these variables I've discussed give you the idea that producing conformity or nonconformity in a child is a complex and unpredictable business, then you have the correct impression. There is no neat way in which you can definitely bring about one or the other attitude. But I've made at least one generalization here that should give you some comfort: Children tend to grow up with basic attitudes that are similar to those of their parents. And that's what most of us want as parents, whether we admit it or not.

At the end of this discussion I want to take a somewhat different direction. I suggest that, whatever the parents' own attitudes may be, they should not wish their child to grow up to be either a confirmed conformist or conservative, a confirmed nonconformist or radical. For there is often a rigidity—and to that extent a weakness—in these extreme positions. The individual who is excessively conventional in social outlook and behavior, or so conservative in political views that she or he is outraged by any talk of change, is really a frightened person, condemned to live an uneasy and somewhat unhappy life. For the world is always changing.

And the individual, let's say a woman, who must always dress in a bizarre manner or run her home and family in outlandish ways that irritate her neighbors is, at the least, a bit of a nuisance and is a captive of her own compulsion. The man who is so dogmatically radical that he can always be counted on to disapprove sourly of everything that is happening in the country is not only a bore but is usually the person who is not effective in bringing about change for the better.

I think that valuable citizens are somewhere in between. They should be inwardly secure enough not to feel threatened by changes in life-style (such as the hippie appearance and philosophy) or by reasonable proposals for political and social change. They should be able to work actively for a

cause such as the environment or civil rights when they have
been convinced that there is peril or injustice. They are freer
than those at either end of the spectrum to respond to the
realities—human and material—that surround them.

This secure personality in children is produced by parents
who not only avoid some of the specific traps I've discussed
here but who also establish a generally loving and respectful
relationship between themselves and their children. This is
what all parents should try to do anyway, whatever their
views.

:: **10** ::

Grief Needs To Be Felt and Expressed

Death means different things to different children, depending on their age, whether someone they know has died, how
close they were to him, their parents' religious beliefs.

We can learn something about the capacity for grief in
very small children if we will think of situations in which they
are merely separated temporarily from their parents. Even
at six months of age a baby (let's assume throughout this
discussion that the bereaved child is a girl), will be depressed
for a while if her parents go away, and her recovery will
depend on the parents' prompt return or on her acquiring
loving substitutes. At one and a half years a child will sadly
miss any absent member of the household, let's say the
mother, speak her name, go to her room or to her picture.
If it was the person who took most of the care of her, the child
may also show symptoms of anxiety, as if she already realizes
the desperateness of her dependence at this age. By two or
two and a half a child in a hospital is very clear about the
cause of her anxiety and grief. She keeps wailing, "I want my

mommy." If she sees another child crying, she explains insistently to the nurse, "He wants his mommy."

Children in the three-to-six-year-old period understand a lot more. They can be partially reassured when a parent is just temporarily absent. They insist on knowing what death is if they hear it referred to. They have progressed from a dependent love to one that is also warmly outgoing. So when a member of the family dies, a father or grandfather, for example, a child misses him as a whole and well-appreciated person. She can express her sorrow in words occasionally and she can define her anxious questions in words. This ability to communicate is a great comfort. On the other hand, her mind is now much more complex. She has a vivid imagination that easily turns morbid. And she can suppress her feelings to a remarkable degree or disguise them. At this age a child who has had no experience with death will become worried about the idea of death, just because of her curiosity and fearfulness.

By the time a child gets beyond the age of six she is apt to be more realistic and to have more control over her feelings. With the help of her parents and friends and her religion, she has probably figured out some explanation of what happens to one after death. Whatever her beliefs about the soul, she probably faces the reality that the body has no feelings after death. She would be distressed at the possibility of the death of her parents but she knows by now that someone would take care of her, and she might even ask who it would be.

Psychiatrists have learned, through working with adults and children with various kinds of personalities and grief reactions, that whenever a loved parent, brother, friend, or even a pet dies, there is a deep sense of loss that cannot be evaded or patched up quickly. An aching void exists that will only heal gradually over the months as new attachments and interests partially replace the old. It isn't true that the small child who hardly seems to notice the loss hasn't felt it, or that the mother who remains cheerfully considerate of everyone else, or the boy or man with the stiff upper lip, has somehow escaped the blow. A person may, by keeping distracted, postpone the mourning for a while. Or she may build up such a strong dam to hold back the grief and other feelings that she has little conscious awareness of them. Sometimes they may break out again in disguised forms, as in angriness toward inappropriate people, or in phobias or compulsions. When a person manages to suppress her grief altogether she may be unable to feel emotions of other kinds either. For instance, as the months and years go by she may be unconsciously afraid to love anyone deeply because of the risk of being deprived again.

The natural way to respond to the death of a loved person is to grieve—not just for a day or two but for the weeks and months that must pass before the sense of loss has had time to heal. That is to say, the loss has to be faced and eventually mastered.

The tendency of kind parents may be to try to protect their child from the pain of the death of a relative by speaking of him only rarely and by keeping up a cheerful front. But if the child has loved the relative, the only way she can recover from the loss is to mourn. Parents will sometimes attempt to ease a child's grief over the loss of a pet by quickly giving her another. But this implies that the love and the pet are of little significance, a view the child will not really accept. All this is not to say that mourning must go on all day, every day. The normal pattern, for children and adults, is to be distracted a good part of the time by the everyday business of living and occasionally even by pleasant matters. Then some association brings them back to the loss of the beloved. No one can tolerate a constant grief (except the mentally ill person with a deep depression who cannot escape it); it must be coped with bit by bit, usually in the company of other sympathetic family members. Parents can set the example for the children by speaking of their own recollections and sadness when these come over them.

A death in the family involves another emotion that many parents wouldn't think of but that psychiatrists have to deal with often. This is guilt. A young child is apt to feel—unconsciously, at least—that she bears some of the responsibility for the death of a brother (or sister or parent). This is based on magical (superstitious) thinking. The child was sometimes angry at the brother and wished that something bad would happen to him. Then if a death occurs (or illness or accident), her conscience tells her that she willed it. Another reason children accuse themselves is that parents frequently blame illness on bad behavior. Colds are said to come from not wearing rubbers or from staying in the water too long. Skates on the stairs cause broken bones. Mother's headache is due to children's quarreling. It is not that a child will accuse herself in words. The sense of guilt may be largely buried in the unconscious layers of her mind.

Parents should keep the possibility of guilt in mind so that they can recognize traces of it and help to counteract it. It's important during the illness or after the death of a member of the family to make clear to the children what the real cause is. We tend to forget, during those tense days, that the children may have been given no satisfactory explanation. It has to be at the children's level of understanding, of course, not one that will mystify them further. (For instance, "Cancer is a special kind of lump—in an old person, usually—that grows and grows for months, we don't know why, and makes a person feel more and more tired and sick until he dies." "We call it a heart attack when a person grows old and the tubes that carry the blood to his heart muscles get so plugged up inside, like a rusty pipe, that no blood can get through." "A stroke often comes from the same rusty-pipe problem, but in the blood vessels of the head.") Another way to counteract guilt is to keep the memory of the child or parent who died from becoming too sanctified. The natural tendency is to try to recall only the ideal qualities, but this makes the children feel particularly evil for having had mean thoughts or done unkind things occasionally. It's sensible for the parent to recall at times—not resentfully, but understandingly—that the one who died had faults like all of us: "Daddy really had a temper, didn't he?" "Do you remember how selfish Joan was about her dolls?"

By about three or three and a half years of age, any child is apt to develop a sudden worrisome curiosity about death, even though there has been no death of a relative or friend. Her attention may be caught by a dead bird, a funeral, a graveyard, or an adult conversation about death. Sensing what a drastic state it is, she anxiously wants to know just what it would feel like to die, to be buried, to be separated in this way from one's family. This readiness to take death very personally is just one example of the small child's remarkable capacity to identify with other people. This is the principal way in which she grows emotionally and learns about life in this three-to-six-year-old period. It is this empathy with the feelings of others that enables her to grasp both the pleasant and the fearsome aspects of life.

The child of three or four usually wants to know first what *dead* means. Partly she wonders if it feels agonizing in some way. I think the answer, both for parents who do and parents who don't believe in life after death, is that the body doesn't feel anything any more; it doesn't breathe; the heart doesn't beat. This takes away some of the unnecessary fear that the condition of death itself is painful or that burial involves claustrophobia. Parents with a conviction about heaven fortunately can speak about the soul having a good life close to God and about an eventual reunion of the entire family. But I believe that parents who do not have this belief can honestly comfort the child a little by explaining how the spirit of a person lives on in other people's fond memories, and in the kindness and good work he leaves behind. If a child asks whether the same body ever comes back to life on earth, the answer should be an honest no.

When the child asks whether she has to die, she should be told yes, that all people have to die, but usually not until they are very old and tired and don't mind so much. In making points like these, it's good if parents can be serious and honest, but unafraid. To try to be excessively reassuring only arouses suspicion, as we all should know. On the other hand, if the parents try to act quite unconcerned about death, this encourages the child to begin the process of denying her own feelings, which may later make her a more difficult person to live with, for her future family and for herself.

When a child asks whether her parents will die someday, she is thinking primarily of her great dependence on them. They have to admit that they will, though not for a long, long time, until they are very old. It is important to remind the child that by then she will be a grown-up woman with a husband and children, so she won't need parents to take care of her any more.

While we are discussing questions and answers, I want to get back to the general importance of keeping communication open between children and parents. This is partly so that children will not bottle up their feelings and so that they and their parents can comfort each other in sharing their grief. It is also to try to keep the children from developing fantasies about death that are worse than the reality. Even the experienced parent or professional person is being constantly surprised anew by children's misinterpretations. This is particularly true of those under six, but older ones can form weird ideas too. It is not rare for a small child to come to the angry conclusion that one parent's death was caused somehow by the other. Talk of the body can make a child assume that the head is missing. A six-year-old boy fed on television violence may assume that most deaths are due to foul play. Children (like some adults) may think that a person could easily be buried alive.

Should a child go to a funeral? Should he see the body if the coffin is open? I and many parents, I think, feel that for a child to view a body would be unnecessarily frightening at his inexperienced, sensitive stage. This is even hard on many adults. Families have different views about children's attending funerals. I think it would be unwise to take a young child to the funeral of someone he did not know well, because it would stir up distress that had no point. But if a member of the family close to the child has died and if it seems the right thing to the parents, the funeral may even be consoling and inspiring. The sight of all the friends paying their respects and the beauty of the service may enable the child of over three years to see the dignity of death, its relationship to the life that has been well lived and the love that obviously continues on in the friends.

:: 11 ::

Respect for Children

Some parents teach young children to talk about having a girl friend or a boy friend; or urge them in the junior-high-school years to play kissing games or have dates, long before they have the depth of feeling to love seriously; or joke about their children's infatuations as soon as they begin to experience them; or ask them to tell what happened during their dates. In these games the somewhat jaded parents are looking for a bit of vicarious excitement in their children's romances or pseudoromances.

What's the harm? I believe that a child is meant to progress spiritually from infancy to adulthood by one small step at a time. A girl becomes aware of romantic love at three, four, and five years, when she develops an intense adoration of her father. There is nothing humorous or make-believe about this love. It is touchingly sincere and idealistic. Then because of complicated factors in emotional development she must sternly suppress this romantic quest for about six or seven years. The energy that went into it is now diverted and sublimated into impersonal interests such as school learning, nature, science, and tales of heroism. The stricter the standards and ideals of her parents, the more strictly will her romantic and sexual interests be repressed. But even in adolescence, when glandular pressures bring her face to face with the opposite sex in the most turbulent way, the idealism and restraint about love that she has acquired all along from her family will still be exerting powerful influences. It will imbue her devotion to her beloved and her eventual spouse with tenderness, spirituality. It also will continue to provide the main power for her ambition to study and plan for her life work and to pursue it at the most idealistic level.

When a child's upbringing is of this kind, she maintains into adulthood an underlying respect for her parents (even though she may be criticizing them a lot on the surface in her teens), a sense of awe and idealism about love, and a natural dignity in being herself.

In a similar way a small boy develops an intensely romantic attachment to his mother. This is later repressed and transmuted into impersonal, intellectual drives. But in adolescence, when his glands demand that he pay attention to girls again his attitude toward them is imbued with idealism because of his earlier attachment to his mother and the fact that it then had to be repressed and disguised.

At the other end of the scale are the parents who have no particular standards for themselves or ambitions for their children. In these families the romantic and sexual drives of early childhood do not become much diverted into studying, curiosity about the universe, ambition to go far in a constructive or creative field. Instead, sexuality remains a more direct interest throughout childhood, and is expressed as relatively uninhibited and undiscriminating sexual activity from the beginning of adolescence.

So when parents, for their own enjoyment, invite a young child to mimic adult romance they are, at least to a slight degree, cheapening love and diminishing the idealism that their child would have had to invest in his future marriage and career.

There are other types of sentimental exploitation of children. Some parents—more often mothers and grandmothers —cherish babyishness in children. They may go into spasms of delight when a three- or four-year-old girl talks baby talk. They may enjoy seeing a little girl self-consciously showing off in public.

By now you have realized that my brother and sisters and I were brought up by parents who had a horror of cheap romance and baby talk and showing off. When one of us tried to play up to strangers we were sternly admonished, "Don't be a hotel child!" The reference was to the little girl with very artificial curls and fancy clothes who is sometimes seen mincing around the lobby, looking for attention.

To show that I don't imply criticism just of mothers, I'll mention next the father who is so enamored of his daughter —both as a dependent child and as an appealing, small cutie of the opposite sex—that he calls her, "Daddy's little Sweety-kins," and is constantly caressing her, if only with his eyes and tone of voice. It's good for any daughter to know that her father has a special affection for her just because she's a girl; boys get a similar assurance from their mothers. But when a father is too syrupy and cuddly (he owes this kind of ardor to his wife), it's apt to interfere with his daughter's emotional growth and her readiness later to love someone her own age.

A masculine mistake of quite a different kind is when fathers become overinvolved in Little League athletics. I think a majority of professionals in the children's sphere would agree that the level of athletics into which boys themselves feel drawn, beginning somewhere around ten to fourteen years of age, and in which the motivation is a wholesome mixture of fun, competition, and the wish to become skillful, is good for boys. It is also helpful to include an adult who can supervise and referee, as long as he is well liked by boys and sees the game as an enjoyable way of inspiring some sportsmanship and skill. But I think the whole business becomes at least mildly detrimental when fathers or teachers take over, become tense, push the kids beyond their natural inclination, make them feel ashamed when they make errors, give them the conviction that winning is all-important, feature the star players, and neglect those with little skill.

Here's quite another type of exploitation that is becoming commoner as the importance of intelligence and education keeps increasing. I occasionally receive a letter from a mother giving me evidence that her child's intelligence is at the genius level and offering to submit the child to me or other professionals to investigate, test, write up in a professional or popular journal, perhaps recommend for very special schooling. And there have always been lots of parents who are boasting of their children's intellect or their school and college triumphs. It's natural for parents to be proud of any good attribute of a child, whether it's musical or athletic ability, attractive appearance, affectionateness. But when they persistently single out a trait like brilliance for assertive glorification, they are showing a rather egotistical pride in one characteristic for which they are really taking the credit themselves and a lack of appreciation and respect for the child as a whole. It is not only that a child needs to feel loved as a whole person; it is the whole—not a part—that will determine the individual's success and happiness in life.

Once in a while I hear of a situation in which a child, let's say a girl, whom the parents had cherished greatly died and another girl, born subsequently and resembling the first, was named after her and expected to become just like her. This puts an impossible burden on the younger child, not only because no child can be turned into another but also because she will feel somewhat rejected by her parents when she fails to conform.

A sort of exploitation that's not serious in itself is the calling of twins by names that sound almost the same—Ronald and Donald, for instance, or Ellen and Helen. Parents use similar names to emphasize the fact that the children are twins, a phenomenon that fascinates the whole world and that the parents can't help but be proud of. Yet it clearly has no advantage for the twins; in fact, it must be a terrible nuisance because they—and everybody else—will constantly have trouble trying to make out which is being spoken to. Since everyone wants to make a fuss over twins and lump them together and since the problem of so many twins is in ever becoming sufficiently independent of each other, I think that respect for the two individuals should consist in encouraging them gently to be as separate as they are willing to be.

I imagine that a majority of readers will disagree with at least some of the points I've been making. They'll feel that I make mountains out of molehills or am an old scold. It will depend on how strictly a parent was brought up and whether he now wants to use the same methods. There is no one right way to rear children. There are millions of ways of rearing children, and as a result all children turn out differently.

A critic of my position could point out that in one sense all children are exploited by their parents for the parents' satisfaction. That is to say, all parents yearn to have their children be more or less like themselves—in standards and tastes—and mold them constantly in this pursuit. Is this very different from the other examples of exploitation I've been discussing? I agree that the difference is relative. I think it is not only permissible but really desirable for parents to want to see their child turn out like themselves, provided they are thinking in terms of giving the child a character that will adjust him or her happily and successfully to life as they envision it. I have only been pointing out situations in which parents can be on guard against grasping for transitory satisfactions at certain stages of their children's development, and keep their eyes on their children's long-range success.

Chapter III

Teaching Beliefs
and Ideals

:: 12 ::

Idealism Is As Real
As Materialism

There are lots of people nowadays who lack belief in a religion or in a set of values or even in themselves. They assume, because they have no faith in a religion, that there is no real basis for man to be idealistic or spiritual in outlook; they make remarks such as "Sex, after all, is just a matter of glands," or "When a person thinks he's doing something for charity he's really only gratifying his ego." Even among churchgoers there are quite a few who are ready to admit, since their religions were formulated thousands of years ago, before biology, psychology, and sociology revolutionized our ideas about man's motivations, that there is no assurance that any of the old beliefs about man's spiritual nature are correct.

It's not that we are disenchanted about the physical aspects of our civilization. We are proud of the cars and rockets and artificial heart valves we've created. But we have lost much of our belief in the dignity of man. I'll list a number of examples of what I mean. No one of them by itself proves

75

much. There are great dissimilarities between them. But I think there is a common denominator, a thread that runs through all.

The trend probably set in early in the twentieth century, but it became obvious in the wave of disillusionment that swept over many writers, artists, and other intellectuals after World War I. In the 1920s there began the determined debunking of history; writers emphasized the stupid, ridiculous or immoral sides of our heroes. Novels and plays at first became more boldly realistic; in more recent years they have gone on to stress the crude, animal aspects of men and women, as if to say, "This is what people are really like. The nobler images of the past were shams." A recent play that was much admired was composed largely of a husband's and wife's contemptuous revelations of each other's repulsive characteristics.

Adolescents have always responded the most wholeheartedly to the romantic, idealistic aspects of love. Today they are the most sceptical about such matters. Marriage for a lot of people has lost its former meaning of a lifelong mutual devotion. They say, "You can always get a divorce if it doesn't work."

Painting used to show mostly people who were good to look at. Now it has turned increasingly to abstractions; but when it shows human beings, they are ugly or distorted.

Music that serious people compose or listen to has shifted from consonance to dissonance, as if only the unsweet or harsher sounds were meaningful now.

Modern choreographers are apt to shy away from movements that express grace, preferring what in the past would have been called angry or awkward.

In none of these fields am I judging the excellence of the art or saying that what was previous was better. All arts must keep developing or die. I'm only pointing out the common denominator of disbelief in or scorn for the qualities that used to be considered the worthier aspects of man.

People express their regard for those they associate with —and also for themselves—by their clothes, grooming, manners. Since the Victorian age there has been a progressive retreat from formality. More recently there have appeared a pointed disregard for the impression made on others and, at the same time, a disparagement of self.

People's decreased respect for themselves is due partly, I think, to what you might call a sense of having lost their souls. They used to consider themselves unique beings whom God had created somewhat in His image. Some of the respect they had for God they also felt for themselves as God's special creation. But science has made many people feel that they are only slightly different from monkeys and rats, that they are really animals who respond mechanically to sensations and hormones and memories, who fashion their own ethics and deities, as they do their shelters, not out of any inspiration but in accordance with the physical circumstances of local existence.

Another, indirect cause for lack of self-respect may be the superhuman capabilities of our new machines. There is nothing about men and women that seems equally impressive.

Still another factor in a pioneering country like America, I think, is the lack of awe for the older generation and its values. In other parts of the world not only do children feel deep respect for their parents and an allegiance to their parents' convictions, but also the parents go right on revering the grandparents. In America the father says, "Son, if you don't do better than I've done, I won't think much of you." This upside-down deference of the parents toward the children makes for geniality between the generations and for rapid innovation and material progress. But youths today develop merely an affectionate regard for their parents' character and a tolerance for their old-fashioned ideas; when they in turn become adults, they look for no particular respect—from their children or from themselves.

The fact that the Victorian age set such foolishly artificial, stuffy standards of propriety may be another reason why succeeding generations have spurned dignity with such vehemence. Even words like *propriety* and *decorum* set our teeth on edge today.

One reason I feel sad for the various doubters and cynics is that it is easier for people to live serene lives and raise wholesome children if they have definite religious or philosophical convictions. I mean that human beings are believing animals just as much as they are reasoning animals and are apt to feel let down when they lack a basis for belief. Actually, many of the agnostics and hesitant believers are groping today for a deeper meaning to existence. I've been impressed with the way university students and faculty members will fill an auditorium to listen to a renowned mystic, theologian, or philosopher.

But the more important reason I feel sad for people without beliefs is that I think their doubts are based on lopsided concepts of our species, concepts that focus on our crude instincts, our psychological weaknesses, our sheeplike social traits. It is a view which emphasizes our relationship with lower animals—which certainly exists—but which ignores the elements that make us so very different from other species.

I'd put it that human beings are extraordinary, first, in being born with a nature prepared to form high spiritual ideals—such as a courageous loyalty, a romantic, tender love, a dedication to all humanity—which may carry them to great achievement; second, in being able to create forms of art—buildings, gardens, paintings, literature, music, dress, manners, ceremonies—which will give them pleasure and inspire them to live life on a more challenging, rewarding plane. This is exactly how human beings have built civilization.

The original source of these ideals and creations is the

fantastic capacity of young children (particularly between three and six) to adore, be inspired by, and pattern themselves after their parents—not the parents as they really are, but glorified. They believe their parents are the handsomest, wisest, most omnipotent people in the world, and certainly the most attractive. They yearn to be like them in all respects —in occupation, in manner and in having babies of their own. Because they are so very aware at this dependent age of how much their parents' love means to them, they are now inspired with a similar capacity to love others generously. Out of this will eventually grow their devotion to their own children and their altruism toward humanity. (Those unfortunate children who receive no love have none to give— ever.)

Everyone can see that little girls want to play at being mothers and boys play at being fathers. They use a doll or a younger child for the role of baby. Little girls dream and talk, in our uninhibited country, about growing babies inside themselves. It's not as commonly realized that boys at three and four and five eagerly want to perform exactly the same miracle of creation, though a majority of them never state it openly. If they do express the wish and their parents tell them that this is impossible, they will typically refuse to accept the reality for many months, insisting that they can do it if they want to. (We believe that this male envy of the female's creativity is the explanation of the strange custom in some parts of the world called "couvade." When a young woman goes into labor and is taken to the labor hut to be attended by the other women, her husband goes into labor too. He is taken to another special hut, where his men friends hold his hands and sympathize with him while he writhes in apparent pain.) As the little boy grows older he is gradually forced to face the fact that he cannot grow a baby. But we believe that the intense desire to create then seeks other substitute outlets, such as building structures, drawing pictures, composing stories, inventing machines.

A boy in the three-to-six-year-old period idolizes his father as the particular model to be copied in all respects. He spends all day—in his play activity and in his manner—pretending to be his father. At the same time he develops an intense romantic attachment to his mother and idolizes her as his feminine ideal. As such she will strongly influence his choice of a wife when he grows up. This is the age when interest in being married, curiosity about sex and sex play are fairly common, even in the most properly brought up children.

But the boy's possessive love for his mother results, we believe, in an increasing sense of rivalry with his father in the deeper levels of his mind. He fears, with childish logic, that his father is correspondingly resentful of him, and he develops quite an awe of him. (On the surface he continues to get along well with him.) His uneasiness about his father's presumed resentment keeps increasing, and eventually makes him come to repress and deny his possessive love for his mother. There is a real reversal of feeling for his mother—from romantic attraction to romantic aversion—which mounts in intensity from about five to nine years of age and finally makes him leery of all members of the opposite sex. He squirms when his mother tries to kiss him, he groans at love stories on television and in movies, he makes a great point of scorning all girls. But most important of all, this temporary aversion to romance and sex, we believe, is what now makes him turn—with relief and special pleasure—toward impersonal interests such as reading, writing, arithmetic, science, nature. In other words, this is why children are emotionally ready for schoolwork at about six years. This is the emotional basis for intellectual curiosity.

The boy's sense of alienation from his father makes him look instead to heroes of history and fiction and the comics for his idols. It also makes him turn to teachers, to government officials and to God as the highest sources of authority, displacing his father, to a degree. It readies him, that is, for his religious life and for his law-abiding existence as a citizen in a democracy.

Developments in the girl are comparable. In the three-to-six-year-old period she pays her admired mother the great compliment of imitating her all day long, and she forms a romantic and possessive attachment to her father. But in the resulting rivalry with her mother she does not feel the degree of awe that the boy does for his father. Therefore she is not compelled to renounce so much of her physical affectionateness for her father or so much of her natural direct feelings for people in general. But she too becomes fascinated with the 3 Rs, nature, and science.

The emotional development of our species up to the age of five or six is not, in one sense, basically different from that of the higher animals. Like them we love and depend on our parents, learn most of what we know by imitating them. What distinguishes us so sharply from other creatures is the characteristics we acquire after five: our inhibition and sublimation of sexuality, our capacity for abstract thinking, our interest in systems and rules, our inventiveness and creativity, our capacity for being inspired by heroes and spiritual ideals, our urge throughout history and in all lands to define and worship a God. To a great degree these all are outgrowths of the two special kinds of love we feel for our two parents. And it is fascinating that these particularly human characteristics are brought out in us, after the age of five or six, by our having to relinquish our possessive yearning for one parent because of fear of rivalry with the other.

The glandular changes of adolescence force the boy and girl to become abruptly aware of sexuality again. Its pressure is intense. But much of it is still held in check and then transformed into idealistic channels. There will be a continuing investment of some of that energy into studying, into cultural, religious, humanitarian, and creative interests.

The boy's romantic adoration of his mother and the girl's of her father, suppressed for years, veiled, disembodied, now lends mystery and spirituality to their awakening love for young people their own age. Many of them are reluctant at first to recognize their own sexual feelings, especially toward those for whom they feel tenderness and respect, though this taboo lessens with time. They yearn to take care of their beloveds, please them, put them on pedestals, accomplish wonders for them.

This idealization of the opposite sex is a source of further inspiration. It combines with the human drive to create; and these two forces are the source of our poetry, novels, plays, music, painting, sculpture. (Dante was inspired to write the greatest poetry of all time by his lifelong devotion to Beatrice, a woman he had only seen, never known.) In more subtle disguise the combination of idealism and creativity stirs people to design buildings and bridges and machines, to pursue the sciences, to make technical advances.

The glandular and growth changes of adolescence also revive the child's rivalry with the parent of the same sex and raise it to new heights of intensity. This is the cause of the rebelliousness which strains family life at this age but which is necessary to make the young person want to leave home and become independent. Most constructively, this rivalry with the parent provides the power behind the human being's impatient drive to make changes in the world—to put an end to injustice, to introduce reforms, to accomplish goals more effectively, to discover new truths that supersede old concepts.

In adulthood a man's and woman's tendency to idealize certain people, just as they idealized their parents in childhood, is what inspires these admired people to rise to greater heights than they otherwise could have achieved. It is the trust of the multitude which buoys a leader to further greatness. When our spouses, friends, or associates admire our skills and qualities, we are inspired to do better.

In a sense, then, all the beauty and progress in civilization that human beings have contrived, and the nobility they have achieved in their relationships with their fellow beings have sprung from the aspirations kindled in them by their trusting, ingenuous, unrealistic idealization of their two parents in early childhood.

To summarize this more briefly still, we can build a magnificent reality in adulthood out of what was only an illusion in early childhood. This is the extraordinary power of our species. And this is what parents can foster.

The capacity for intellectual development, idealism, creativity, and spirituality is latent in all young children. But they will maintain high aspirations through childhood and into adulthood only if their parents set a good example and high standards. If the parents live only at the level of their bodily needs, even though law-abidingly, their three-year-old children's idealization of them will gradually shrink down over the years to life size and provide the children with little inspiration to go beyond their parents' level. If the parents don't exert any inhibition over their own sexuality or their children's, as happens occasionally in delinquent families here and in a few primitive spots around the world, there will be no interest in their children in learning, in discovering, in building, in advancement.

How, specifically, can parents go about fostering idealism and spiritual convictions in their child? This is a crucial question in our time.

Of course, what influences children most of all is the parents' manner and attitude toward each other. This doesn't mean that all is lost each time there is a quarrel. What is important is that after disagreements (and during, if possible) the parents show that they still respect each other and have pride in their marriage. (It's fatally easy, as a marriage wears on, to fall into the habit of bickering or sarcasm or provocation.) They can let it be evident that they have clear-cut standards by which they themselves live and to which they expect their children to conform. They don't have to be stern in setting these standards, only definite.

Parents can reveal their admiration for their own heroes —whether heroes of fiction or of history or of the present day —and their admiration for such qualities as altruism, courage, loyalty, perseverence, learnedness, or whatever else they esteem. To put it another way: In an age when it's the style among many to appear cynical, it's wise to avoid teaching such an attitude thoughtlessly to children.

Parents can always show, in their own appearance, dress, and manners, that they take pride in themselves as well as treat others with courtesy. This helps their own morale and also sets the tone for their children. They can be sure that their children dress for whatever the occasion is—which doesn't mean to overdress. (I even believe that children should be expected to keep their rooms orderly, for the sake of everyone's spirits.)

It's crucial that parents always require politeness and consideration for themselves from their children. This can't be taught, of course, unless the parents reciprocate. But parental politeness to their children does not mean parental submissiveness to them. There is a profound difference between them.

At most family dinner tables there is discussion of the news of the world and the neighborhood, which sometimes includes the questionable behavior or attitudes of real people —strangers, acquaintances, adults, children. Parents, in making their comments, can resist the temptation to play the cynic. They can show their conviction that the most enduring satisfactions in life come from serving others and from spiritual and creative pursuits without having to be pompous.

Reading aloud to children until they can read fluently to themselves is one of the most powerful ways to stimulate them to be studious and imaginative. If the stories are idealistic, they arouse corresponding aspirations in the children.

As children learn to read to themselves, and to develop tastes in comics and television, it is important for parents to watch their selections and encourage those that respect the moral and spiritual sides of humanity, even though such stories may be oversimplified for children and have villains in them. The parents should forbid stories and shows that glorify or dwell on brutality.

Adolescents are intensely sensitive to the estimation of others. On the surface they show their great concern to please their own group. Underneath they are still looking for guidance from their parents and other respected adults, though they cannot admit this to their parents or even to themselves.

Parents should be respectful of their son's and daughter's inhibitions about sexuality and their inclination to idealize the opposite sex.

The romantic interests of adolescents brought up with high standards will at first be half paralyzed with shyness and almost blinded with idealism. The objects of their early infatuation are often inappropriate (overestimation again), but their feeling of love is just as poignant at the time as love can ever be. Parents ought to repress any inclination to tease, to make fun of their children's loves. On the other hand, I believe parents shouldn't push early dating or suggest kissing games at parties, which cheapen love by encouraging its physical expression before children are mature enough to love truly.

Though adolescence is usually the most idealistic age period, there also may be plenty of expressions of disenchantment. Young people are trying to outgrow their dependence on their parents and find their own identities, so they want to discover characteristics and ideas of their parents about which they can feel critical or disillusioned.

There's evidence that the job of adolescents and youths is easier if the parents have no hesitation in expressing their own beliefs and telling their children what behavior they would like from them as long as they live at home, whether or not they are willing to comply. Young people are not really bothered by such definiteness—far from it. They may come around, sooner or later, to some of their parents' views and reject others. In either case, it helps them to steer their own course if they can see their parents' standards.

:: 13 ::

Child Psychology Can't Substitute for Morality

Juvenile delinquency has increased markedly since World War II. So has the prevalence of venereal disease in adolescents. Illegitimate births have tripled. Youths from well-to-do families have gone out to steal or destroy property for excitement.

I don't think that the picture is predominantly dark. A great majority of young people behave responsibly. There are many more serious students in high school and college and graduate school than there have ever been before. Tens of thousands have risked jail in working against discrimination and an illegal war. But I don't believe we can shrug off the signs of trouble.

A lowering of standards of behavior in children presumably reflects either the same process in adults or at least a great uncertainty in parents about what the standards should be. I'm sure that the factors responsible are many and complex.

A basic one has been the increasing acceptance of a scientific and naturalistic view of man's place in the world, and a weakening of the authority of religion, discussed in the last chapter. Another factor has been the prosperity of the past thirty years; it is unfortunately true that human beings generally behave better in adversity than in affluence.

In any case, I want to single out for discussion now certain ideas current in child psychology in the past generation or two that I think have made trouble for parents in their teaching of morality, because parents have accepted them too literally. The concept that children naturally want to be good and will grow up right if they only have parents who show them the right kind of love has made parents feel it was their fault, not the children's whenever the children misbehaved. There's been the fear—mistaken, in most cases—that if a parent is strict, the children will not love her or him or will be traumatized. There is the oversimplified belief that sexuality is just a wholesome instinct that should not be repressed too severely. There has been the strong American emphasis on social adjustment, which some parents have interpreted to mean that when in any doubt they had better let their children go along with the crowd. There's been the reassuring principle, generally but not always true, that children will absorb their parents' moral standards just by living with them, without having to be preached at all the time. Reinforcing these new concepts has been the drive, which has persisted since the turn of the century, to throw out the prudery, the stuffiness, the insincerity, of the Victorian period.

The emphasis in child rearing in the past fifty years has been so heavily on the psychological factors that it has almost crowded the moral aspects out of sight. The effect of all this has been to make many parents doubt their own standards and to dilute them—quite drastically—as they have passed them on to their children.

Some manifestations of current moral attitudes are ambiguous. For instance, surveys indicate that quite a large percentage of young people consider it not very wrong to cheat on school and college examinations. Many people feel that it is all right to cheat large institutions such as the government and insurance companies. Yet person-to-person honesty and considerateness are still highly valued. Young people in fraternities and sororities, for instance, have had the courage and humanity to end racial discrimination, which most of their parents and grandparents accepted quite smugly. Adults in small, stable communities will still go a long way to be helpful and generous to neighbors in trouble. Service clubs strive for the same spirit downtown.

This contrast indicates, I believe, that the units of industry and government have become too large and too powerful, by far! They don't just make people feel small and insignificant and subtly resentful. They effectively control people's lives, without giving people any compensatory control over them. In small towns and rural communities, morality is quite personal because everyone knows almost everyone else.)

My belief is that some parents have lowered, too abruptly, their expectations of how children should behave, partly in response to the idea that since our species is closely related to other animals we should not be held to arbitrarily high standards of behavior, but mainly due to new psychological concepts that have been lopsided, incomplete, incompletely understood, or one-sidedly applied.

But I think that the underlying convictions of most citizens have not changed as much as the lowered surface standards would indicate. As a result there is a cruel discrepancy, for young people who transgress, between the tolerant attitude they believe exists and the reality. The girl who has an illegitimate child or the boy who gets caught in vandalism finds that our customs and laws and a majority of our citizens are almost as stern as they used to be.

The most impressive evidence that standards have slipped in a maladaptive way comes from guidance clinics. The increasing numbers of children who are growing up in families of reasonably high standards but with too little restraint, too little sense of moral obligation, are likely to be miserable in childhood, to get into trouble in adolescence, and to be unhappy and ineffectual in adulthood.

It is the nature of man, when he grows up in a stable family in almost any culture, to want to share in the aspirations of his community, to cooperate in its work, to have its approval. Conscientious parents have always tried to teach these attitudes. When this rearing process fails to work right, when individuals turn out as adults to lack a sense of direction or to be impulsive and irresponsible, there is distress in them—though they may deny it—and in those who are close to them.

Parents often find it particularly difficult nowadays to know how much direction to give their children about sexual matters. In this respect it is helpful to keep in mind that sexuality is not a simple instinct in human beings at all. Its roots are strong and primitive. It is molded by the parents' sense of propriety, by the idealized image that children gain of their parents, and by the ideals the parents teach specifically. In this elaborate process a great part of the sexual longing is transmuted into such spiritual attitudes as tenderness, altruism, marital devotion, love of children, creativity in the arts and sciences, and even of the drive to study.

Good parents should stop worrying, I feel, about whether the strictness of their standards will alienate their children's love or cause maladjustment. Children are made more comfortable in having been kept from wrongdoing or in paying for it. Underneath, they feel grateful to their parents. Naturally they won't say thank you; they grumble or sulk temporarily; but this doesn't mean they have been disciplined unwisely. All children, being lawyers at heart, will experiment once or twice with trying to make parents feel guilty for some disapproval or punishment. If the parents are unable to fend off such a reproach, children will surely bombard them with more—not because they are ruthless but because they can shield themselves in this way from guilt.

I'm not assuming that there is only one right set of morals. Morals will always be quite different in different countries, at different social levels even in the same community, and somewhat different in every family. I'm only encouraging parents to be clear and firm in passing on the set of morals and ethics which they themselves believe in.

Though it's true that children who are loved want to be good, they are also tempted frequently to get off the narrow path. They need to be reminded regularly of what is expected, and corrected when they have misbehaved. If their parents feel the guilt themselves instead of making their children feel it, the children will be stimulated to create more trouble the next time and the next.

We have learned in child guidance work that parents are often more tolerant toward one child than another; they will be surprisingly lax in what they expect of one child without being consciously aware of this. So different children in the same family may end up with different morals. Therefore it clarifies matters—for the parents as well as for their children —when they speak explicitly of the standards and behavior they expect. I'm quite convinced that not only the best-behaved children but also the happiest and most successful ones are those whose parents present their beliefs unequivocally and leave no doubt that they expect their children to live up to them. I don't mean stern parents. I mean affectionate but firm parents.

At the top of the list of expectations, if it were my children, I'd put a strong sense of obligation to be helpful, generous, honest, and gracious—not only toward the people they'll know but also to those they won't know.

Children of one year should be kept from biting their parents or pulling their hair. By two they should, for example, be helping the parent to pick up their things, run small errands, say thank you. By three they could help with table setting. By four they could lend a hand with the dishes and the yard work and be making their own greeting cards. These may sound like petty gestures. But the child who acquires genuine considerateness is more likely to become the dependable worker, the well-beloved friend, the deeply responsible citizen of the community and of the world.

:: 14 ::

Children's Understanding of Religion

Religion means different things to children at different ages. Children under six years of age are bound closely to their parents with ties of love and admiration and dependence. They play house much of the day, pretending to be fathers and mothers and babies. When they see animals they want to know which is the daddy and which is the mommy. So family relationships provide the main structure and content of life. Children under six get their concept of God directly from their parents and think of God as somebody like a faraway grandfather, somebody the parents know.

If the parents think of God as being on the stern side, that is how He will be presented and visualized. If the parents think of Him as kindly, the child will too. Children assume that God loves them and wants them to be good. So the parents in a natural way use God to reinforce their own philosophy of morality and discipline.

I envy the parents who see God clearly and concretely, because they can then explain Him in a way that is easy for a child to understand. I suppose that my own religion is a form of humanism, which invokes and tries to strengthen the spirituality and idealism of women and men but has difficulty conceiving of God more definitely than as a spirit or as the mysterious Creator. I am inspired by the teachings of Jesus, especially the emphasis on love and understanding.

As a psychologist, the only advice I have for Christian parents who believe rather literally in the Bible is to go lightly on the hell-fire and on the vengeful aspect of Jehovah when speaking of religion to a small child. (I will not discuss Judaism specifically, but many of the basic principles will apply to Jewish children as well as to children of other religions.) I say this because children under six easily acquire morbid fears by misinterpreting what is told them. And they don't understand, as adults do, that their religion offers them forgiveness and salvation if they believe in God. I mean that when young children hear of divine wrath and punishment they imagine literally that these will strike them, because they always feel a little bit guilty.

In the six-to-twelve-year-old period children want to be less close to their parents. They'd like to get over some of their slavish admiration for them. They prefer to get their information and their ideas about truth and morality from other authorities. This is all a part of their instinct to become somewhat independent of their parents now so that they can begin their adjustment—as future adults—to the outside world.

As six to twelve year olds try to free themselves from the immediate, watchful discipline of their parents their consciences grow stricter and they become more interested in, and more sensitive to, general rules and laws. They take them all very literally; they want to know if the mayor has to obey the president and their father has to obey the mayor.

Children's concepts of right and wrong are very arbitrary —black is black, white is white and there is no place for gray.

They scold their father for driving thirty-eight miles per hour in a thirty-five-mile-per-hour zone. They have a compulsion to step over cracks in the sidewalk because to step on a crack might mean breaking their mother's back.

It's easy to see, then, why children of this age are apt to be interested in religion and in God. Not God as a grandfather any more but as the final authority on right and wrong, an authority way above his parents, or even the president. The Catholic Church has recognized this readiness for at least some aspects of religion by making five or six the age of first communion.

The age period brings problems for parents who are humanists or agnostics, for when their children hear other children talking about God they ask their parents, "Do we believe in God?" If the parents explain about their belief in the spirit of God but not exactly in a man-shaped being in the sky who is watching the behavior of each individual, or if the parents try to explain their honest uncertainty about what one ought to believe, the child is very apt to feel that this vagueness is quite unsatisfactory.

In answering such a question about God my own inclination as a parent would be to take into account the child's desire for something definite. If I believed in spiritual values and could accept the idea of God as the symbol of man's aspirations, I'd tell my child, "Yes, I believe in God." My reservations can wait several years, until the child is ready for greater subtleties. If the child asked, "Do we believe in hell?" I'd say, "No, we don't." If he asked about heaven or life after death, I'd reply that I believe that everything kind and good that a person has done for others goes on helping them after he dies; in this sense a person never dies.

If I were an atheist or such a thoroughgoing agnostic that I could not honestly express even a tentative belief in God, the spirit, I'd just say that I am not convinced there is a God but I recognize the fact that many fine people are convinced and that every individual will decide for himself as he gets older. In other words, I'd let six-to-twelve-year-old children feel that they don't have to separate themselves from, or become an adversary of, the religious people of this world just because of their loyalty to me.

And if my children had an inclination to go to Sunday school because their friends did, I would encourage them—as part of their quest for their own solution.

In the adolescent years the psychological situation is apt to be quite different. Children are now engaged in the effort to make a much more profound separation from their parents and they are groping for their own independent identities. This search goes much deeper than looking for answers to such questions as what occupation, what religion, what kind of spouse, they should choose.

Most basically, identity is a sense of being able to function as a separate person but with close relationships to others. As adults most of us take this achievement for granted. For many adolescents the transition, while they are cutting themselves partly free of emotional dependence on parents but before they have gained an inner assurance of being able to function independently, is quite frightening. It is somewhat comparable to the feeling of being truly lost in the woods, or going under an anesthetic, or having a nightmare in which the danger is intense but mysterious.

Quite a few adolescents at this stage reach out to religion for support—to their family's religion or another. It is partly a search for certainty; this is why a child brought up in a Protestant denomination or without any religion may turn to the Catholic Church, which confidently offers such concrete answers. It is also partly a search for a personal relationship with a firm but compassionate God who offers a parental kind of love, guidance, and support. To turn to God in this way saves adolescents who are temporarily unsure of themselves from having to run to their parents for guidance, which would seem like an admission of immaturity.

A very few adolescents become so insecure that they are totally obsessed with religion. On the one hand the parents can take comfort from the fact that religion is giving the child something to hang on to. On the other hand such a child can be in a shaky state, and it may be advisable to get a psychiatric consultation.

In the adolescent years parents and children may be able to talk profitably together about their religious concerns and questions. Adolescents never want to be told authoritatively what beliefs they should or should not hold. The impatience with which they sometimes explode when they think their parents are trying to impose their own opinions on them may scare the parents out of ever again opening their mouths on the subject. But the fact is that young people need to know and want to know what their parents' views are—in all the important departments of life—though they rarely admit this openly for fear of admitting their immaturity or of inviting too much parental interference.

The parents' cue is to express their beliefs as applying to themselves only, and to listen to their children's ideas with the same thoughtfulness and respect with which they listen to a favorite friend's views. The temptation of parents, as soon as they have got the drift of their child's thought, is to explain just where the child is mistaken—as I remember from being a parent and, before that, being a child.

If you can show your children not only that you respect their right to have their own opinions but also that you really understand what they are saying and see the point of it (you don't have to agree with it), you flatter them that they are becoming adult, you reassure them that you are not going to steamroller them, and you put them in a mood to consider your beliefs seriously.

:: 15 ::

Preparing a Child for a Good Marriage

In the nineteenth century such a title as this might have implied steering a son or daughter toward a marriage that was financially or socially advantageous. My mother, who was a highly idealistic and moralistic woman, would have meant a marriage to a person of fine character.

But I have in mind a marriage that will succeed and keep succeeding, preferably on a joyful level. This implies a good adjustment in the physical, social, and spiritual aspects of the relationship, which in turn depends on a healthy emotional development from earliest childhood.

The fact that America's divorce rate is one of the highest in the world suggests that we probably aren't preparing our children as well as we could for marriage.

In saying this I'm not implying that I'm against divorce; I think it's the wise course if sincere, prolonged efforts to make a go of a marriage fail. But I also believe that many marriages fail unnecessarily for a variety of reasons. The couple may have married before they were mature enough to know what they needed in the way of a mate and, more important, what they should have to offer a mate. Or they didn't have enough chance to get to know each other in advance. Or they changed too much subsequently. Or they didn't try hard enough to salvage their marriage. Or they never realized that marriages don't succeed all by themselves, but must be cultivated with devotion. Or they formed, from childhood, an unworkable image of marriage.

The most powerful influence on children's concept of marriage, of what they will want in a mate, and of how they will relate is the image they form when they are only three, four, five years of age. At that period nature (in the sense of the instinct system developed in our species during the countless centuries of its evolution) expects them to acquire most of the basic mental images by which they will be guided and patterned as they mature—not only in regard to marriage but also to work, social relations, parenthood. They get these images primarily from their parents, by watching them —intently and admiringly.

In the son's unconscious mind, the kind of person his mother is and the kind of relationship she has had with him and with her husband will play an important part in forming his romantic ideal, in guiding him to his eventual wife, and in shaping his marriage. A small girl forms her masculine ideal from her father, and eventually will shape her marriage, to one degree or another, after the marriage of her parents.

The cue, then, for parents is to measure up reasonably well to their own ideals of what men and women should be (which varies, of course, among different groups and individuals) and to conduct their marriage in a predominantly loving, cooperative, happy manner.

This is a lot easier said than done, as anyone who has been married knows. But fortunately it is not necessary to achieve perfection. Small children (unlike adolescents) have a strong tendency to overestimate the good qualities in their parents and to minimize their faults—partly because children sense that they need their parents' virtues to give them their own emotional strengths. Also they are impressed primarily by the general qualities of their parents and by the spirit of their marriage more than by the small details.

In this connection parents shouldn't worry excessively, as they sometimes do, about the effect of their quarrels. Since marriages are made by two people who have grown up in different families with different ideals and customs, there are bound to be sharp differences in points of view and some angry feelings. In fact, if there were any children who had been brought up by parents who were magically immune to quarrels, these children would be shocked when they themselves inevitably got into quarrels with their own spouses and would assume that their marriage was doomed.

You might say that children have to learn from their parents how to quarrel constructively—to see them visibly striving for mutual understanding and showing respect for each other no matter how outraged their feelings are. In other words, couples should try to avoid the mere trading of insults, which are designed not to find a solution but to hurt and enrage.

For the sake of the children as well as the sake of the parents, every marriage has to be cultivated continually. Like a garden, it will deteriorate rapidly with neglect. Each partner, in addition to carrying out her or his own jobs and responsibilities, has to be thinking of the emotional needs of the other. Each partner must show visible affection and appreciation, give boosts to the other's ego as needed, and occasionally offer unexpected help or presents or treats.

A husband or wife shouldn't have to strain to remember to carry out these manifestations of love. They should come easily, if the spirit is right. The act of pleasing another is enjoyable in itself (you know the excitement of choosing a fine present), and there is further reward in the response of the other person.

A second vital factor in raising children to make a good marriage is to help them to become cooperative people—not begrudgingly, but happily cooperative. This means letting them be helpful from earliest childhood. I say letting rather than making because children begin to have the impulse to be helpful by the age of two, and the parents need only to be appreciative in order to reinforce this impulse. This is in contrast to demanding or even asking for helpfulness. To imperiously demand good behavior is generally an inferior method because it tends to harden children's hearts and put them in the opposite mood. To ask politely for help is a better idea (if the children themselves don't spontaneously see the opportunity), for it benefits them to experience being helpful, even if this is on request.

But what children are most intensely proud of is taking the initiative in being grown-up—in any respect—and having this recognized. Children of two years get the idea of helpfulness because they have learned to appreciate their parents' loving helpfulness and because they are so imitative. If their mother dusts, they want to dust. If she sets the table, they want to set the table. All she has to do is let them help —and then compliment or thank them. (Of course, she also has to resist the impulse to say, "No, you might break something.")

But if small children forget their helpfulness at times—or never start it—their parents can and should ask for it. The crux of the request is to put it graciously, in the voice one would use to a respected friend. That kind of request is a compliment in itself. We can go on to say that to prepare children for marriage—and for success in all human relations —adults should show them respect as people, for as much of the time as they deserve it.

To put it the other way around, we should resist the impulse—which persists in adulthood in most of us as a hangover from the way we were treated by some adults in our childhood,—to humiliate them with a condemnatory or belittling attitude when they behave badly. Even in correcting children it should be possible to speak with politeness to their more mature side, asking for control over the other side, which has gotten off the track.

Just as important as showing respect to a child is to ask respect from her or him. The first without the second can create an unattractive, unhappy person. When a parent is too self-effacing or apologetic or guilty to ask respect, the child senses that it is an expression of submissiveness and is stimulated to treat the parent badly. The extreme example is the arrogant brat. But common, mild examples are the children who don't bother to pick up their things or to speak politely or to give adults a chance to talk.

Physical affection between the parents and between parents and child is a basic factor in readying a child for the various kinds of physical affection in marriage. I'm thinking of hearty kisses and hugs on greeting and departure, arms around waists when walking, cuddling together when talking and reading aloud. Children, especially in the three-to-five-year-old period when they are beginning to have sexual feelings, may make very gradual sexual advances during cuddling periods and parents have to find tactful ways to slip out of these situations. And parents shouldn't get involved in erotic embraces and caresses with each other when with their children.

As children come into adolescence they pay more attention at the family dinner table to news and gossip about romances, marriages, and divorces—local and national—and particularly to their parents' attitudes on these matters. At such times it's important for parents to show their respect for marriage (not to make cheap or cynical jokes about it) and to show their belief that it has to be treated tenderly to succeed. This is to counteract the idea, so prevalent in this country, that falling in love is something like lightning that magically strikes two people and ensures that they will live happily ever after.

The parents, even before their children begin falling in love, can indicate in a sympathetic spirit how rapidly teenagers change, in personality and life aims, into their twenties, and how these changes often bring to an abrupt end romances that were intense initially. This kind of talk doesn't need to be deadly serious or kill-joy in spirit. It is important for adults to show that they respect the intense infatuations into which adolescents often plunge; it is insulting and unfair for parents to refer to these feelings as puppy love.

It is difficult for parents with strict standards about love, sex, and marriage to know what attitude to take on these matters in discussions with their children—especially in view of the extraordinarily permissive climate that has come into existence in the last few years. I think that the change has been wholesome in that it has diminished the hypocrisy, secrecy, and guilt of earlier generations. But I happen to believe that the protest against the prudish past has carried current attitudes to the opposite extreme, and that strict parents have the right to state a middle-of-the-road position.

I don't mean that they should take arbitrary, righteous stands, implying that their view is the only correct one. That would encourage their children to rebel indignantly. Parents can show that they are always ready for reasonable discussion on an adult-to-adult level. They should listen thoughtfully and sympathetically to their children's views, which, incidentally, may turn out to be as conservative as their own.

Parents can show that they realize that their children, especially in later adolescence when they are less and less under the immediate supervision of parents and teachers, will be guided increasingly by their own judgments and convictions anyway. And parents should show confidence in their children's good sense and good morals. But at the same time, on the basis that their children are still inexperienced (though they should not rub this fact in), parents can and should make clear their own views and standards.

I myself would take a generally conservative position, as I did in my book *A Teen-ager's Guide to Life and Love*. I'd explain that it is normal for children raised in families with high aspirations to feel inhibited about sexuality in adolescence, that it's through this partial inhibition and the sublimation of the sexual drive that civilization has been built and all the arts have been developed. This does not diminish the pleasures of romance and sex when one is ready; quite the opposite.

Early dating and experimentation, before one has the capacity to love deeply, may get sex off to a bad start. It's sensible to stick to group dates and perhaps visits to each other's homes until one is fifteen or sixteen or seventeen. A considerable majority of college students advise no intercourse before eighteen, and then, they say, only if there is a deep, generous love, the sort that may lead to marriage.

Children, no matter what they say, certainly want to hear their parents' views and will be influenced by them. But of course they won't always follow these recommendations, as we all remember from our own adolescence. That doesn't mean, though, that the advice was not helpful, just the same.

From my strict point of view, it wouldn't be wise for a mother to send her daughter, as she prepares to go to college, to the gynecologist to be fully equipped with a contraceptive device or pill, as is sometimes done today. I feel that this expresses the mother's expectation that her daughter will have casual affairs. This would be a devaluation of love on the mother's part, however slight.

On the other hand, I think parents should make it clear that if their sons or daughters ever do fall deeply in love and decide to have intercourse before marriage, they should take the serious responsibility of consulting a physician and preventing a pregnancy that would be harmful to all concerned, including the baby. I would never imply to a son that I expected him to be casual about love.

I think it's all right for a mother to suggest to her daughter that, if she wishes, she might consult the family's gynecologist about these matters. This distinction between the parent deciding that a daughter should be equipped, and leaving most of the responsibility to her, may seem a small one, but I think that it is an important one.

Sex education in the more formal sense is discussed in another chapter.

Discrimination Hurts Everyone

This discussion applies to all minority groups who are discriminated against on the basis of race, religion, or ethnic origin. The discussion also concerns the harm done to children of the discriminative groups. We are apt to think of whites as being the discriminators, but, of course, some minority groups discriminate against others too.

Children are affected by discrimination in various ways. Psychological studies have shown that by four or five years of age black children in America become convinced that they are inferior people because of the color of their skin. The belief will come partly from what their parents must tell them about discrimination directly or indicate to them indirectly, partly from the treatment they receive from white children and adults. What this really means is that black children become prejudiced against themselves, at the start of life, by accepting the white man's prejudice against them. At a later age, experiments involving black and white students who take tests in one another's presence show that a black student, let's say a girl, who actually scores just the same as a white student will characteristically rate her own performance as inferior. This unrealistic sense of inadequacy gets expressed, of course, in low expectations for herself in school and career. It also follows that the black student comes to think less well of her family, her friends, and her race than they deserve. And they, in turn, have less esteem for her. So there is a vicious circle in operation that keeps the self-confidence of all members of the race depressed.

Human beings are strongly influenced by what others expect of them. This has been demonstrated in a variety of natural situations and also in experiments. When people feel that others expect them to behave well or to achieve highly, they tend to meet the challenge. If others expect them to be delinquent—even though they are really high-principled—they let down their standards to some degree. It's bad enough, for instance, when the community expects further delinquent behavior from a particular youth (of any color) who has already served time in a training school, because this helps to discourage him and make him cynical. ("What's the use of trying if that's what they think of me!") There are many prejudiced white people who expect most minority youths to be lawless. This surely increases to some degree these youths' temptation to misbehave. The main reason the great majority of minority youths don't succumb is that they are actually brought up with high standards. I've always noticed as a physician that conscientious black parents instill a greater obligation regarding lawfulness and politeness than white parents do. They must do this, they explain, because blacks will be blamed first whenever there's trouble.

To me, it seems remarkable that most minority children grow up so conscientious and friendly. It speaks for the parents' maturity and their forgivingness that they haven't instilled a fierce hatred of the groups that have deprived and humiliated them. How do they manage to teach their children that God is in heaven and that human beings are generally trustworthy? I doubt that I could have done it if I had had to prepare my sons for what minority youths must face.

What I said about the effect of the community's expectations has also been shown to be clearly true of schoolwork. If a teacher believes that certain students—of whatever group —are stupid, even though they really have a satisfactory aptitude, not only will the teacher's impression of their performance be poor, but their actual performance in that classroom will be poor by objective measurement as well. They will also appear dull to a visitor to the class. They are not dull. They are reacting to the teacher's explicit or implicit depreciation with a conviction that they *are* inadequate. Experimental projects carried out by the Bank Street College of Education in New York have shown that some of the most withdrawn and indifferent black pupils can respond dramatically to teachers who like them, believe in them, and will go halfway to find their interests.

It is easy to see why racial discrimination undermines minority children. But it's also true—through not as easily visible—that it is harmful to those who discriminate. If they are told, for instance, that they must avoid any group because they are dirty or diseased or bad, they are really being taught that they must be afraid of them. Such fears are harmful to children's personalities.

There are parents who don't teach a specific fear of any minority group but who show by their manner that they feel more uneasy, for example, if they find their children playing with a black child whom they don't know than with an unknown white child. In discussing the news of the day they may use a tense tone in mentioning that a black family has moved into the neighborhood. These vague expressions of apprehension are as disturbing to children as specific fears, sometimes more so. Children have had less experience with the world, so their imaginations are less realistic, more morbid.

We must go a step further and recognize that the mere fact that a white child's parents don't meet socially people from minority groups will give him a slight sense of strangeness and uneasiness, a feeling which most of us realize is still in us in adulthood when we try to overcome this social barrier.

We have plenty of evidence that children turn out most successful—occupationally, socially, academically, emotionally—if they can grow up feeling that there are no ordinary situations that they can't cope with adequately, no people that they can't deal with agreeably. For their own sakes they should be able to feel this way about people of different races as well as about people of different backgrounds and manners.

Another harm to the child in learning prejudice is that it gives him a scapegoat for his own inadequacies. When I hear an adult sneer at Jews or Catholics I feel embarrassed for him that he has revealed so publicly his insecurity about his own worth, and that he has to take such a childish and spiteful way to try to overcome it. The capable and confident person doesn't need to boost himself by trampling on others. It's healthier for children to grow up believing that they must prove their capabilities rather than that they can claim superiorities that have no basis in reality.

Some parents who say they don't want to teach their children prejudice and who regret the damage that discrimination does to minorities are still opposed to integration of schools because they fear its effect on their own children.

This fear is based primarily on the knowledge that black, Mexican American, Puerto Rican, Indian children *on the average* have lower scores on intelligence tests and show less academic aptitude than average white children. In truth there are very bright children from these groups as well as average and dull ones—the same range as for white children. But there is a larger proportion of minority children in the lower-score brackets, and this is what brings the average down. There is no proof, however, that they are innately less endowed with gray matter. Most psychologists believe that the intellectual and academic differences are explained by the cultural deprivation of these groups in the U.S. I agree with this view. The study that particularly impressed me— regarding the power of environment to influence intelligence—happened to involve a group of white children. They had been born illegitimately to mentally retarded mothers but were adopted into above-average families. They developed levels of intelligence roughly similar to those of their adopting parents. The majority of blacks, Mexican Americans, Puerto Ricans, and Indians are up against multiple cultural disadvantages: poor education, irregular and low-paying jobs, poverty, crowded living quarters, little intellectual stimulation, little hope for betterment, the constant humiliation from the white world. A white child would be just as unlikely to develop good intelligence if brought up in such an environment.

There is no evidence that the social traits for which some black people of low economic levels have been criticized, such as lack of middle-class strivings, are inborn. Sociologists are convinced that such attitudes, along with the poor environments in which these black people must live, are the accumulated result of three centuries of slavery, discrimination, and humiliation. Everything I've learned about personality development in children makes me believe so too. (Slaves had little incentive to be ambitious. Also they were forbidden to marry, and the men were discouraged from developing any sense of responsibility toward their women and children.) Black children born or adopted into highly educated black families develop the same personalities as their white counterparts. Present-day black people in Africa who are reared with cultural advantages are bright, proud, and determined.

Other ethnic groups in America's past—Germans, Swedes, Hungarians, Poles, Italians—started from poverty and slums, but they were able to escape as soon as they learned American ways. Black people, because of their skin are faced with a slippery incline. They must struggle more intensely than white people to climb upward, and if they or their children are not able to persevere, they'll slide more easily to the bottom again.

Actual studies of the effects of integration of schools in American cities show academic improvement for the black children and no academic disadvantage for the white children. The improvement in the black children was anticipated because a great majority of black schools in the past have been inferior—in equipment, in the level of training of their teachers, in the morale of teachers and pupils, as well as in the cultural background of the pupils. Integration provided better teaching and new hope.

As to why the school progress of the white children was not slowed, there are several explanations: Since the work of the black children improved, the gap between them and the white children was minimized. When children (of whatever color) with widely different aptitudes do go to the same school, as when central city children are bused to suburban schools, they will usually become separated into more advanced and less advanced classes.

Of course, any classroom will have children with a moderate range of aptitudes. That's why in many school systems each class is divided into subgroups. Even when children of widely different aptitudes are combined in the same class, it has been shown in experiments that a good teacher can move them all along at their different rates, provided there isn't too large a total in the class. This was the system in the little red schoolhouse of hallowed fame.

The most effective way to overcome discrimination in schooling would be to integrate neighborhoods. But residential racial integration is often opposed by conscientious parents in a so-called better neighborhood for fear that the supposedly lower behavior standards of black children may prove contagious to their own. This is the most unlikely danger of all. For instance, black parents have at least as high standards for their children's behavior as white parents of the same educational and economic level. Few of the black children who are involved in delinquency are those whose parents can afford to buy homes in "better" neighborhoods. They are predominantly from the lowest economic level, as are the white children who become delinquent.

The social tensions and the harm to adults and children that result from segregation are not stationary today—they are increasing.

Because automation is eliminating the unskilled jobs upon which minority groups have had to depend, there is now chronic, demoralizing unemployment for many of them, which contrasts more and more glaringly with the mounting prosperity of the rest of the population.

These excessively disadvantaged people are the least able to inspire in their children a conviction about the value of schooling. Their children are further alienated if their teachers are uninspired or prejudiced or antagonistic. They drop out of school in adolescence, find no work, lose hope, and get into trouble because there is no other way to spend their time or relieve their feelings. There is a downward spiral in operation.

The pools of demoralization and resentment that are enlarging in our inner cities will not stay confined there while the white people withdraw to the suburbs.

Minority groups are declaring more and more emphatically that they are no longer going to accept the rank unfairness in jobs, housing, and education or the everyday humiliations. I think it is fortunate for all of us that the minorities are taking this firm stand. But minority groups and government cannot bring about the changes all by themselves. The rest of us must do our part. We should support the groups in our communities that are working to open schools, residential areas, and jobs to minority people. We must be quick to communicate, when racial issues arise, with our school and municipal officials and our legislators. We should make our views known to local papers, banks, and real-estate people. The news reports show clearly that those who are aroused to fear and antagonism at the prospect of integration are quick and vigorous in expressing their feelings. It is the people of good will who most often fail to speak up.

What can parents do to protect their children against some of the harm of discrimination? Minority parents are taking a constructive course, I think, when they themselves participate in the fight for equal rights. By finding a way at last to take action against a humiliating situation, they dispel part of their long-pent-up anxiety and resentment. They gain a greater self-respect. These changes in their inner feelings make them better parents.

I don't know just what minority parents should say to their children about prejudice, never having had to tell my own children anything nearly as difficult. How do you break the news to a small child who trusts you and who still trusts the world that he'll be considered second class and objectionable all his life, no matter how admirable he is, because he has inherited your skin? It must seem like hitting him in the face. It's also admitting that you can't protect him, and that's ignominious. But there are general psychological principles that have at least some application. The most basic is that it is healthy for a child to be able to talk with his parents about anything that worries him and them.

I know, from published observations, that black children will have developed real concern about color by the age of four or five, whether or not they have ever alluded to it directly. Yet I know that many, many black parents postpone a discussion for a long time because the topic is so painful. The trouble with delay is that when parents try to ignore a subject that is truly bothering the whole family, the child's apprehension and misunderstanding become even worse than they have to be. All experience in child psychiatry tells us that.

A major problem, I should think, would be how to explain the prejudice, the deliberate or thoughtless cruelty, of such a large number of people. I remember when my children were small having to find a way of explaining to them occasionally the puzzling behavior of some one person such as a religious prophet carrying a sign predicting the end of the world or a perverse individual who had been trying to strike up a friendship in a children's playground. I'd say casually, "He doesn't think the way you and I think." I'd explain in simple terms his line of reasoning and why I thought it was mistaken. What impressed me and encouraged me was that my children never seemed bewildered by this kind of explanation. It worked in the case of eccentrics, but I admit that I never had to make clear why tens of millions of people think so differently or behave so cruelly.

When children become eight, ten, twelve, they want explanations that are more penetrating. Black parents can then get into such topics as the history of slavery, the readiness of human beings to fear and hate those who seem different, their suspicion of anyone who they imagine might take their jobs or their lovers away, their need for a scapegoat when they feel insecure.

I think it is theoretically preferable for minority parents not to show helpless rage, though they must have felt that reaction at times, for it implies to their child that they have accepted the position of passive victims. And better not to teach blind hatred, though they would have plenty of justification for doing so, because it would signal to the child that they see no constructive solution. To put it another way, the child who learns nothing but hatred won't have the self-discipline to work to overcome the obstacles of prejudice, or to educate herself or himself for a good job.

On the other hand, it should relieve the parents' resentment and help the child to understand her or his own feelings if the parents admit that they sometimes get plenty angry at the nonsense and arrogance of discrimination. That is to say, there's nothing wrong with justified anger as long as it doesn't rob a child or adult of their capacity to achieve and doesn't sour them about human nature in general.

It's good, for minority children's sakes, to believe that

some people are fair, that progress is being made, though it's painfully slow, that their own eventual efforts in the rights struggle will contribute. These beliefs give them a basis for hoping and working, allow them to retain their sense of worth and dignity.

How can white parents and parents of other discriminating groups talk with their children about prejudice and discrimination? And at what age? Children can be expected to begin making occasional references to blacks or other minority groups at four or five or six, depending on where they live and what their experiences are. The fact that the struggle for rights is now so much in the press, on television, and in parents' conversation draws it to children's attention earlier than previously. The time for the parent to begin explaining is when their child asks a question or quotes a neighbor child's mistaken or prejudiced view. Young children will require much simpler explanations than will older ones, of course.

Young white children most need to be reassured that minority people, despite their differences, which may be startling to them at first, are also kindly and affectionate to children. As they grow a little older they need to know—to counteract the prejudice they hear—that minority people are as intelligent, healthy, and well behaved as well. Later they need to understand some of the historical and psychological reasons why minority groups have been oppressed, feared, and deprived.

It aids the perspective of adolescents to realize that there has been little antiblack feeling in France, for instance; that prejudice has arisen recently in England when people from India and the West Indies began to compete in significant numbers for jobs and housing; that in the United States the apprehensive men who have viewed with horror the possibility of black men marrying white women have thought nothing of relationships between white men and black women—

in other words, their concern is not really for the "purity of the race" but is an unconscious expression of that common human attitude, sexual jealousy.

On the positive side, children of all ages should hear—at home and in school—about the contributions to the arts and sciences made by blacks (in Africa and the U.S.), Puerto Ricans, Mexicans, and Indians.

Within the family there may be uneasiness if a youth of one color wants to invite one of another color home for a meal or a party or a vacation. Parents should first make the effort to think youthfully and tolerantly, as their children do. If they feel that their own tolerance is too small, better to say so and not blame it on the conventional neighbors. If the guest is of a different sex from that of their own child, they shouldn't assume that marriage is imminent.

The school has a large part to play in the teaching of appreciation of other races. As children get beyond the age of six, it is their nature to begin to question their parents' ideas about what is correct and to turn instead to authorities in the outside world, particularly their teachers. In their instinctive need to get over their former conviction that their parents are all-wise, they quote teacher's opinions whenever they think they might counter their parents' opinions. So the teacher, if she or he has the general respect of the class, has an audience that is looking for new concepts.

Another aspect of school-age children is what might be called their clannishness. This can be used in constructive or destructive ways. In their desire to clarify what is proper and improper behavior and to strengthen their own convictions, they associate with those whose standards are similar to their own. This is one of the reasons they love to form secret clubs with their pals. Then they can easily agree that the members are right and that nonmembers are misguided. They tell the latter, "We have a club but you can't belong." If children are left to their own devices or if they are taught prejudice by their parents and teachers, they can become intensely intolerant at this age. But if a respected teacher shows them that it is fairer and more grown-up to appreciate the qualities in those from different backgrounds, they can take to this sort of ideal with just as much enthusiasm. There is material for teaching such appreciation in political history, literature, and the histories of science, technology, and art.

Better still if the school can include pupils from a variety of backgrounds so that the children can learn appreciation in practice as well as in words. I think that all parents should work for well-integrated schools, not just because it is morally right, not just because it will benefit those who have been discriminated against, but also because it will broaden and make more flexible the attitudes of all children.

In the same sense it will be better preparation for life if all children grow up in neighborhoods that contain people with a variety of backgrounds and skin pigments. In fact white people should be becoming aware of the fact that they are a rather small and unpopular minority in this world. They'll have to learn to get along agreeably with the others or face steadily increasing resentment and retaliation in the decades to come. It is much easier to learn such habits in childhood.

The best way that individual parents could influence their children would be to remember to include people of other backgrounds when they ask friends to join in family activities.

Chapter IV

Control of Children

:: 17 ::

It's Not a Question of Strictness or Leniency but of What Is behind These Methods

I want to discuss several different styles of parent-child relationships and their results in child behavior. To cover such a wide range in one piece the discussion will have to be oversimplified, even to the point of glibness.

A few children are permitted to call their parents by their first names. (Both my children came to this by themselves at about the age of three, and I didn't object.) Many people are at least mildly shocked by this, feeling that it represents a lack of respect on the part of the children and a lack of self-respect on the part of the parents. Sometimes this proves to be true, other times not at all. I'd say, in retrospect, that my sons were too afraid of me, rather than underrespectful.

Some children who are treated leniently turn out to be brats. They fight constantly, interrupt visitors or glare at them if they don't happen to like them, defy their parents' requests or call them names. Other children raised leniently are quite charming. I've known a lot of them.

Though it's often assumed that children raised strictly will be well behaved, some of them turn out to be distinctly disagreeable or downright mean.

It is plain from this brief listing that there is no simple, predictable relationship between the style of rearing and the result.

The father who encourages his son to call him by his first name *may* want to be just a pal to him. If questioned, he may explain that as a child himself he felt too much in awe of his own father, afraid of him, perhaps hostile to him. He wants his relationship with his own son to be much warmer and more affable. Whether he can achieve this without producing a slightly spoiled child will depend on whether he can be not only a pal but a parent too. For it's impossible to turn out a well-adjusted child unless the parent is willing to lead, to approve of some behavior, to disapprove of other behavior.

As children grow they have to keep exploring the limits of what their parents will allow them to do, which will require the parents to make new restrictions frequently. And they have to keep testing their parents' firmness, patience, self-respect, to see how much they will be permitted to impose on them. Parents who are trying to be just pals will be forced to the wall sooner or later. They have to become firm parents at least for the time being, or, less satisfactorily, they must finally lose their patience and become angry; either of these reversals will make the child temporarily resentful. But if the parents are then overcome with guilt for their strictness or their outburst, they will soon be acting apologetic and thus will be inviting the child to overstep the limits again.

Actually a justified parental firmness, though it may make children a bit resentful for a short time, does no harm to their personality nor to their long-term relationship with their parent. Quite the contrary. Children know they are inexperienced and that their security depends on their parent's guidance. All psychiatric experience proves again and again that a child is made uneasy by chronic parental indecision, comforted by parental firmness. A child is not satisfied by a parent who is only a pal.

To go back for a moment to the question of a child's being allowed to call the parents by their first names, I'd say there's no harm in it at all if this appeals to the parents and if they are quite ready at the same time to give strong leadership. But if it's a sign of a wish to dodge the usual strains of the parent-child relationship, it can be a trap.

I'd sum up this point by saying that it is really normal for children to carry at least a mild degree of impatience, grumpiness, or criticalness toward their parents intermittently throughout childhood, adolescence, and youth. This impatience is part of what eventually makes them leave home and chart a course for themselves through life.

In the uncommon case of the individual who grows up with an *intense* resentment toward one or both parents, the explanation is not simply the ordinary parental firmness. The relationship must have been complicated by other parental attitudes, such as unusual meanness or vacillation; also parents who tend to feel guilty on slight provocation may invite a child to be excessively reproachful.

I suppose it is only in the U.S., with its tradition of relatively uninhibited children, that prompt obedience and politeness suggest parental severity. Sometimes that is the case. But I've seen extraordinarily well-behaved children who have never been intimidated, who have grown up with a high degree of spontaneity, originality, and creativity. It simply isn't true that pleasing manners must go along with a spiritless conformity in personality. I do admit, though, that it takes parental skill to raise charming children by means of a light touch. The parent must have a very pleasing personality too—to set the example and to make the child want very much to please in return. The parent must know what he or she expects from the child. The parent must be able to stay pretty well on an even keel, in order not to need to crack down irritably at one moment or to subtly invite the child to get out of hand at another. Few can reach such perfection. (I never could.) But it helps other parents to know clearly that neither permissiveness nor harshness is necessary theoretically for a good result.

It is not really mysterious why some children treated with more-than-average leniency turn out to be brats and others to be quite appealing. Actually the spirit of the discipline is distinctly different in those two cases, however much they may appear the same on the surface. When the child is spoiled—slightly spoiled or infuriatingly spoiled—it means that the parent is afraid to be firm, afraid of arousing antagonism. This fear is usually combined with parental guiltiness and submissiveness toward the child.

You may think that I'm overdoing this theme of parental hesitancy, but I think it's the commonest problem in child rearing in America today. It manifests itself as parental timidity about toilet training in the second year of life and as parental fear of being definite about what they expect of their children in adolescence. It's commoner in college-educated parents than in others. It isn't the parents' fault; the most conscientious parents are the most susceptible. It's predominantly the fault of all the psychologists, psychiatrists, and pediatricians (like myself) who, with the best intentions in the world, have been preaching to American parents for the past half-century about the importance of love and understanding, about the problems that sometimes result from excessive repression or hostility. This kind of advice has proved in practice to be too intimidating to parents. Another contributing factor, I believe, has been the general tendency, in a nation settled by pioneers, to revere the children and expect them to surpass their parents. The net effect of this emphasis is often to make parents subordinate their wishes and pleasures to those of their children, or even to belittle themselves. In other parts of the world parents assume that they are wise and good and they ask that their children look up to them.

By contrast, when children who are being reared leniently prove to be delightful people, you can be sure that the parents have a clear picture of how they want them to behave. But they guide them back into line so promptly, so deftly, the very first second the children start to get into trouble or to be difficult, that there never have to be shouts, scoldings, slaps. (I don't mean that such parents have to be constantly on guard either; it's all done without conscious effort.) The system works like a sensitive thermostat that keeps the room temperature within one degree of the optimum all the time, in contrast with an inefficient thermostat that doesn't go into action until the temperature has fallen five degrees.

There are at least three quite different types of parental strictness, however much they look the same on the surface. In one type the parents are badgering the child constantly, because they resent him or her for some conscious or unconscious reason or because they are chronically resentful about something else entirely but find it easy to take out their anger on the child. This makes for a hostile, mean child who may show open antagonism to the parents if they permit this, or bottle it up in relation to them and take it out in cruelty to brothers, sisters, or playmates.

In another case the parents are not mean but merely too dominating. They must be constantly directing, controlling the child (let's say it's a boy), running his life, shaping his every reaction. They may make him quite colorless or at least passive in childhood. But there's a good chance that in adulthood he'll eventually get around to a full identification with his parents and become quite a bossy person himself.

In a third case the parents' firm leadership does not spring either from hostility or need to dominate but only from an unusual exactness in their picture of what correct behavior consists of. But they may be quite willing to let their child's basic personality, flavor, and originality develop in its own direction as long as he or she is conforming in manners. In other words, the area of parental domination is actually quite narrow and superficial.

Before closing I want to give my usual plug and express my own preference for firm leadership, whether it's obvious or subtle. This makes for a better-behaved child and a more peaceful family life as well as for a happier child.

The real point I've been making is that you shouldn't be fooled by superficial similarities or differences in the child rearing in different families. A considerable majority of parents are loving and reasonably firm underneath; on the surface they may appear either lenient or strict in style. The style is not very important. The results will be much the same and will be good.

:: 18 ::

Three Styles of Discipline

Some fascinating experiments were carried out many years ago to show the different effects of authoritarian (external, arbitrary) discipline and democratic (internal, responsible) discipline. Activity clubs were set up for several groups of boys of the middle-childhood years. The boys were to work at hobbies in after-school hours, under the leadership of the psychologists conducting the experiments. Other psychologists, concealed behind screens and armed with pads, pencils, and stop watches, kept careful track of what went on.

In the group designed to demonstrate the effects of authoritarian discipline, the leader took charge from the beginning. For example, he announced to the boys that this was a carpentry club and that they were going to build bird-houses. He told them where to get the materials and what the design was to be as well as how to use the tools. The leader was agreeable enough in manner, but he left no initiative or choice to the boys and he maintained order efficiently.

The procedures in the democratic group were quite different. When the leader first spoke to the group he explained that it was their club and they could choose their activity. Typically in such a situation, as everyone knows from adult groups too, all kinds of projects may be offered, from sensible to totally impractical. One boy may suggest building a real plane in which they can fly, and he wins a couple of backers. The democratic leader doesn't squelch anyone or try to impose his ideas. He just keeps the discussion fairly orderly and perhaps reminds the group of certain realities if they forget them.

If the group should finally settle on birdhouses, the leader shifts the discussion to the questions of how to find or make designs, secure materials, borrow tools. Committees may be elected to divide the work. When building time nears, there are more matters to discuss and decide, such as the sequences, the methods, perhaps even different committees of boys to saw, to sand, to nail, and to paint.

You can probably guess some of the results of the experiment. In terms of efficiency—the number of hours and days necessary to build a certain number of birdhouses—the authoritarian approach is way ahead. To a visitor the proceedings look better organized.

The other side of the picture becomes evident if the leader leaves the room for a while. The boldest spirits kick over the traces first and begin horsing around; then the less-courageous ones follow, until there are only a couple of worried goody-goodies still sticking to business. (I was always one of those timid ones, myself.) The reason is that under tight discipline people have no outlet for their spontaneous ideas and individual wishes; resentment builds up under the surface. It doesn't break out, though, until the leader leaves the scene.

In the democratic group the work goes on almost as well with the leader out of the room as when he is there. This is because the boys feel that the project is their very own (not assigned by the leader); they've decided ahead of time how it should be carried out; they have no pent-up hostility to vent by abusing the premises.

A third type of discipline was also used in these experiments—laissez faire, or excessively permissive. The leader was there with the boys, he answered questions, he gave individual help when asked but he offered no leadership. His group never accomplished anything. From time to time the boys would tire of fooling around and try to get organized on a project. But no one of them was a strong enough leader to hold a group this size in line, and the disruptive behavior of the least responsible members was enough to sabotage the constructive efforts of the more mature ones.

It was interesting that the laissez-faire group accomplished slightly more when the leader was out of the room. It was as if the children were embarrassed or extradisorganized when they had an adult present who didn't know how to act like an adult.

I think it was wise for the experimenters to include a laissez-faire as well as a democratic group, because there are lots of people (of the sort who incline to the authoritarian approach) who believe there are only two methods of bringing up children: an authoritarian way that produces well-behaved children and a permissive way that produces brats. I agree that overpermissiveness or laissez faire—which really means submissiveness on the part of the adult—often results in ill-behaved children. I believe, furthermore, that you can bring up polite, cooperative children by either the authoritarian or the democratic approach—but the character that results will be quite different.

Authoritarian discipline is one that is imposed from the outside—like the leash on a dog. The child or adult who has been accustomed to it obeys well enough while the authority is present—whether parent, teacher, or boss—but tends to throw off the restraint and behave at a less mature level when he gets the chance.

A democratic discipline is not based on the leader's strength or presence. It is based on the example of his very evident sense of responsibility. It is based on his respect for the dignity of others. It is based on his visible trust that others have a sense of responsibility too. These attitudes are just what inspire the growth of a corresponding sense of responsibility and cooperativeness in the characters of those he is leading. These attitudes become permanent traits in his followers that increasingly govern them from within, whether or not an external authority is present. These attitudes are what equip them to be conscientious citizens, in childhood or adulthood, and resourceful subordinates; eventually they may become leaders who will be independent in their thinking and who will inspire others in turn. These are the qualities that are particularly valuable in making democracy work.

There was another significant observation made during this study—not about the value of this or that form of discipline, but about what happens when a child is transferred from one form of discipline to another. After a number of weeks each group of boys was shifted from the type of discipline under which he started to a second, and later to a third, to find out, among other things, what the effects of different transitions were. On the shift from democratic to authoritarian discipline there was a lot of grumbling among the boys, as you can imagine, but it wore off before too long. The transition that was really difficult was the one in the opposite direction, from authoritarian to democratic. All the resentments that had been piling up in the boys' feelings for weeks came pouring out for a while in the form of hostile behavior toward the democratic leader, despite the fact that he was taking such pains to show respect and consideration.

I learned the same thing when I was on the medical advisory board of a children's convalescent hospital that shifted from a harshly authoritarian type of discipline to a moderately democratic, kindly one under a new superintendent. All Hades broke loose, and it took a long time to build a good atmosphere.

What this means in ordinary life is that when a new teacher runs into disciplinary problems on taking over a class, or when a new housemother has trouble in an institution, it may not be a sign of inadequate leadership. After a while it may become clear that a truly constructive change has been made. For another example, when a racial or ethnic minority that has long been badly treated—by the police or an employer or a professional organization—is given more consideration, its members may temporarily become not less but more demanding and angry. After their accumulated resentment has been expended, they will gradually come around to an appropriate responsiveness to the new fairness being shown them.

:: 19 ::

The Need To Control Aggression

Is it good or bad for boys to play with toy weapons? For many years I emphasized its harmlessness. When a thoughtful mother expressed doubt about letting her son have guns and other warlike toys—because she didn't want to encourage him in the slightest degree to become delinquent or militaristic—I would explain how little connection there was between these toys and the development of an aggressive personality. I used to say that in the course of growing up, children have a natural tendency to bring their aggressiveness more and more under control, provided their parents encourage this. When children are one to two years old, for instance, and angry with another child, they may bite each other without hesitation; but by the age of three or four they have learned that crude aggression is not right. However, they like to pretend to shoot a pretend Indian. They may pretend to shoot their mother or father, but they grin to reassure the parent that their guns and their hostility aren't to be taken seriously.

In the six-to-twelve-year-old period boys will play an earnest game of war, but it has lots of rules that limit aggression. There may be arguments and roughhousing, but real fights are relatively infrequent. At this age boys don't shoot at their mother or father, even in fun. It's not that their parents have become stricter; their own consciences have. They say, "Step on a crack, break your mother's back," and try to avoid stepping on the sidewalk cracks—which means that even the thought of wishing harm to their parents now makes them uncomfortable. In adolescence, aggressive feelings become much stronger, but well-brought-up boys sublimate them into athletics and other competitive activities, or into kidding their pals.

In other words, I'd explain to parents, playing at war is a natural step in the disciplining of the aggression of young boys. Most clergymen pacifists probably played the same games. An idealistic mother doesn't really need to worry about producing a scoundrel. The aggressive juvenile delinquent was not distorted in personality by being allowed to play bandit at five or ten years of age. He was neglected and abused in his first couple of years, when his character was beginning to take shape; he was doomed before he had any toys worthy of the name.

But nowadays I'd give parents much more encouragement in their inclination to guide their son away from violence. A number of occurrences have convinced me of the importance of this.

One of the first things that made me change my mind—several years ago—was an observation made by an experienced nursery-school teacher. She told me that her children were crudely bopping each other much more than previously, without provocation. When she remonstrated with them, they protested indignantly, "But that's what the Three Stooges do." ("The Three Stooges" was a children's TV program full of violence and buffoonery that recently had been introduced and immediately had become very popular.) This attitude did not signify a serious undermining of character. But it certainly showed me that watching violence can lower a child's standards of behavior.

What further shocked me into reconsidering my point of view was the assassination of President Kennedy and the fact that some school children cheered about this. (I did not so much blame the children as I blamed the kind of American parents who will say about a president they dislike, "I'd shoot him if I got the chance!")

These incidents made me think of other evidences that Americans have often been tolerant of harshness, lawlessness, and violence. We were ruthless in dealing with the Indians. In some frontier areas we slipped into the tradition of vigilante justice. We were hard on the later waves of immigrants. At times we've denied justice to groups with different religious or political views. We have high crime rates. We have a shameful history of racist lynchings and murders, as well as of regular abuse and humiliation of black people. In recent years there apparently has been a rise in the frequency with which infants and small children have been taken to hospitals with bruises, fractures, internal hemorrhages, and fractured skulls caused by gross parental brutality.

Is it a coincidence that a great proportion of our adult as well as our child population also is endlessly fascinated with dramas of Western violence and brutal crime stories in movies and on television?

Of course, some of the phenomena I have described are characteristic of only a small percentage of the population. Even the others that apply to a majority of people don't necessarily mean that we Americans, on the average, have more aggressiveness in us than the people of most other nations. I think, rather, that the aggressiveness we have is less controlled, from childhood on.

To me, it seems very clear that in order to have a more stable and civilized national life we should bring up the next generation of Americans with a greater respect for law and for other people's rights and sensibilities than in the past. There are many ways in which we could and should teach these attitudes. One simple way is to show our young children our own disapproval of lawlessness and violence in television programs and in play.

I also believe that the survival of the world now depends on a much greater awareness of the need to avoid war and actively to seek peaceful agreements. There are enough nuclear arms to utterly destroy all civilization. This terrifying situation demands a much greater stability and self-restraint on the part of national leaders and populations than they have ever shown in the past. We owe it to our children to prepare them, very deliberately, for this awesome responsibility.

When we let people grow up feeling that cruelty is all right provided they know it is make-believe, or provided they sufficiently disapprove of certain individuals or groups, or provided the cruelty is in the service of their country (whether the country is right or wrong), we make it easier for them to go beserk on provocation.

But can we imagine actually depriving American boys of

their pistols or of watching their favorite Western or crime programs? I think we should consider it.

I believe that parents should stop children's war play or any other kind of play firmly when it degenerates into deliberate cruelty or meanness. (By this I don't mean they should interfere in every little quarrel or tussle.)

If I had a three- or four-year-old son who asked me to buy him a pistol, I'd tell him—with a friendly smile, not a scowl —that I didn't want to give him a gun for even pretend shooting because there is too much meanness and killing in the world; that we must all learn how to get along in a friendly way together. I'd ask him if he didn't want some other present instead.

If I saw him, soon afterward, using a stick for a pistol in order to join a gang that was merrily going "bang-bang" at one another, I wouldn't rush out to remind him of my views. I'd let him have the fun of participating as long as there was no cruelty. If his uncle gave him a pistol or a soldier's helmet for his birthday, I myself wouldn't have the nerve to take it away from him. If when he was seven or eight he decided he wanted to spend his own money for battle equipment, I wouldn't forbid him to. I'd remind him that I don't want to buy war toys or give them as presents, but that from now on he will be playing away from home more and more and making more of his own decisions; he can make this decision for himself.

I wouldn't give this talk in such a disapproving manner that he wouldn't dare decide against my policy. I would feel I'd made my point and that he had been inwardly influenced by my viewpoint as much as I could influence him. Even if he should buy weapons then, he would be likely to end up —in adolescence and adulthood—as thoughtful about the problems of peace as if I'd prohibited his buying them, perhaps more so.

One reason I keep backing away from a flat prohibition is that it would have its heaviest effect on the individuals who need it least. If all the parents in America became convinced and agreed on a toy-weapons ban on the first of next month, this would be ideal from my point of view. But this isn't going to happen for a long time, unless one bomb goes off by accident and shocks the world into a banning of all weapons, real and make-believe. A small percentage of parents—those most thoughtful and conscientious—will be the first ones who will want to dissuade their sons from war toys; but their sons will be most likely to be the sensitive, responsible children anyway. So I think it's carrying the issue unnecessarily far, for those of us who are particularly concerned about peace and kindliness, to insist that our young sons demonstrate a total commitment to our cause while all their friends are pistol toters. (It might be practical in a neighborhood where a majority of parents had the same conviction.) The main ideal is that children should grow up with a fond attitude toward all humanity. That will come about, basically, if this is the general atmosphere of our families. It will be strengthened by the attitudes we specifically teach toward nations and groups.

I feel less inclined to compromise on brutality on television and in movies. Although children have their own fantasies of violence, the sight of a real human face apparently being smashed by a fist has a lot more impact on children than what they imagine when they are making up their own stories. I believe that parents should flatly forbid programs that go in for violence. I don't think they are good for adults either.

Young children can only partly distinguish between dramas and reality. Parents can explain, "It isn't right for people to hurt each other or kill each other and I don't want you to watch them do it." If children cheat and watch such a program in secret, they'll know very well that their parents disapprove, and this will protect them, to a degree, from the coarsening effect of the scenes.

:: 20 ::

The Child Who Tries To Control His Parents

A father wrote to me, "Whenever my wife and I try to have an adult conversation at dinner, our three and a half year old interrupts with: 'Talk to *me.*' My wife says we *should* include him, but I feel if he's old enough to eat with us, he's old enough to learn that he can't have all the attention all the time. What do you think?"

I think that a child shouldn't be allowed to interrupt his parents' conversation at any meal (or between meals), whether he's three or thirteen, nor be impolite in any other way.

Some people may say that there is no particular significance in what this father reports, that all children are a little bit jealous of their parents' attentiveness to each other and that children shouldn't be expected to know what politeness is at this age. A few might even say there is no proof here that this child really is jealous or spoiled or demanding; maybe he just wants a little legitimate attention, like everyone else.

I believe that children as young as a year and a quarter can show clear-cut jealousy of a younger baby, and by two years may be bothered by a mother's attention to her husband, or even to a friend on the telephone. And I believe that if a child as young as one and a half is allowed to assume that his wishes come first, he can develop into quite a tyrant in a short time. I remember a boy of this age who was left in the care of an adoring maiden aunt, who enjoyed catering to his whims, when both his parents had to be away from home for three weeks. He found that by pointing at any chair his aunt was sitting in and firmly saying, "Chair!" he could make her vacate it in his favor; so he practiced this lordly game frequently, with increasing authority. When his parents came home he demanded that they too give their chairs up to him, and he shouted indignantly when they didn't hurry to do so. They explained firmly that they liked to sit in their own chairs and liked boys to be polite. In a couple of days he stopped trying to bully them. This showed me how readily a small child will take command when an adult surrenders it.

The fact that a father feels he must ask a professional person whether there is any justice in his own belief that a child shouldn't be allowed to interfere with his parents' conversation, and the fact that the mother feels that the child should always be included, if he wishes, in all family talk, shows how far we have gone in America in emphasizing the rights of children and limiting the rights of adults. I doubt that such a question could have been asked seriously in any other country in the world—or even in America in earlier centuries. Whatever happened?

I don't know for sure, and it would take too long at this point to speculate on all the possibilities. I'll mention only two important factors. One, I think, has been the striving among the pioneers and immigrants in a new country to focus on the future and the children: "We want our children to have what we never had." The other has been the influx of new concepts in child development that have come from psychologists, psychiatrists, educators, and pediatricians. American parents have accepted these much more avidly than parents in other parts of the Western world, perhaps because American parents did not have such deeply engraved traditions. In any case, these rather startling new concepts have made many parents feel that when in doubt they'd better let the child have his way, rather than run the risk of distorting his personality with the wrong management. This point of view has been unfortunate. For none of the new knowledge, important as it has been, has contradicted the common-sense philosophy and methods that good parents have always used. And it is better for good parents to be confident of themselves—even if they are technically somewhat mistaken—than for them to be hesitant and submissive.

When I say that I don't think it's wise for parents to let their child control their conversation, I want to be sure I'm not misunderstood. I'm not saying that I think there is only one proper degree of conversational participation for children that applies to all of them. Every parent will have at least a slightly different viewpoint, which is as it should be. Such differences are what lead to the variety of personalities that children develop and carry into adulthood and that make the world go round. And I'm not worrying about all the children who interrupt their parents' conversation not because they think this is their right but because they get so excited about wanting to tell their own experiences or ask questions. I'm disagreeing only with what I think is the far-out position taken by this mother. I'm doing so not simply on the basis of my own personal taste or preference but because I've seen a lot of troubles pile up when parents let a child go on for years being as dominating as this.

There are reasons why children between one and six years are particularly sensitive about being left out when they're with both parents. At one and two they're becoming very aware of their separateness and their rights as an individual. These are aspects of their growing independence. At the very same time they're becoming increasingly aware of their dependence on their parents, particularly in the sense of missing them when they're away, wanting to keep track of them and get close to them at times when they are home, feeling possessively jealous when a parent pays attention to a new baby, to the other parent, even to an acquaintance on the telephone.

Sometimes children who are anxious about separation from their parents, in the sense of not wanting them to go out in the evening, for example, and not wanting to be left with a sitter, especially an unfamiliar one, will use their anxiety to increasingly control their parents. If a child sees that whimpering or crying as the parents prepare to leave will make them hesitate, explain for the tenth time that it's just for the evening and delay their departure for another quarter of an hour, the child may put up more and more fuss on each succeeding occasion. In a couple of months you can perhaps see that the anxiety has now become minimal and that controlling the parents is the main issue.

The same transformation may occur when a child is being left in nursery school or kindergarten for the first time—or for the first few days each fall. The child clings and cries. The parent postpones leaving, perhaps stays for the whole school session. In a few days it becomes apparent that no progress is being made, in fact the child is making more fuss than at the start.

A third variation is the two year old who begins to show anxiety when the parents say good night and leave the room, perhaps repeatedly asking to go to the bathroom again and to have another drink of water. If the parents respond with a sympathetic concern, the child may keep them busy for an hour—and for a longer period each night.

In these examples, I'm not implying that there was not genuine anxiety to start with, but that the anxiety was exploited for the satisfaction of controlling the parents and eventually became the dominant motive. And I don't mean that the parents should become harsh when they eventually come to this realization. They only need to say good-by or good night in a cheerful but firm manner as if they know for sure that there is nothing to be scared of, and leave without looking back. Their assurance helps the child to overcome his anxiety.

A very simple type of controlling—without anxiety—is when children find that they can make a doting grandparent

play a game twenty times in succession or read twenty stories. It's very clear that to control an adult, after having
always been the controlled person before, is endlessly fascinating.

Beginning around three years of age, children's feelings
for their parents, which were predominantly dependent
before, in the sense that they needed them and leaned on
them, now become more outgoing and generous. By the age
of three and a half or four, a boy's romantic attachment to his
mother has become strong and possessive enough so that he
begins to sense a rivalry with his father. The psychoanalyst
gets the most clear-cut evidence of this: When a young boy
is playing in the doctor's office with a family of dolls, he may
have the father doll go away on a trip and get lost, or be killed
in a plane accident; whereupon the boy doll takes over, to a
greater or lesser degree, his father's place and his authority
in the family. A boy's guilt about having a boy doll supplant
the father doll often shows up in such a story when he has the
father doll come back to life and punish the son severely.

Parents who have heard that children at this age are apt
to become romantically possessive and jealous will often spot
evidences of it in their children's casual talk. A little girl will
tell her mother, without being conscious of the full implica-
tions of what she's saying, "Mommy, why don't you go away
for a long, long time. I'll take good care of Daddy."

Some parents, having studied child development and
learned that a child this age is likely to suffer from jealousy
of a parent and from guilt and fear about this, assume that it
will be kinder to him or her if the parents hide a lot of their
affection for each other (so as to stir up less jealousy), or even
to let the boy have opportunities to imagine that he is as
important to his mother as his father is (for instance, let him
sleep in his father's bed when his father is away), or that a girl
is as important to her father as her mother is (let her take a
trip with him, to make up for the fact that the mother took

an earlier trip with him). Psychiatric experience with cases such as these shows that a child who is encouraged to imagine that he is a successful rival of the parent of the same sex has more rather than less trouble with jealousy.

I think it is quite possible that, because of his age, the child referred to in the letter is jealous, at least unconsciously, of his father's position as husband. And his demanding behavior suggests that his parents have been so politely deferential that he does believe his right to converse with his mother is at least as great as his father's.

But whether such a boy is specifically jealous of his father in the romantic sense or whether he is really jealous of both parents, irrespective of sex, I think it is a mistake to let him come to think that he deserves to have a place in every conversation and is entitled to demand it. His parents' submissiveness to his orders inevitably encourages him to become increasingly tyrannical. When he moves into the outside world—whether to nursery school at three or four or to school at five or six—he will find himself quite unpopular. If he is flexible enough, he may be able to learn how to be more cooperative and agreeable. If not, he will have a social (and marital) handicap all his life.

There is also a chronic tension between spoiled children and their parents throughout their childhoods. For even though something obliges the parents to be submissive, they can't really accept children's assertiveness and rudeness. They will show a persistent irritation or disapproval and they will explode from time to time. When children sense that they are displeasing their parents, though their parents seem unable to stop them, they feel guilty. And their guilt is apt to make them be more provocative in their behavior. It's as if a child is saying, "How far do I have to go, how angry must I make my parents, before they will take control of me?" To put it another way, children really don't like to be allowed to rule the roost. They have a deep awareness that they are basically helpless and that they have to depend on their parents' wisdom and strength. Instinctively they use provocative behavior as a means of getting parents to assert the control that has been lacking. But all this makes for tensions and crises and storms.

When parents become convinced that they have been too submissive to children—that they have let them lead them around by the nose—they are apt to have a strong revulsion of feeling. They develop a slightly resentful, revengeful attitude toward the children. They tend to jump on them when they ask for any privilege, whether it's out of line or legitimate. This is a natural reaction, and it may help not only the parents but the children to turn over a new leaf.

In the long run it isn't necessary to be at all harsh to children to make them be reasonable and polite. In fact, parental aggressiveness stirs up counteraggressiveness in children—whether or not they dare to express it openly— whereas parental warmth, serenity, politeness, help to induce reasonableness. If I had a small son who tried to keep me from conversing with my wife, I'd merely explain to him that fathers and mothers have lots of grown-up things to talk about so they can't always talk to their child or listen to him; he'll just have to be patient.

It may temporarily frustrate children who have been used to bossing their parents to hear that they can't do it any longer. But once they have learned this, it is no hardship on them to have to be considerate, provided their parents are considerate of them in matters in which consideration is their due, if parents show children affection, enjoy them, provide them with friends and activities, are polite to them. Children want to be as much like their parents as possible and they want their parents to love them. These powerful forces (along with plenty of reminders, of course) will keep them in line if their parents set the example.

Chapter V

Children Who
Could Benefit from
Psychotherapy

:: 21 ::

For Which Problems?

I've received a number of letters asking how parents would
know when a child needs psychiatric treatment.

The simplest answer would be, "When parents are dis-
satisfied with some aspect of a child's behavior and haven't
themselves been able to find the reason for it." This implies
that it doesn't matter whether the problem seems great or
small, and I go along with that. If the parents are unhappy
about even a relatively minor matter, this will continue to
sour the parent-child relationship and may lead to other troubles. Besides, a parent can't always tell what is major and
what is minor. Peskiness or rebelliousness that is driving the
parents crazy may be found to be due to something as simple
as overpermissiveness. Whereas a tendency to withdraw,
which doesn't really bother anyone and which only makes
the parents wonder a little, may prove on investigation to
need a lot of treatment. So it's sensible for parents to go
ahead and ask for professional assistance in at least the evaluation (diagnosis) of any persistent symptom. Next comes the

question of whether treatment is advised, and whether the parents will want to go along with it.

But this simple rule doesn't cover all the cases that would benefit from psychiatric attention. The main reason is that parents sometimes don't sense a problem that may be quite apparent to others.

I will now try to give a list of symptoms that generally would justify at least an evaluation. But so much depends on how intense the symptom is, what the age of the child is, and most important, how the child gets along in other respects. Take bed-wetting, known as enuresis. It may mean nothing at three years of age in a child who's generally well adjusted or it may be a temporary expression of jealousy of a new baby. At six or eight or ten, enuresis always has significance, but the significance may be great or small; it can be an indication of one kind of tension in one child, quite another in another. If I had a son who was wetting the bed at the age of six or eight, I'd prefer that someone look into the situation. If I lived two hundred miles from a psychiatrist and the child got along well with brothers and sisters, friends, teacher, and schoolwork and showed no other symptoms, I'd feel he could wait, if necessary, for the consultation. But if he had trouble competing enjoyably with other boys and had a number of fears, I'd travel the two hundred miles. Somewhat the same rule goes for fears. Quite a number of four and five year olds who are otherwise well adjusted have transient fears. But if fears persist, are severe and are accompanied by other signs of tension, they should be looked into. Phobias about going to school should be investigated promptly, because they often become more difficult to overcome the longer the child stays out of school. As far as social adjustment is concerned, children should be able to play more and more cooperatively as they grow past three years of age, should have fewer fights and should settle most of them with little violence. A child who can't make or keep friends by six, or who is aggressive or cruel or timid with other children, should have help.

It is normal for the two year old to have difficulty separating from his or her mother, but most three year olds can separate for a half-day of nursery school. On entrance to kindergarten and first grade there are only a few children who can't let their parents go. If they don't adjust soon, they need help.

When parents have real difficulty in managing or controlling their children, they need assistance.

Telling imaginary tales occasionally as if they were true is normal at three and four. The sense of reality and the obligation to answer truthfully should be pretty well established by five or six. The child who is regularly lying after that is under great strain or has a serious personality problem. Stealing and fire-setting after the age of five certainly need looking into. The boy who wants to be a girl or always to play with girls and the girl who is chronically resentful that she is not a boy can more easily be helped at a young age than later.

It is normal for preschool children to try to get into sex play occasionally (though I personally think they should be gently discouraged). After six, children brought up in a family with high standards try to repress their sexual curiosity and impulses most of the time, though these may occasionally reappear when they feel that secrecy is assured. The child who persists in sex play despite prohibition, especially after six, and the child who is always trying to involve younger children needs help.

The child who stutters or who is highly excitable or who is always sad or who is ready to explode with anger needs evaluation. A pupil who is having any persistent trouble in school—whether it is with reading, math, paying attention, or in getting along with teachers or classmates—should receive special help in school or outside.

Thumb-sucking, as far as I know, has no special significance in itself; you judge the child by how he gets along in other respects.

Nail-biting when a child is under temporary tension, as in

a scary movie, means nothing. If he bites his nails frequently, it means that he is under a certain amount of strain; it may or may not be of importance.

Nail-biting is a good example of a type of symptom that is merely a direct and natural reaction to a stressful situation. It doesn't imply that anything has gone seriously wrong in the development of the individual's personality. Other symptoms that are natural reactions are, for example: the poor appetite of a child who has been urged much too often to eat; the meanness of a small child who is temporarily feeling displaced by a new baby; the dislike of school by a child who is failing there for some reason. Theoretically, you only have to change the environment or management somewhat or help the child to understand (as in the case of jealousy of the new baby) that the danger is not nearly as great as he or she imagined.

At the other end of the scale are the symptoms which indicate that because of the long-continued effect of unfavorable influences, emotional development has been definitely delayed (as in the case of a school-age child who demands constant attention from the teacher, can't sit still, can't concentrate on the work to be done), or emotional development has progressed in an unfortunate direction that is likely to cause the person unhappiness for years (as in the case of a child who has become basically hostile toward everyone, or passive, or deficient in conscience). Children in these categories need not only a change in environment but also direct psychological help in straightening out their inner feelings so that they can get back on the right track. Of course, most of the symptoms children show are not at one or the other extreme end of the scale; they partly represent a reaction to the present situation and partly a disturbance of personality from accumulated pressures of the past.

How do you go about getting psychiatric diagnosis for a child and, if necessary, treatment? In a large city there will be child psychiatrists in private practice and child-guidance clinics. Both will be prepared to adjust the fee to the family's ability to pay. But because the clinic usually receives some support from the Community Chest or from government, it is able to care for more cases from families with less-than-average income.

Because there is always a demand for more child-psychiatry services than exist, there are waiting lists. Usually there is a waiting list for evaluation (diagnosis), and there is apt to be a longer wait for treatment for those cases for which it has been recommended. There are some conditions that are considered greater emergencies than others, and children suffering from these may not have to wait so long.

Many cities and towns that do not have a child psychiatrist or a child-guidance clinic do have a family social agency; sometimes there is a Catholic, a Jewish, and a Protestant family service agency. This would always be a suitable place to first raise the question of what is upsetting a child and what needs to be done. A psychiatric social worker takes a full history of the problem and of the background, from the parents, on a number of occasions. Another social worker may see the child, and there may be psychological tests.

If they find that this is a case within their professional range—for counseling the parents and perhaps for working with the child too—they will do so. If they consider it one that will require more elaborate diagnostic or treatment services, they will refer it to a child psychiatrist or clinic. Because of their regular contacts with such other services, they may be able to get the family to the most appropriate one in the shortest possible time.

What exactly do the child psychiatrist, the psychiatric social worker, and the clinical psychologist do? It is easier to tell first what goes on in the average child-guidance clinic. The mother, in several sessions, tells a social worker about the special difficulty and also about the child's adjustment in various respects since infancy; and she tells something about the family setup in which the child lives. The father gives his picture of the situation, which sheds additional light. The child psychiatrist may see the child once or twice, to gain a firsthand impression, and the clinical psychologists will give him tests, as required, of emotional attitudes, personality makeup, and intelligence. Then in a conference the staff members involved fit the pieces of the picture together and come to a tentative diagnosis and tentative recommendations, which are subsequently discussed with the parents. In one case the parents may be told that the problem is a relatively superficial one and are advised, over several sessions, about how best to manage it themselves. In another case the trouble is seen as more deeply ingrained. Then it is recommended that the child come regularly for treatment (psychotherapy), perhaps once a week for months; and usually one or both parents continue to visit the social worker for counseling.

The child psychiatrist in private practice has the job not only of treating the child directly but also of counseling the parents. This in some ways is more difficult than having the parents work with a social worker, because it takes the child a longer time to develop trust in the psychiatrist—until he becomes convinced that the psychiatrist is not spilling his confidences to the parent.

What goes on in psychiatric treatment? This is the part that seems mysterious to most people. It will depend, of course, on the problem, on the personalities of the child and parent, and somewhat on the particular philosophy of the therapist. Roughly speaking, the job is for the patient, parent, and therapist to use their three kinds of knowledge to discover what went wrong. The child or parent talks about what he consciously remembers from the past and how he feels about things right now. The therapist has been trained to understand the influence of painful past experiences (like being worried in early childhood that some bogeyman was after you or that your parents might disown you) and also to understand the influence of forbidden desires (such as to get even in a drastic way with a brother or a parent), both of which are apt to be repressed into the unconscious layers of the mind. The patient and the therapist work at the slow process of fitting these two aspects of the problem together. The parent and social worker may be trying to figure out why the parent automatically reacts in a manner that rubs the child the wrong way. This business of fitting bits of the truth together isn't the rational, intellectual process I've made it sound. The truth comes to the surface in indirect, unexpected ways or is blurted out in angry reproaches, some of which are quite illogical. When the child and the parent each have come face to face with what it was in their unconscious minds that has been making them respond to each other in self-defeating ways, they will be able to handle their daily relationships more sensibly.

A small child can't begin by talking about what bothers him or her, the way an adult or an adolescent may. The therapist usually has a collection of dolls (representing parents, policemen, children, and so on), dolls' furniture, cars, blocks, and pistols, with which a child will usually be quite ready to start playing out imaginary situations. With time and with increasing confidence in the therapist, the child's play themes will get closer and closer to his own worries. He also will learn to express his feelings and discuss how to live with them, in words.

The psychoanalyst is a psychiatrist who has had special training in the concepts and methods first worked out by Freud. He may want to see the child three to five times a week (rather than once a week, which is the commonest scheduling in child-guidance clinics), and he deals more intensely and exclusively with unconscious levels than does the psychiatrist who is not a psychoanalyst.

In recent years a new form of therapy, family therapy, has been developed to tackle the kinds of behavior problems that involve two or more members of a family—which is a large proportion of the behavior problems. Having various members of the family in the room with two therapists often brings about a more rapid and dramatic facing of the problems by all concerned.

When a child's difficulty is first brought to attention in regard to schoolwork, the first step will probably be to use the school's diagnostic and guidance facilities, if any. There may be a psychologist on the staff of the school system to give tests for school achievement, intelligence, and aptitude. Perhaps there is a guidance counselor (a teacher or assistant principal trained to look into the meaning and solution of school problems) or a school social worker who works with parents and child and keeps in touch with the teacher. If the school counselor or psychologist finds that a child's problem goes deep enough to require it, he or she will refer the parents to a child-guidance clinic. In a few large cities there are fully staffed child-guidance clinics within the school system, equipped to take on any type of psychiatric problems that come to light in the school.

:: 22 ::

Do Parents Cause the Problems?

A discussion, such as the one in the last section, about symptoms that could be helped by psychotherapy is apt to make conscientious parents, even those whose children show no signs of trouble, feel at least a little bit concerned about what they have done to their children—or left undone—in rearing them. I think it's important that parents get a different and wider perspective on this whole subject. It's true that personalities are formed from the impact of the environment—of which the parents constitute a very significant part—on children's inborn temperament. But it is a basic mistake to assume that all parental influences are either definitely good or definitely bad in themselves. To be sure, parental lovingness is absolutely essential, and its influence is on the favorable side as long as it is a sensible and balanced love. It is also true that parental neglect, in the sense of indifference to the child's welfare, is always detrimental. Excessive and consistent harshness is unfavorable. However, most parental characteristics don't fall into such simple moral categories. Take, for example, parents' ambition for their children. It sometimes puts an unusual strain on a particular child and thereby produces symptoms. But it's essential to realize that parental ambition in the broad sense is what has accounted for all the advances in civilization. Parents who are not ambitious raise children a majority of whom are simply not ambitious. I don't think it's bad to be unambitious—it is just one of the conditions of man; it has provided all the people who are satisfied to work at chores that ambitious people consider intolerably dull. Parents who are ambitious for their children are only carrying out one of the obligations built into them during their own upbringing. And when this process occasionally misfires a bit, it's usually because of minor quirks in parent or child that no one could have anticipated ahead of time.

Another area to think of is the development of rationality or intellectuality. A majority of parents of an intellectual bent tend to control the feeling side of their own nature to a greater-than-average degree. Their mental self-discipline actually suppresses some of their emotional responsiveness. They also tend to do the same thing to their children's feelings, without ever having decided to do so, without even noticing it. They do it by example as well as by deliberately teaching self-control. When this process happens to go beyond a certain point, in the rearing of a boy, for example, this may have the effect, when he is grown up, of interfering with comfortable relationships with his spouse or children or coworkers. An extreme, comic-book example of this is the absent-minded professor who not only doesn't know when his wife is wearing a new dress, he also doesn't know when she's miserably unhappy. Yet if there were no parents who suppressed their children's emotions to a degree, and diverted that energy into intellectual and academic channels, there would be no one to attend universities.

When parents emphasize right and wrong, especially at certain stages of development, it sometimes helps to produce a compulsive (overscrupulous) personality in a particular child. But unless there is a majority of moralistic people in every country in every generation, there can be no justice. In fact, there can be no society.

So in a sense, many of the disturbances we are discussing are accidental by-products of the human striving to create a more civilized world. To put it in more personal terms to parents, there is no point and no justice in their reproaching themselves because some of their efforts misfire in certain respects with one or another child. All parents are separate and special people largely created by their own upbringing, over which they had little control. They do their best in raising their own children. A certain characteristic of a parent may help one child to achieve a generally good adjustment. In a second child it may play a part in creating a quirk of personality that does him no particular harm or good. In a third child it may foster an unusual combination of personality traits that enables him to make a particularly valuable contribution to the world—in the arts, for instance. Both parents have a thousand traits that are making countless impressions on their children, each of whom responds on the basis of a thousand individual traits. There is no controlling such multitudinous interactions.

A characteristic that seems like an asset at one stage of development may get in an individual's way later. (Great athletic success in high school or college occasionally distracts a man from making a real contribution in later life.) And what seems like a weakness or a distortion in a child may be the core around which she or he succeeds in building a personality of unusual strength and productivity. (This is seen clearly in the lives of certain great novelists, artists, scientists, and political leaders.)

Parents have no way of knowing in advance how their own personalities will mold their child or how each characteristic of the child will contribute to her or his final destiny. Naturally it is safer for parents to try to cultivate in themselves what are generally considered to be virtues and to suppress what are usually considered vices. They can try to be honest in recognizing their more obvious shortcomings. Certainly they all have to work hard to impress their standards on their offspring. But beyond that they have little to go on. It would be completely unrealistic for them to think that they can make their children turn out ideal according to some preconceived pattern, as a perfect cookie cutter presumably could turn out perfectly shaped cookies.

If, after having done their best, parents see that a child of theirs is showing the effects of some strain, they can ask for professional help in locating the source and counteracting it. There are two good reasons why they should still try not to reproach themselves. They did not knowingly create the problem. And when parents do become guilty, it makes for further difficulties in the management of the child. Most important of all, young couples at the threshold of parenthood should resolve to fight against becoming guilty ahead of time—worrying in advance that they won't be able to do a perfect job, as so many conscientious American parents do nowadays. They only make their job twice as difficult as it needs to be.

It would help American parents to realize how easily they become guilty about the rearing of their children if they could see the contrast with parents of another country. A Frenchwoman who is a child psychiatrist in Paris wrote a revealing paper on how differently American and French parents act when they first come to her office. American parents typically begin, "We realize that we must have caused the problem and that it's probably we who need the psychiatric treatment." They are like dogs with their tails between their legs. French parents have no such guilt; they have indignation. They say to the psychiatrist, "We've given this child all the advantages—good home, good clothes and schooling, fine family. Yet he shows no appreciation. He is bad. We have scolded him, deprived him, spanked him. But nothing does any good. Now *you* make him behave."

There is another aspect of child rearing that should keep American parents from feeling so bad about every unexpected turn in a child's development. Children are not born with personalities like a soft, formless lump of putty that can be shaped any which way by the parents. They arrive with internal patterns of emotional development just as definite as the physical pattern locked in a chrysanthemum seed. This is apparent even in the newborn nursery. Some children are energetic, others quiet. They can be aggressive, gentle, outgoing, withdrawn, imperturbable, sensitive, balky, compliant, open, mysterious. One kind of parent can enjoy and manage wisely a gentle kind of child and be rubbed the wrong way by an aggressive one. And there's another parent —male or female—who loves the kind of child he or she can call "Butch" but doesn't quite know what to do with one who is gentle and inactive. Few adults would claim to be able to get along easily with all other types of adults. Yet parents have to put up with what they receive in the way of children; it's a great credit to them that they get along at least reasonably well with most of their children.

Chapter VI

Sex Education

:: 23 ::

The Fundamentals

Fifty years ago, after Freud had shown the connection between various neuroses and the frightening, guilty ideas that some children acquire about sex in early childhood, many of the professionals who wrote and lectured for parents had high hopes that such neuroses could be prevented. They felt that if parents could be helped to understand the need for wholesome and thorough sex education, it should be possible not only to prevent children from developing sexual neuroses but also to improve greatly the sexual adjustments of men and women.

The psychological disturbances that these sex educators had in mind were, for instance, the obsessive and compulsive neuroses, the phobias, the hysterical paralyses and anesthesias, frigidity in women and impotence in men, homosexuality and other perversions, and lesser sexual imcompatibilities of many kinds.

Better and more wholesome sex education could be achieved these educators believed, if parents would talk with greater frankness and naturalness about the sexual facts of life with their children, beginning at an early age.

Time and experience have shown that those hopes of half a century ago were too high and ingenuous. To be sure, we do have a more comfortable attitude toward sex nowadays and there may have been some reduction in certain of the neuroses most directly related to excessive anxiety about sexuality. But there is still a great deal of neurosis, perversion, impotence and frigidity, as well as maladjustment to sex and to marriage.

The principal way in which the early educators misjudged was in assuming that the neuroses and sexual disturbances to which Freud referred were caused mainly by simple, intellectual misunderstandings about sex by children who had not had things explained to them correctly. Actually the more significant causes of these neuroses lie deeper in the unconscious mind—in disturbed feelings, particularly those of children toward their parents. A typical example would be an abnormally close and possessive relationship between a child and the parent of the opposite sex and an exaggeratedly antagonistic, fearful, guilty attitude toward the other parent. Lopsided relationships like these become interwoven with children's early sexual feelings. When they grow up, their mixed-up feelings may repeatedly get them involved in out-of-kilter, unhappy relationships with other people or produce neurotic symptoms, or both.

Another way in which the early sex educators misjudged was in assuming that once children got the facts straight, they would be on the right track for good. Anyone who has had young children who ask questions and state their own views about the facts of life knows that no matter how carefully they are straightened out each time, they are forever developing new, unrealistic notions. A parent's first thought is that another child is feeding them misinformation. Occasionally that's the explanation. But more often it's that the children themselves are dreaming up new facts of life—having fantasies of their own on the basis of their own particular feelings about parents, other people, and themselves.

One of the most instructive and amusing articles I ever read was by a magazine writer who held an open discussion about the facts of life with the children of a kindergarten class. The class was made up of children from well-to-do homes where the parents obviously had done their best to provide correct information. The children were quite free and unembarrassed in their remarks, but all of them were mixed up about the facts. One child thought a new baby descends from heaven to the hospital, where the mother has a sort of appointment to meet it. ("She almost didn't get there on time.") Another thought new babies are on display at the hospital and can be bought—rather expensively. ("My father said we didn't have enough money to get one.") Another thought the doctor brings a baby to the mother, who goes to the hospital to get it when he has one ready. Another explained that the mother eats a seed and the baby soon pops out through a little hole.

These five-year-old children also got cause and effect and terminology jumbled. One said sadly that her parents couldn't ever get a new baby now because they had given away the old bassinet; another said that his dog couldn't have puppies because her neuter had been taken out.

Perhaps you think I'm defeating my purpose by playing down the effectiveness of sex education right at the start of this discussion. But I want not only to give you a realistic view, but also to put you more at ease. I want to prevent your getting the idea that in order to keep your children mentally or sexually healthy you must given them a perfect course of sex instruction—or at least give them perfect answers to their questions. You'll do a better job if you don't take it too seriously. I also want to be able to point out what, by contrast, is really the important part of sex education.

I feel quite sure that the most crucial aspect of sex education for any child is not the factual explanations they hear from time to time, but the picture they form of the over-all relationship between their parents and between each of their parents and themselves. If their parents love each other, respect each other, show an appropriate degree of physical affection for each other, then the children will have a basic image laid down which will be a powerful guide for them as they grow. They will strive always to be like the parent of their own sex. They will hope to have, to cherish, and to help a future spouse of their own as they see their parent doing.

In addition, it is necessary for each of a child's parents to enjoy the child as boy or girl—whichever the child is. A boy, in order to be ready to play a man's role as husband and worker, should have felt his father's general approval, affection, and firm leadership. A father who has been consistently standoffish makes an unsatisfactory guide. The same applies between the mother and daughter.

The parent of the opposite sex should be able to enjoy the child as a member of the opposite sex. (I don't mean that the parent should be seductive to the child.) This, plus the child's own romantic attachment to the parent of the opposite sex, prepares him or her to fall in love with, to win, to be a good lover to, to take care of, to live comfortably with, an appropriate member of the opposite sex—someday.

Whether or not children hear the most approved explanation of the physical difference between the sexes or of where babies come from or of how human beings mate is of secondary importance. To stretch this point, even if children get most of their information from ignorant playmates or from literature that parents disapprove of, nevertheless, if their feelings are right, they'll be little harmed by this misinformation.

In Victorian times some highly protected girls didn't receive any sexual instruction, didn't consciously know about intercourse, until marriage. But if the relationships they had had with their parents were sound, they soon made as good marital adjustments as the knowledgeable girls of today.

On the other hand, I have worked professionally with adult patients who had had instruction from parents, read approved books on sex, received hygiene lectures at college, had long, explanatory talks with friends. Still they were fearful or unresponsive or resentful about sex or about man-woman relationships in general. The fault was that their parents had had badly distorted marriages—I don't mean occasional quarrels—or the child's relationship with the parents had been miserably unhappy. Usually the two maladjustments go together, for they are apt to have a common cause.

Am I saying that there is no importance at all to sex education of the specific, verbal type through childhood? No. I think it is definitely worthwhile. It helps, if only in a secondary way, to give children—gradually, as they grow—a more correct and wholesome view of things.

Discussion about the facts of life is also valuable in giving children the feeling that it is all right from time to time to ask their parents more questions—until children think they know more than their parents. This will keep children from having as strange fantasies, or being as puzzled by other children's morbid ideas, as they might otherwise.

To have occasional casual talks with their parents also keeps children from imagining that their parents are sternly disapproving about any sexual interest—a feeling that children are likely to have in the absence of any mutual discussion.

:: 24 ::

The Specifics

Children's first questions—usually about why boys and girls
are shaped differently—are apt to come when children are
somewhere between two and a half and three and a half
years old, depending partly on the experiences the children
are exposed to. They'll come earlier if children see other
members of the family undressed.

Many child psychiatrists believe it's better for children
not to be deliberately allowed to see their parents undressed.
The relationship of young children to parents is so intense—
in attraction, in rivalry, in awe or fear—that regular exposure
of parents' bodies heightens such attitudes to an uncomfortable degree. An occasional glimpse by accident is inevitable
and not nearly so disturbing.

Seeing the anatomies of brothers and sisters generally is
not too upsetting, and in most cases is considered soundly
educational for preschool children. The same goes for the
anatomies of friends as seen in toileting at home or in nursery
school. I'm not suggesting letting children play naked or play
doctor—that's too stimulating in our usually dressed society
—but allowing them to look when they make brief trips to
the toilet or are being changed into bathing suits, for instance. Children of school age have a desire for modesty and
this should be respected.

The most crucial aspect of the small child's questions
about sex differences is to realize that both boy and girl are
apt to draw anxious conclusions from sex differences. A boy
is likely to jump to the conclusion at two and a half, three,
or three and a half that a girl was meant to have a penis like
himself and that some injury has deprived her of it. His next

thought may be that the same accident could happen to him. This thought is instinctively alarming to all males.

A girl seeing a boy's or man's penis for the first time is apt to wonder why she was deprived or injured. Psychoanalysis reveals that the little girl is most likely to conclude that her mother didn't love her enough to make her right. So a parent should be sensitive to the likelihood of such assumptions in both boys and girls, and try gently to counteract them. "All boys and men are meant to have penises, like Daddy, Uncle Harry, Charlie. Girls are meant to be different. Girls aren't meant to have penises. Mommy and Aunt Harriet and Linda don't have penises. Instead, girls have a place inside called a uterus, to grow a baby in. And girls have breasts to feed a baby with. Boys don't have a uterus or breasts." Often small children show by subsequent direct or indirect questions that their fearful assumption about injury to the penis has stuck in their minds better than the parents' effort at reassurance. So be prepared to repeat the reassurances, in various forms.

Psychiatrists have discovered that when a small child has a worry, it's better to focus on the worry for a minute before trying to remove it. When your son asks his first question that shows his anxiety about loss of his penis, try to remember to say something like, "Some boys think a girl is meant to have a penis too, and when they see she hasn't got one, they think maybe something bad happened to it. But that isn't true. Nothing bad happened. A girl is meant to be made different from a boy. A girl is not meant to have a penis. No girls have a penis," etc. Similarly, in speaking to a daughter you can say, "Some girls, when they see a boy's penis, think they were meant to have a penis too, and they think that maybe something happened to it." And then continue with the explanation.

What about children who reach three and a half, four, or four and a half without ever asking a question? Child psychiatrists, from long experience, doubt that such children have never had their suspicions raised. It is much more likely that they were sufficiently upset by noticing the difference so that they didn't dare inquire. Or that they asked a question that embarrassed their parent just enough so that they decided it wasn't a safe topic. But children concerned about such a problem can't help referring to it indirectly. They'll ask, "Is a dog a boy?" "Is a cat a girl?" "Is a frankfurter a boy?" Or they will too persistently try to spy on their parents or to get other children to undress, despite parental disapproval. Then a mother can show that it's all right to wonder and ask questions by saying, "I think you are worried a little bit about why boys are made different from girls, about why girls don't have a penis. Perhaps you think that girls were meant to have a penis and that something happened to it."

Children's next question is likely to be concerned with where babies come from. The easy, straightforward answer is that the baby grows inside the mother's tummy or abdomen. Young children know that the tummy is the place where food goes after it's eaten and that some of the residue comes out from the anus. It's a child's natural assumption, then, that a mother eats a tiny baby or a seed and that the grown baby comes out through the anus. So the parent needs to do a little discriminating by the time a child asks subsequent questions about entrance and exit. The baby grows in a special place, not where the food goes. When it's big enough it comes out through a special hole, the vagina, not where the BM comes out. And if the child asks and the parent feels ready to answer, the seed comes out of the father's penis, when he puts his penis in the special hole. In most cases the child doesn't get to the seed question for weeks or months after the first questions about where the baby comes from, so parents have practice with the easier answers before tackling the ones that are likely to make them more tense.

Young children are good at putting their parents at ease in regard to the facts of life. They ask the questions in the most matter-of-fact way and are intensely interested in the answers and not embarrassed by them.

In the six-to-twelve-year-old period children prefer to get at human concerns through an impersonal, abstract approach. They no longer play family or mother their dolls or talk about having babies of their own. They try to cool their feelings about their parents. So they more easily show interest in how animals reproduce than human beings. And when they do get around occasionally to human beings, they like talk with a scientific flavor. This is why many schools go in for animal keeping in kindergarten or first grade and later take up human reproduction in nature study. But it's good for parents to be helpful also by showing that they still are willing to answer all questions to the best of their ability. The subject of the growth spurt that accompanies puberty, and how widely the age of the onset of puberty varies, should be taken up by school or parents by the fifth grade.

In the adolescent phase, children become intensely though secretly interested in knowing a lot about sex. It would be fine if they could turn to their parents at this time and if their parents could answer comfortably and fully. But this usually doesn't happen, for several reasons.

A child's first romantic love, at the age of three to five years, is for the parent of the opposite sex. From the age of six to about twelve, the child comes to feel that this love was dangerous and forbidden. These two facts, together with the acute awareness of sexuality that comes to boys and girls during their teen years, makes them unbearably embarrassed to admit their own sexuality to their parents or to think of their parents as sexual beings. The embarrassment of children is quickly communicated to the parent who tries to talk with them.

The distress is apt to be particularly great between son and father, daughter and father. I can remember how carefully I picked a private occasion to bring up the topic with each of my sons and how each said, in instant alarm, "I know all about it already." It is fairly characteristic of girls at the time of first menstruation to beg the mother not even to mention this to the father. Some girls can talk fairly comfortably with their mothers. And mothers often have an easier time than fathers when they bring up the topic with their sons, if the mothers have given up hope of the fathers' ever getting around to it.

Even in these enlightened days a great majority of adolescents get their information or misinformation about sex from pals, older brothers or sisters, books, or school because of the embarrassment between them and their parents. Perhaps this is inevitable. I would still advise parents to try if they can. If it's too hard to get started, a parent can give the child a book and indicate willingness to discuss any aspects of it.*

In any case, it's good for parents to know that they aren't abnormal—or even unusual—if they find talk of sex difficult with their adolescents.

There are several general aspects that are worth mentioning here. It's sound to start out in a cheerful, positive tone by explaining that preoccupation with sexual thoughts at this age is nature's way of making a person grow up (it's not abnormal). Nocturnal emissions or wet dreams are an expression of physical readiness. Menstrual periods are part of the preparation of the uterus each month and don't need to inconvenience or discomfort most girls. There is a natural impulse to masturbate and almost every teenager does it—occasionally or often—and it does not cause physical or mental disease. I think you should get around to mentioning venereal diseases, but toward the end of the discussion, explaining that they do not come from sexual relations themselves but from relations with an infected individual, who is usually a promiscuous person. Important to make clear, too,

*E.q., *A Teenager's Guide to Life and Love*; Benjamin Spock M.D.

that acne does not come from masturbation or sexual thoughts, as adolescents often fear.

Parents should be prepared for adolescents' less direct questions and arguments about dating, use of make-up, rules about the hour for coming home, the permissible age of marriage, and so on.

Even in discussions of anatomy and physiology, I think it is important to integrate the spiritual and romantic aspects of sexuality; otherwise sex is made to seem mechanical and animal-like. This means that sex should be discussed in school, not so much by the school doctor or nurse, gym teacher or biology teacher, but by any and all teachers who are mature emotionally, who are respected by the students and who feel comfortable talking about sex.

Courses in literature, drama, history, all involve sexuality in the broadest sense. They invite classroom discussion of the romantic relationships of the people in the books, and also lead the adolescent students, if they trust and like the teacher, to bring up their own personal concerns about romance and sex. All this discussion and questioning is good. Sex is related to every other aspect of life and can constructively be discussed by counselors and by teachers in all subjects in which it comes up, as long as the spiritual aspects are included.

:: 25 ::

Embarrassing Birthdays

Several mothers whose babies were born less than nine months after marriage have asked me whether it wouldn't be better, for the children's sake, to change the date when their birthday is celebrated so that later—adolescence, for instance—when they are wise enough to put two and two together, they won't discover the awkward relationship between the wedding day and their true birthday. (Or as an alternative they suggest they might falsify the month of their marriage.) The difficulty, as experience has often shown, is that sooner or later children are likely to learn of their true birth date—from their birth certificate, for instance, or from a slip of the tongue on the part of a relative. (The same would apply to a fictitious wedding date.) When children in adolescence or in adulthood find that the fact that they were conceived before marriage has been deliberately concealed from them, they may take this premarital conception to be a more significant, a more shameful matter than they would have if there had been no deceit. And more important, they lose some of their confidence in their parents' truthfulness.

On the other hand, I don't see any reason why the parents need to call children's attention to the close relationship of the two dates, at least until they raise the question themselves or until a parent is discussing sex and conduct with them in adolescence. Such a compulsive truthfulness would not benefit children at an age when they were too young to understand the real significance of the situation. It would only indicate that the parents have made no progress over the years in outgrowing their guiltiness. If the parents have been reasonably open and honest in answering other questions about life, children will probably feel free to ask about the date relationship if it ever strikes them, which won't be likely before their teens, anyway. Then the parents can answer according to their beliefs.

I myself would not want my adolescent child to get the impression that I thought a pregnancy outside of or before marriage was of no importance. I would want him or her to believe that sexual intimacy is better saved until a couple are married or are at least definitely committed to marriage, after many months of ever-closer companionship and the discovery of more and more shared ideals. (I'd put the emphasis on "many months" because any courageous adolescent at the start of each new infatuation is sure that this time it's the real thing.) I would like him or her to feel that even after a couple have decided on marriage, they show a degree of irresponsibility toward the good name of their relatives and of their own future marriage and of their future child if they carelessly conceive a child premaritally.

What can parents say when their adolescent children bring up the question of why they were born so soon, or when the question evolves out of their parents' discussions with them about the facts of life? I would say something like the following: "We had been very much in love for a year and had decided to get married. We thought it better to postpone the wedding until Daddy had a job and we could have a home. We began to have intercourse but we were careless about birth control. That was not right, because it upset our parents when the wedding had to be hurried and you were born so soon. If people decide to have intercourse before they are married, they should be very responsible about it. But we loved you very much when you were born, and our parents forgave us."

The foregoing line of reasoning is based on two assumptions on my part that may have little appeal to some parents. The first is that honesty with one's children is of great importance—in building trust between parent and child and in building integrity into the child's character. If a child finds that his parents have lied about an important matter, he loses some of his faith in them and he loses some of his conviction about the importance of honesty itself. On the other hand, there are many parents who do not set such great store by strict honesty; they use false threats to make their children behave, feeling that this is well justified if it works; they use frequent lies that they'd call white lies to cover up, excuse, or explain matters that would otherwise be troublesome or embarrassing; some even enjoy leading a child on with tall stories, just to see what he'll make of them. A child brought up this way doesn't stay fooled for long. He learns that his parents often don't mean what they say and he eventually learns to tinker with the truth himself, for practical or playful reasons. It's not that one philosophy is right and another wrong, only that they are different, and they result in the formation of different types of personality.

My other assumption is that to make the world better, parents should try to instill in their children morals and standards at least as high as their own, certainly not lower. This is a difficult assignment in today's materialistic and per-missive atmosphere.

Now I'll go on to some other problems, applying the same philosophy.

What does a mother say to a child who was born illegiti-mately, whose father she never married and whom she or the grandmother is raising (that is to say, the baby was not placed for adoption), whether or not she later marries another man? In the first place, I think it is better for the child to be ac-knowledged as the mother's child, rather than passed off, as is sometimes done, as having been born to the grandmother. For experience shows that almost always children discover the truth sooner or later—from neighbor children, for in-stance, from an absent-minded relative, from old letters, or from a birth certificate. And when children discover a secret of this importance that had been withheld from them, experience shows that it can sometimes be a shattering emotional blow, even though their mother and grandmother have been kind and devoted to them all along. Second, it disillusions them about the honesty of their relatives. Third, when mothers and other relatives are keeping children in the dark about their parentage, this makes for a constant insincerity and evasiveness in the adults' manner toward children that will bother them underneath and interfere with the development of their security and sound characters.

Even if a mother marries another man who wants to raise the child as his own, I believe it is better for the child to know he or she had another father, the real father, first, even though the child may not remember him. It may seem very foolish to some people not to take full advantage of such a generous and affectionate offer from the stepfather, especially if the true father is considered no great shakes. But again, the chances are great that the child will discover the truth sooner or later and react with shock and disillusion. My own preference would be to let the fact come out casually, from the beginning (from two and a half, three, three and a half years of age, when children begin to ask questions and to get the idea of relationships), that the child had another daddy, that he and Mommy found they couldn't get along so they decided not to live together any more. Then Mommy found another man that she could love and get along with very well. And this man loves the child and wants to be like a daddy to him always.

Some might say that such a story would make the child assume that his mother had been actually married before and that this would be a partial untruth which would one day have to be faced. True. But I think that this untruth is much less harmful to the child than the other and so is the lesser evil (Certainly there would be no point in trying to explain illegitimacy to a young child.) I do think that the mother should later be prepared to answer candidly about not having been officially married before, if and when the child at ten or fifteen begins to ask searching questions about his true father's name and whereabouts. But she does not need to stress the lack of marriage or be dramatic or tragic or defensive about it, for the unconventional aspect of the affair is not what is most important to the child, as it might be to an adult.

But honest answering should not mean calling the true father a scoundrel, a dirty dog, if the mother considers he was. For any child needs to think of both of his parents as being worthy people; otherwise he believes himself to be partly worthless by inheritance. So, for the child's sake, the mother should speak of the child's father's good qualities. She should also speak of their love for each other, so that the affair will not seem entirely meaningless and sordid. In many cases it would be appropriate to mention that both father and mother were too young to know what was best.

If the natural father lives near and is mature enough to be willing to visit the child regularly (just as a divorced father should), it would be very valuable for the child. For if a father (or mother)—because of shame about his failure in a relationship, or painful associations, or fear of being scolded by the ex-paramour—fails to keep in contact with his child, the child usually feels unworthy of love. This is not good for his character.

Chapter VII

Adolescence
and Rebellion

:: 26 ::

The Many Kinds

Parents and society have always been concerned about adolescents. This may be as much a reflection of the worrisomeness of parents and of their jealousy of their children at this age as it is of the conduct of youth. But it is the nature of young people constantly to challenge their elders, and they also secretly enjoy scaring them a little. Disciplinary problems—at home and in the community—have existed throughout history.

Psychoanalytic experience has taught us that adolescent rebelliousness doesn't consist of just an impatience to be more independent of the parents, in rights and privileges, though it feels this way to the youths themselves. In the deeper, unconscious layers of the mind it has more of the quality of a resentful rivalry with the parent of the same sex. This is like the rivalry of the little boy at four, five, and six years of age, when he felt resentful inside that he couldn't be as big, smart, rich, and powerful as he imagined his father to be and that he couldn't compete on an equal basis for the

attention of his mother. The little girl at that same age resented, in her unconscious mind, her mother's seemingly
fabulous privileges and clothes, her possession of a fascinating husband, her ability to grow real live babies.

The adolescents' rivalry with their parents is much
sharper than that of the small child because now they have
nearly full-sized bodies, and aggressive and sexual instincts of
high intensity. This is especially true of the boy. He realizes
that he soon will be a man, with a job, wife, and home of his
own, and it riles him to have to submit still to the indignities
of being his father's child. The girl realizes that it will now
be her turn to be the beautiful woman who attracts the men,
chooses a husband, and has the babies. This gives her the
impulse to push her mother aside, though she may be too
polite to express this directly unless she is very angry.

Rebelliousness and rivalry in adolescence take many
forms, depending on the society to which the individuals
belong, their personalities, their particular relationships with
their parents, and whether they are male or female. In the
remote mountains of Tennessee and Kentucky, for instance,
where life is relatively uncomplicated and where independence is highly valued, a boy of fifteen or sixteen may graduate to manhood abruptly in one day. When his father angrily
orders him to do something that he doesn't want to do he
may suddenly, unexpectedly lose his temper, knock his father down and then walk off to the nearest town to find a job.
I heard a number of examples of this pattern when I was a
psychiatrist in the Navy.

At the opposite end of the educational scale is the son of
an urban professional man. Ever since he was a small child
he has accepted the obligation to do well in school as an
essential part of the process of becoming a professional man
himself, not only in order to meet his family's expectations
but also to be able to rival his father's achievements. In this
kind of family the father characteristically tries to be a rea-

sonable, generous, and encouraging leader to his son. If he feels anger or impatience, he tries to tone it down. These attitudes in the father make it difficult for his son to feel conscious anger toward him or to rebel beyond a little grumbling. To hit his father or even shout at him would be almost inconceivable. Psychiatrists learn that the rebelliousness is there but it finds indirect outlets and quiet forms. Many such boys remain respectful toward their fathers and shift all their irritation toward their mothers. They frequently criticize their mothers' appearance and behavior, blow up noisily when their mothers scold them or remind them of their duties.

A fairly common sign of rivalrousness in the same group, but one that doesn't look anything like rivalry on the surface, is school failure—in high school or college or graduate school —by a boy who has the intelligence and the motivation to do well and who has done well in the past. Sometimes this occurs when the boy first studies a subject that is related directly to his future lifework, especially if he is thinking of following in his father's footsteps. Psychoanalysis may show that in the unconscious mind the academic failure represents in part a fear of competition with the father. Interestingly enough, the hidden fear may be either that he won't be able to do as well as his father or that he may do so much better that his father will be furious. School failure also serves another unconscious purpose. It tortures the ambitious parents; but they can't punish the boy, and he won't feel too guilty, as long as he is consciously trying hard.

This uneasiness about competing with the father may show up in another way. When a boy at sixteen or eighteen is asked what occupation he's heading for he may answer that he doesn't know yet; the only thing he is sure of is that his father's field doesn't appeal to him at all. Then at about the age of twenty a doctor's son, for instance, may casually drop the remark that he will be taking quite a lot of chemistry this year. "Why?" asks his father. "You have to have it for medical school, of course," the son answers. "But I didn't know you were going into medicine!" exclaims the amazed and delighted father. "Didn't I tell you?" asks the boy in real perplexity. The boy has grown up enough by twenty so that he no longer is afraid of the competition implied in entering his father's field, but there is enough embarrassment left over from the past to make him forget to tell his father about his change of heart.

When a youth from a family with low educational expectations gets into trouble at school (aside from slowness because of mental limitations), it's more likely to be from sassing a teacher or principal because he can't submit any longer to the correcting and nagging, especially when the lessons mean nothing to him anyway; or he defies the authorities by staying away altogether.

When we study the serious delinquencies, we see that there is a large element of rebelliousness and rivalry in them. But they also are based on a deprivation of love from early infancy. Before we discuss these, however, it's important to point out that the word *delinquency* is the loosest kind of term. It means different things in different states and municipalities. It is anything for which a youth has been judged guilty in juvenile court. It may include parking a car too long, dumping trash cans on Halloween, running away from home, stealing a few boards from a building site, or shooting a filling-station attendant while trying to rob him. The last example is a crime usually committed only by an aggressive, unprincipled character. On the other hand, studies have shown that a great majority of the leading citizens of any town took part in some kind of mischief in youth that would have landed them in court if they had had the bad luck to be caught.

In the more serious delinquencies of boys such as vandalism, stealing, armed robbery, sexual assault, and brutality, investigation reveals that throughout childhood there was a great lack of parental love and concern, with a lesser or greater degree of cruelty. In adolescence the father (if there is a father still in the home) and the mother are apt to exert little control over such a youth's aggressiveness, and it is then directed mainly against the civil authorities. Serious delinquencies occur much more commonly among poverty-stricken, disorganized families, but they exist also in well-to-do neighborhoods.

The delinquencies of girls usually have much less aggressiveness in them. One of the commonest is running away from home. In doing this a girl will cause great distress to her parents. She also makes the neighbors wonder whether her parents treat her badly. She can indulge her own immature fantasies of finding lovely substitute parents and perhaps also a Prince Charming. Another fairly common, and more serious, problem with girls is sexual delinquency of a promiscuous or provocative type—they flaunt their misbehavior. Psychiatric investigation shows that though defective parental morals and insufficient affection may be part of the background, the more immediate factor is the girl's impulse to shame and enrage her parents because of an angry rivalry with her mother or a resentment that her father doesn't show her enough attention.

Even in many of the quiet, illegitimate pregnancies at various social levels it becomes clear that the girl was not really carried away by passion or by infatuation; she involved herself rather cold-bloodedly, without consciously knowing why, because of resentment against her parents.

The central problem of older adolescents and young adults, as Erik Erikson has made clear, particularly in his books *Young Man Luther* and *Identity: Youth and Crisis*, is to find their individual identities—what kind of people they want basically to be. While growing up through childhood they have been molded in their parents' image—particularly in the image of the parent of the same sex—partly through the parents' efforts, but even more by their own efforts to be like their parents. To become effective adult human beings, however, they must break off most of their dependence on their parents, not just to become free enough to leave home but to develop ideas and aims of their own so that they can help to solve the problems of the society in which they will live the rest of their lives. An underlying rivalry with the parent of the same sex, which began way back in childhood but which is much intensified in adolescence, is the main source of youths' rebelliousness against their parents and their parents' beliefs. The feelings of impatience and critical-ness come first; they put youths on the lookout for the new ideas with which to differ from their parents and other authorities.

The fact that youths have an emotional bias in favor of revolutionary ideas doesn't prove that their ideas are either wrong or right. They may be unsound, partly sound, very sound. Many of the advances of civilization—technical, scientific, artistic, and spiritual—have come about by means of the impatience of the young with the concepts of their elders.

Erikson pointed out that a few youths and young adults get stuck, in their striving for a separate identity, in a pattern that he called negative identity. They feel an unusually vehement need to be completely different from their parents. But they seem unable, for a considerable period, really to disengage themselves emotionally, to find or be reconciled to their own true characteristics and drives. The individual whose parents are neat, clean, organized, and purposeful makes a great point of appearing slovenly, dirty, and disorganized, and he may appear genuinely baffled about what he wants to accomplish in life. This is a way of saying, "All I know is that I want to be the opposite of my parents." To a casual observer this may look like a form of independence, but actually it is a sad kind of dependence against which the individual is fighting constantly but ineffectively. I'm not describing here the young person who may be eccentric in appearance but who has a sense of direction and is moving toward a goal; he may be a bit obsessed with the need to show his separateness, but he is in fact establishing a satisfactory independence.

In many primitive societies around the world, adolescents are welcomed with great ceremony into adult society as full-fledged members at a relatively early age. In the Western world that we know, their existence as a separate group, suspended between childhood and adulthood, is prolonged for years and years while they acquire more education. This persistent exclusion from the adult world reinforces and prolongs the feeling in youths that they are really a separate group. They deliberately accentuate the contrast between themselves and adults by developing vocabularies of their own, clothing styles of their own, games and dances of their own, entertainers and heroes of their own. Then if it turns out that these styles bother their parents, they become even more useful and pleasing to youths.

It's quite apparent that most youths balance their need to appear different from adults by their need to appear very much like one another—in the same matters of appearances, tastes, beliefs. I don't mean that there aren't some differences from neighborhood to neighborhood; and there are a few individuals with the independence to stand out from the crowd. But let's put it this way: Most human beings are more afraid of seeming different from their peers in adolescence than at any other stage.

:: 27 ::

How Parents Can Cope

Rebelliousness against parents is a natural, built-in aspect of all adolescents. It assists them in giving up the comforts and security of home and achieving real independence. They must also become sufficiently critical of their parents' ideas and ideals to be able to reject those that would be inappropriate for them, or for the times, and to take on others of their own. But all this doesn't mean that parents should take their children's objections and demands at face value—far from it. The successful rearing of children to adulthood and the transmission of family values has always depended on the parents' still acting as parents throughout adolescence, being understanding but watchful, assuming that their own experience and wisdom still have something to offer, making their standards and wishes and rules clear even though the rules have to be modified with each successive year of maturation and even though the rules aren't always obeyed, being ready to become firm and occasionally even indignant when gentle persuasion doesn't work.

In Europe, Latin American, and parts of Asia, youths in general and university students in particular have usually been in the forefront of radical protests and social revolutionary movements, though most of them have become considerably more conservative within a few years. It's an old saying in such societies that if a man wasn't a radical in his youth, he'll never have much independence or spunk. Visitors to America have often asked in the past why the great majority of students were so politically or ideologically docile here. (From the end of the depression of the 1930s until a decade ago, about the only trouble students caused was a few panty raids on girls' dormitories.) My interpretation is that American students have been up against relatively little that stirred them to vigorous rebellion. In most other parts of the world young people are held down much more by the authority of parents and grandparents, and their wishes are subordinated to the family's needs. This gives them issues to feel resentful about and an impulse to rally to the cause of the underdog. Anthropologists from abroad have been struck by the way in which most American parents will give their daughters and sons anything they have; and ask for no particular respect for their seniority.

When parents are quite definite in their beliefs, adolescents know which ones they are rebelling against and which they accept. They also will be clear about which ones they later come back to and which ones they continue to reject for life. But when parents are uncertain or vacillating, they don't hold up standards and concepts that their children can grasp. The children still will have the impulse to differ, but they will have trouble deciding what the issues are. They will be left somewhat bewildered. I think that this is at least part of the explanation why a few of the youthful protest groups have given the appearance of looking around for a cause—and of having trouble finding one of sufficient significance.

Student groups have complained particularly that in the huge universities of today there is little sense of human relations between faculty and students. I think that there may be another underlying reproach, in this confused period we live in: that teachers, like parents, are not expressing sufficiently definite beliefs—religious, spiritual, philosophical, or ethical —for youths either to adopt or reject. I think that all human beings crave beliefs that they can adhere to not only as individuals but in common with others. After adults settle down with their jobs, spouses, children, and neighbors, these realities of living can, to a degree, make up for a lack of religious or philosophical certainties. Youths have no such props.

In American more than in any other country we parents,

especially of the college-educated group, have lost a lot of our conviction about how much and what kind of guidance to give our children. The more we have learned about children, the less certain we have become. We have paid much more attention than Europeans have to the new concepts of child development derived from Freud and Dewey, and to the teachings of psychotherapists, educators, and pediatricians generally. This is probably because we have come from many countries and backgrounds and have few common traditions; we don't respect our elders; we move from place to place. We seem to have become particularly fearful that we will make our children resent us or will distort their personalities if we exert too much authority over them. This parental hesitancy has been more marked in relation to adolescent children than to any other age group.

Of course, it is the instinct of adolescents to try to emancipate themselves by continually pressing, reproaching, and nagging their parents for more freedom and privileges. However, parents should not assume that because youths ask for more freedom, they necessarily want it. In fact, half the time when they appear to be demanding it, they are really debating inwardly about whether they are ready for it. But they won't admit this, even to themselves. I've known adolescents to make particularly preposterous requests—to borrow the car to drive to a rather disreputable joint and stay late, for instance—and it became evident that unconsciously they asked for much too much in order to be sure they would be turned down. I recall several cases in which adolescents were going through a painfully shy stage and felt unable to attend certain social functions, though their parents were prodding them to do so. Yet these young people earnestly complained to me that their parents were keeping them tied to home. Sometimes adolescents whose parents are too permissive actually tell a school counselor that they wish their parents would make definite rules for them as their friends' parents do.

I'm not saying that youths wouldn't like to be able to master all worldly challenges at a young age, and I'm not saying that they never want to be given permission to try something more grown-up. I'm only saying that they still count on parental guidance, and that often when they demand and complain, they don't really mean it. They certainly resent being talked down to or being bossed arbitrarily. Parents can be reasonable in tone, willing to discuss all the issues, to talk adult to adult. They can show confidence that their children have good morals and good judgment and at the same time act quite sure that the kind of rules and behavior they are outlining are for their children's own protection and good name.

As for those youths—predominantly males—who run into study blocks despite high motivation and intelligence, the first step is to discuss the situation with the school personnel and get their recommendations. This often includes psychiatric consultation. The psychiatrist usually advises psychoanalysis or a less intensive but prolonged course of psychotherapy. (Quick unblocking is uncommon.) Enlightened universities are now permitting students who have run into a blank wall or who have lost their sense of motivation to withdraw for a year or two without damaging their academic records, and then to return when there is evidence that they are back in gear.

Is political radicalism a sign of youthful maladjustment that might be eased by psychiatric counseling? Of course, my view is that with the injustices existing in America today— poverty, inadequate medical care, mounting pollution, rankling discrimination—all of which are entirely unnecessary and continue to exist only because of greed and indifference, we are fortunate to have even a few youths who work in movements for fundamental change. They seem the realistic people to me and we are fortunate to have them. On the other hand, there are individuals who use rebellious attitudes not to work for reform, but just to provoke and irritate the people around them, and this is neurotic. Such individuals usually have enough other problems of adjustment so that they can be encouraged to seek counseling on the basis of finding the causes of their general unhappiness, more easily than they can be convinced that their politics are crazy.

Chapter VIII

Drug Use –
Particularly Marijuana

:: 28 ::

Some Misunderstandings

I'm writing about drug use—primarily marijuana. Parents of college-age and high-school-age youths are the ones most immediately concerned. But parents of small children, and even future parents, can't help worrying a little—about what the dangers amount to and how they themselves will cope with them when the time comes.

The impulse of some people is simply to condemn all drug use and to demand severer laws in the hope that the whole problem can thus be made to vanish. They fear that to raise any questions—about the validity of current attitudes or about the wisdom of our methods of control—means a giving in to drug use, if not approval of it. To others, including me, this seems like an ostrich approach; for, despite horrendous penalties, the use of drugs has spread like wildfire. Better, we say, to look at the situation as objectively as possible; then at least we'll know where we are and whether there are any possible solutions.

Let me say at the start, to avoid misunderstanding, that

I'm not advocating or even in favor of the use of any drugs, including alcohol and tobacco. The ideal society would be one in which people got such fulfillment from their jobs and relationships and recreations that they didn't need to intoxicate themselves. But drugs are already in wide use in our society today—that is my reason for examining them.

The drug I'm principally concerned with here is known as cannabis, after the plant that produces it. In the leafy form it is called marijuana, pot, or grass; in the concentrated, solid-gum form, hashish. But I'll also mention briefly heroin, barbiturates, LSD (acid), alcohol, and tobacco.

In order to get a perspective on marijuana, it is essential to talk first about some contrasts and misunderstandings. For a dramatic example of how we tend to react to the subject of drugs with emotion rather than reason, you have only to compare our feelings about the dangers of tobacco, alcohol, and marijuana with the actual, proved dangers from these three substances.

Tobacco (through cancer, heart disease, and emphysema) and alcohol (through cirrhosis of the liver, pneumonia, and traffic accidents) play a large role in the death of no fewer than one million Americans each year. Marijuana has not been proved to be responsible for any deaths. There is agitation about the possible role of marijuana in highway accidents. But the only data so far, from simulated driving tests, show that moderate intoxication from marijuana does not impair judgment and skill the way moderate intoxication from alcohol does.

The alcoholism of an estimated six million individuals in this country results in the occupying of tens of thousands of hospital beds at any one time by people suffering from permanent brain damage and delirium tremens. It also causes great economic, emotional, and social distress for the millions of families involved. Marijuana hospitalizes extremely few. Though it plays a part in the dropping out of certain young people from school and society, it does not incapacitate fathers and mothers of previously well-established families as alcohol does.

Yet a majority of people, except perhaps of those under twenty-five, think of marijuana as the more dangerous drug. Here are some other comparisons.

Those who take heroin and other opiates, such as morphine, and many of those who intensively abuse alcohol become physically addicted, in the sense that they cannot then refrain without severe bodily and psychic distress and even death. LSD and marijuana are not physically addictive; this is why they are not called narcotics. They are said to be habituating for some, in the sense that these individuals may become psychologically dependent.

Marijuana and LSD are psychedelic, or consciousness-expanding, drugs; that is, they change and enhance sensations—sight, sound, touch. They are hallucinogens—hallucination producers (LSD commonly, marijuana rarely, depending on the dose). Marijuana, in the overwhelming majority of cases, produces a pleasurable mood. With LSD the reaction may be pleasurable or terrifying—there is no predicting.

Amphetamines, sometimes called speed, are stimulants used by many people to keep them awake while studying or driving, or for weight reduction. Larger doses are used by some individuals to achieve feelings of self-assurance and exhilaration. These drugs are most dangerous when taken as frequently repeated intravenous injections to sustain a sense of ecstasy for several days. These highs are followed by depressions, which then must be overcome by further ingestion or injection. The abuse of amphetamines causes aggressive, impulsive behavior, physical exhaustion, malnutrition, and paranoid mental illness.

Barbiturates are considered rather harmless sleeping capsules by most people. But they are used excessively by some individuals to produce a state similar to drunkenness; they may cause an addiction that is difficult and dangerous to overcome. These drugs are also dangerous in that the differences between a useful dose, an intoxicating dose, and a lethal dose are relatively small. Twenty thousand people a year die from them, suicidally or accidentally.

Now to focus on marijuana. So far no agreement has been reached that permanent damage to the brain or mental functioning results from misuse of marijuana. Occasional individuals react with symptoms of anxiety. A heavy dose may produce transitory hallucinations.

The old accusation that marijuana incites individuals to violence, crime, and sex is now flatly denied by professional people familiar with its effects. Unlike alcohol, which sometimes produces belligerence and assaultiveness and which is implicated in half the convictions of robbery, rape, and murder, marijuana induces a mood of passivity, contemplation, and sometimes amusement.

The common assumption and fear that the use of marijuana disposes people to go on to more dangerous drugs is considered unjustified by a number of thoughtful investigators—and they have convinced me. These investigators calculate that only 2 percent of those who have used marijuana ever try heroin and fewer than 1 percent of them become addicted to heroin.

The reasons for the initial use of any drug are psychological. A person so constituted as to be willing or eager to use a drug as dangerous as heroin naturally will be likely to have tried marijuana first; in fact, 80 percent of heroin users have done so. But there is no evidence that the use of marijuana induced them to use heroin. There were heroin addicts for many years before marijuana came into popular use.

How extensively and intensively is marijuana used? Surveys have shown that at least half of all college-age youths have tried marijuana at least once. Experimentation and regular use have been increasingly frequent at the high-school and junior-high-school levels too. There is, of course, every degree of frequency in its use, from people who try it gingerly "just once to see" to the infrequent individual who is stoned an appreciable part of the time—the pot head.

Since there is no addiction to marijuana and no proof as yet of any physical harm from its use, the most significant distinction, it seems to me, is not between the person who smokes once a week and the person who smokes once a day. It is between the person who maintains his drive and effectiveness, even if he smokes one or more times a day for diversion, and the person who loses some or all of his interest in his work and his ability to function. For the second kind of person, the main focus of his life is his psychedelic experiences.

The pot heads are a small percentage of those who use marijuana. They may be able to cut down on or stop smoking marijuana without distress if they find a renewed sense of purpose and direction.

There have always been people, particularly young people, who during their quest for identity have lost, at least temporarily, their sense of purpose and their relationship to the workaday world. In past generations some of them took to narcotics and some to drink. But now marijuana, with its relative cheapness, availability, and physical harmlessness, makes an obvious appeal to dropouts and potential dropouts. In place of emptiness or tension it gives such people a source of pleasure, a compatible social group, and a definite if meager focus for their lives.

It is probably not true that pot heads were ever well-adjusted personalities who were led astray by encountering marijuana; rather, they were people with serious problems who found a solace. We have no way of telling whether, if there had been no marijuana, they all would have dropped out in other ways—through the use of narcotics or alcohol, through mental illness, or drifting—or whether some could have carried on fairly well.

A study at one college showed that marijuana smokers on the average do not have lower academic grades than non-smokers.

Why are so many young people drawn to drugs, especially nowadays?

Drugs are first of all a means of easing tensions, forgetting frustrations, overcoming feelings of emptiness, as users of tobacco and alcohol realize. The turn to marijuana occurred at a time when young people were becoming acutely aware of a number of tragic injustices—an illegal, immoral war in Vietnam in which they were expected to do the killing and the dying, harsh discrimination against blacks and other minorities, rapidly increasing pollution, widespread poverty in the midst of unprecedented wealth. Young people, with high enthusiasm and courage, became active in the struggles to overcome these wrongs. But when, eventually, progress appeared to them to be unattainable, many turned in their frustration to drugs, music, the search for individual salvation through a revolutionary life style, and mysticism.

Young people have always yearned to try all experiences to the degree they dared, driven partly by the instinct to know and to master, partly by the need to find their identity. Those of today, who have been raised with remarkably little fear of the unknown and of the authorities, are less afraid to experiment than their forebears. And at their age the fascination with burning the candle at both ends and the need to prove their courage by taking chances are at a maximum.

Youths also have a deep need to be thought well of by their peers. This means that dares often are accepted instantaneously, without question.

The young always are tempted to rebel against the laws of society and the rules of their parents. Their consciences more readily allow them to rebel if they can detect hypocrisy in their elders' attitudes. Is there hypocrisy about drugs? The government not only condones but also profits from the use of alcohol and tobacco, two of our most devastating drugs. And a majority of parents indulge.

And when parents are driven frantic by their offsprings' taste in music, hair styles, or drugs, their children feel an added inducement to persist.

If people above the age of youth had been in the habit of thinking of tobacco and alcohol as drugs, which they surely are, and of themselves as drug users, they wouldn't have been so shocked by the sudden popularity of marijuana. A majority of them, after all, had indulged in tobacco and alcohol in their youths and never thought of them as ruining their health or their characters if used in moderation.

Finally, there's the simple matter of style. Styles change in clothes, in music, and even in intoxicants. And it's most often youths, in their rebelliousness, who set the new patterns.

In summary, it seems clear to me that marijuana is a drug that is much, much less harmful than heroin, the amphetamines, the barbiturates, LSD, alcohol, and tobacco. By that I don't mean that it surely has no dangers. It blots out concern in a small percentage of people who already are evading problems.

But we don't know whether, in providing solace, marijuana leads astray any appreciable number who would not be withdrawing in some other way if marijuana were not available. A particularly serious aspect of this question, still unanswered, is whether adolescents in high school and junior high, at a particularly stressful age, are deflected from solving their developmental problems by the use of marijuana.

:: 29 ::

Prevention and Control

It seems clear to many people who have looked into the problem of marijuana—including myself—that most government attempts to prevent its use have done much more harm than good. In 1937 Congress officially named marijuana a narcotic (which it is not), and its sale and possession were made felonies punishable by long jail terms.

This law was based on unsupported allegations by narcotics agents that marijuana leads to crimes of violence and to mental and moral degeneracy. No scientific evidence was presented to the congressional committee, only hearsay, and the only doctor to testify was called uncooperative because he disagreed with the agents' testimony. The states soon followed the congressional example with equally unsound, harsh laws.

At any one time nowadays there are two hundred thousand people in jail in the United States for marijuana offenses. Most of these are young people. Some of them are serving terms of twenty and forty years just for possession of marijuana. Sale is punishable by death in one state.

These harsh penalties have not stopped the use of marijuana; in fact, its use has skyrocketed. Yet citizens and legislators ignore the evidence. They insist on severe penalties, particularly for sellers, not recognizing that the great majority of sellers are students in high schools and colleges who are simply accommodating their acquaintances and providing for their own marijuana requirements at the same time.

When the government calls illegal what millions of people consider harmless and their right, the result is a growing

disrespect for law, as older people remember from Prohibition days. The great majority get away with infractions, but
there is the tragic fate of the small minority, the people who
have the misfortune to be caught and jailed.

Another injustice is that it is all too easy for unscrupulous
police to frame long-haired youths, radical leaders, militant
blacks on drug charges, as I know from the experiences of
friends.

The worst effect of all from harsh penalties is that the
youths jailed by the hundreds of thousands are not rehabili-
tated. In most prisons they are embittered by their treatment, taught criminal attitudes and techniques by fellow
prisoners, and often abused sexually.

I am one of those who have been convinced that the best
course would be to legalize and at the same time control
marijuana, at least until and unless some permanent physical
or psychiatric harm is proved.

An age limit of eighteen or twenty years could be set, and
licensed dealers could be held responsible for not selling to
those below that age. This would not stop the use of
marijuana by the young, but it would keep them out of jail,
undercut illegal dealers, and decrease the hypocrisy. If
marijuana is not legalized, I believe that at least the penalty
for its use should be eliminated or reduced to a small fine.

Heroin, however, is an extremely serious problem because addiction occurs quickly, the cure by withdrawal is
painful, and few addicts have the will and the courage to go
through with it. Of those who do, a majority relapse.

In Britain the problem of the individual user has been
taken out of the hands of the police and given to special
medical clinics which give regular injections of heroin or
methadone. This seems immoral to many Americans. The
purpose is to keep the addict from committing crimes to pay
for his drug and to keep out of business the illegal dealer, who
is also the pusher who involves new victims. In Britain there

has been a moderate increase in heroin addiction in recent years but nothing like the tremendous increase in the United States.

I believe that since the attempt to control heroin by the police has been a failure from every point of view in America we should adopt the British approach as a first step.

In some places in the United States a synthetic drug named methadone has been dispensed legally to addicts as a less harmful substitute for heroin. Since it creates a permanent addiction too, it is only a partial solution.

There are organizations of ex-addicts who believe earnestly, on the basis of practical experience, that most addicts can be and should be gotten off the drug through the rehabilitation of each individual—psychologically and occupationally—by group methods, and the rehabilitation of the neighborhood where he lives. I agree that every such effort that offers hope of cure should be utilized.

Residential treatment facilities of high quality, whether run under psychiatric auspices or by group-therapy organizations such as Synanon, are desperately needed all over the country for those heroin addicts who themselves want help in overcoming addiction. These facilities must be staffed by people who show deep concern. To prevent the quick relapse of addicts there must be job-finding services (employers are wary of addicts) and long-term social and emotional support. (Addicts Anonymous is one organization that gives such support.)

Experts agree that the smugglers of heroin and the adult dealers in the drug should be hounded by the authorities. So should the illegal manufacturers of LSD. But there also should be much stricter control of the legal manufacture, distribution, prescription, and sale of the amphetamines and barbiturates, a large proportion of which are prescribed carelessly by doctors or sold without a doctor's prescription.

Prevention of drug abuse by education also sounds like a

good idea and there are laws in some states prescribing school courses along these lines. But you can't expect a few formal warnings to counteract all the powerful social and emotional forces that have lured millions of youths into drugs.

For one thing, the warnings of danger stir up that adolescent feeling: I have as much courage to risk danger as the next man! Admonitions that adopt the tone of "We adults know what's best for you," whether printed in a textbook or spoken by a kill-joy type of teacher, will have a restraining effect only on the docile students in the class. Admonitions will be provocative to the bolder and more rebellious types.

Factual information, without condescension or exaggeration, will be worthwhile. If presented for class discussion by a well-liked, sympathetic teacher, it will do still more good. It would also be valuable to have junior-high and high-school drug-study projects involving library research, perhaps a classroom talk by a cured addict or a visit to a treatment center and subsequent discussions and conclusions worked out primarily by the pupils themselves. They can create their own educational posters.

More crucial than any one course on drugs would be a total school curriculum so challenging and taught by such an inspiring and sympathetic faculty that the students were deeply and enthusiastically absorbed in their work and in their extracurricular activities. This would be real prevention. For drugs are used to overcome feelings of emptiness, aimlessness, tension, frustration, and alienation. These are the conscious or unconscious reactions of many young people to what they consider to be dull, oppressive schools, processing them for slots in a grim society.

The premature deaths of revered entertainers like Jimi Hendrix and Janis Joplin, which were not preachments in books but facts of life, may get through to youths directly and help to turn the tide.

What attitudes can parents themselves take? It shouldn't be necessary for them to introduce the topic of drugs arbitrarily. It will probably be mentioned from time to time by children as young as ten or twelve because of talk or gossip in school.

Parents can listen to their children's information and misinformation, draw out their opinions, gently correct misinformation, explain not only the dangers of drugs but why people seek these particular pleasures and solaces; parents can then work around to their own conclusions, which can be expressed clearly and firmly. And if the parents smoke or drink, they must be ready to discuss their reasoning for going on with these, or resolve to give them up. Mutual discussions of this kind will impress children more than denunciations and warnings.

Parents should take care to be informed about drugs because the chances are great that their children will know a lot these days. And I'd suggest that parents carefully avoid exaggeration of the dangers—the real dangers are serious enough. Otherwise their children thereafter will discount or disbelieve everything they say about drugs.

I'd say to my children that most of these drugs—including alcohol and tobacco—have serious physical or mental dangers. Then I'd admit that marijuana is much more benign. But I'd warn that the legal penalties are severe. I'd point out that in the age period between twelve and twenty many young people find life confusing; they may lose some of their ambition or have difficulty studying or doing anything else. Marijuana and other drugs provide such a pleasant escape that getting back on the track is made more difficult.

I'd conclude with words to this effect: "I would like you to put off the use of alcohol and marijuana—even though they are socially acceptable—preferably until you are twenty but at least until you are eighteen and have greater experience and more sense of direction. Even then treat them with great respect."

Throughout the period when the children are between twelve and twenty years old I'd act willing to get back into a relaxed discussion of drugs any time they brought the subject up. But I would not force the topic into the conversation or take too excited or too arbitrary a position, because that might imply that I was afraid my children had not taken my previous advice seriously or that I did not trust their morality or their strength of character.

Parental trust is extremely important in the guidance of adolescent children as they get further and further away from the direct supervision of their parents and teachers. I don't mean that trust without clear guidance is enough, but guidance without trust is worthless. (The adolescent says, "If my parents assume I'm misbehaving, why bother to behave?")

I wouldn't be seriously shocked or disillusioned if I heard through the grapevine that my adolescent child (under eighteen) had gone against my advice and tried marijuana once, or even occasionally. In today's drug climate that wouldn't mean to me that he was a pot head or a delinquent or that my advice hadn't helped him or that basically I couldn't trust him. After all, a majority of us parents occasionally smoked tobacco or drank beer before our parents gave their permission.

If I found, however, that my son was smoking marijuana daily before he was sixteen or seventeen or even that when older he was a pot head or was using any of the addicting or physically harmful drugs, I would assume that something was wrong in his adjustment, in his character, or in our relationship. I would not evade or delay as if I were afraid to bring up the subject. Nor would I jump on him as if he were a criminal or as if I were about to disown him.

I would instead show a deep and devoted concern—on the assumption that he was as worried as I was. I would tell him that together we needed professional help—from the school counselor or from a guidance clinic or from a psychiatrist in private practice, first to evaluate the problem and then to work on it. (I would have made inquiries previously to be sure that the person we were to consult would have had a lot of experience of this sort and was not condemnatory in attitude.)

The strongest bulwark against drug abuse in any family is a reasonably adjusted personality in the child and strong family ties. These are two sides of the same coin, of course. In this sense parents are preventing drug abuse when they are maintaining a good marriage, caring for their children from infancy, hour by hour and year by year, showing them affection, facilitating their friendships and their hobbies, expecting their help, respecting them and asking their respect.

A matter of some help or harm is the parents' use of drugs. If they drink liquor regularly, even though temperately, if they ignore the dangers of lung cancer and heart disease by smoking cigarettes, they make it easier for their children to use drugs, and to excuse themselves by calling their parents hypocrites. Studies show also that the children of parents who frequently use medication—stimulants, sedatives, pain-killers, tranquilizers—are themselves much more likely to use or misuse drugs.

I'm not saying that parents must give up all their comforters for their children. Children have to accept the fact that parents reserve for themselves such privileges as late hours, more expensive clothes, cars, and sex. But parental abstention from drugs might make a difference in prevention and could be a real help in curing a child who already was in trouble.

Outside the home a sound approach to many of our social ills—including the misuse of drugs—would be somehow to restore a sense of real community to our so-called communities. In simpler societies neighbors of all ages know one another, live close to one another, work together on common tasks, play together, help one another. In our industrial civilization many people work far from home, on assembly lines or in office jobs that give little or no satisfaction; and they compete with one another. They live in more or less isolated homes. They restrict their social life to those they consider their social equals. And when they need assistance they have to buy it from professional people. This is a spiritually impoverished life, compared to what our species was designed for.

Chapter IX

:::::::::::::

Divorce,
Widowhood, and
Remarriage

:: 30 ::

How To Help the Child

A majority of the men and women who divorce eventually remarry. Whether the children involved make a good or not-so-good adjustment to the remarriage will depend in part on how tactfully the matter of remarriage is approached, especially in the preliminary stages.

In fact, it is important to realize that long before there is even a question of another marriage, the children will be concerned about any dates their parents may have, so we will need to discuss dating too.

There are two major stumbling blocks that may interfere with children's acceptance of their parent's new date or new partner or new spouse. The first one is jealousy. This is naturally commoner for an only child, who has had the parent all to himself or herself since the separation. It is also commoner if the child lives with the parent of the opposite sex, because of the romantic element in the love of a son for his mother and of a daughter for her father.

The second stumbling block is children's continuing loyalty to their other natural parent—the one who, as far as they know, is not having dates or planning to remarry—and their wish that their two parents be united again. This loyalty and wish for reunion are often very difficult for a parent to sympathize with because they run counter to the parent's own feelings, so I should take some time to explain.

To make the situation easier to discuss, let's take the example of a six-year-old boy living with his mother, who has been divorced from his father for half a year. The boy is expected to spend part of his Christmas and summer vacations visiting his father, who now lives in a distant city. Such a child may act troubled or even shocked if his mother tells him she is going on a date with another man. Though he knows in actuality that a divorce has occurred, in his feelings there may seem to be just an unfortunate separation that he still hopes will end in reconciliation. In his own feeling his mother and father still belong to each other, and his mother would be unfaithful to go out with another man. His mother, on the other hand, though she may have hesitated about a divorce in the beginning and though she may have doubts in the future if life doesn't work out as expected, is probably now quite satisfied to be finally and totally free of a distressing marriage. She would consider herself a neurotic fool if she were to sit at home moping over a broken marriage when she could be enjoying a bit of social or romantic life again, for these pleasures are often hard for a divorced woman to come by.

There is another, still more basic reason why a parent—in this example the mother—has difficulty sympathizing with her child's wish to have the departed father back in the family again. During the long, painful, quarrelsome period when mutual love was changing to mutual resentment, each parent tried to ward off a sense of guilt about the failure of the marriage by exaggerating the faults of the other and minimizing her or his own.

From the time she decides a divorce is inevitable, a mother wants to see the father of her child as completely, unchangeably impossible to live with, whether his main fault is irresponsibility or meanness or unfaithfulness. She wants her friends to agree that the father is the difficult one and she really would like to have her children agree with her too, though she realizes it would not be fair to ask them to say it. So when the children want their father back or mention his good points, it undermines their mother's main line of defense.

Now we should think again of why children keep hoping for a reunion. They have spent their entire life until the divorce with their father and mother. They have sensed all along that they need both parents; each one has served the family in quite a different way and each one has satisfied quite different emotional hungers in the children. The thought of getting along permanently without one or the other will be frightening to them, at least until they become well accustomed to the divorce and its consequences.

Children may be able to agree with their mother that their father has certain faults. But if they sense that she is exaggerating the faults in order to justify separation or divorce, they will feel a strong urge to minimize them in order to justify their parents staying together.

There is another important reason why children will feel like sticking up for an absent or divorced parent. They sense that they are made up of their two parents—physically in the sense of having come from their bodies and carrying their features, psychologically in the sense of having assiduously patterned themselves after them since infancy. If one parent is bad, they themselves must have some of that badness in them. Child-guidance work with children of parents with criminal records show how common this assumption is.

You may have heard of children who kept begging their mother to find a new daddy for them. I've known a number of such cases. This behavior doesn't contradict the concept of loyalty to a father. It is more apt to occur in a young child (under six) whose father now lives too far away for regular visiting or who has quit trying to keep up any contact. So the child feels a rather desperate need for a day-to-day father just like the other boys have.

Actually a very young child would not feel any inconsistency in wanting an ever-present daddy in the neighborhood and also feeling loyalty to a faraway one who appeared only at infrequent intervals. A school-age child, by contrast, has enough imagination to keep the father's image vivid and also a strong sense of loyalty and propriety.

So for the children's benefit, a divorced mother and father must show the maximum possible respect for each other in speech and in action. But I know from professional experience how hard it is to persuade parents to follow this course. Springing to their own defense and warding off guilt, they immediately cry out, "How can I possibly show respect for such a louse (or cheat, liar, bitch, bastard, tramp)?" I have to keep reminding such parents that we are not talking about justice to the former spouse but to the child: "Tell the child about the qualities that drew you to your spouse in the first place. Speak of the good times you had in the first years of the marriage. Admit there has been a failure but try not to apportion the blame. Admit bitterness, but admit that the ex-spouse is bitter too and try not to ask the child to agree with your bitterness."

(Needless to say, a widow rarely wants to run down her dead husband. If anything, she is apt to go to the opposite extreme, to forget all her husband's defects and exaggerate his virtues. This may make him out such an angel or phenomenal success that his son feels inferior all his life by comparison. Better to admit from time to time that the departed was only human.)

Now we can get on with the practical matter of how

divorced parents can best handle dating and the prospect of marriage. It isn't necessary, of course, for a mother to cut herself off from social life or from the possibility of a good remarriage; in the long run that would do the child more harm than benefit. But if she anticipates the likelihood of feelings of loyalty in her children toward the father, she can be tactful. This not only will be a kindness to the children but also will put them in a frame of mind to respect their mother's choice when and if she wants to remarry.

Even during the process of the divorce, when children ask dozens of questions as they try to visualize what their future life will be like, their mother can explain in a casual, matter-of-fact way that it's possible that she and the child's father may someday fall in love with other people and want to marry them. Then the idea will be in the back of their minds, in advance of the reality, for them to mull over at leisure.

It is important, I think, for the mother and father both to be aware of and on guard against the fairly common impulse of the newly divorced person to rush headlong into one or more shallow romances; these relationships are usually brief because they are not based on any common interest other than sex. One explanation is that a person who has just failed in marriage—let's take the husband—and has been told a thousand times by his wife during the breakup how utterly unattractive he is, sexually and otherwise, wants to prove to himself and to the world that he is still considered appealing by the opposite sex. He also may be excited by the idea that he now can have an affair without being unfaithful.

It is preferable, I think, for a mother not to have any obviously romantic dates for a few months after the divorce, while the children go through a period of mourning for their departed father and while mother and children get accustomed to being the whole family. This doesn't mean that a working mother cannot have lunch with a man or see him occasionally in the evening in the home of mutual friends. I only mean that out of respect for her child's feelings she should not give the appearance of immediately becoming involved in a new, heavy romance, as if the previous one had meant nothing.

When she does begin having dates it will help the children see them in a wholesome perspective if the mother does not seem to be swept off her feet right away. It is better also not to have romantic dates with a number of men simultaneously and to avoid demonstrations of physical affection in front of the children until the friendship is several months old and the children show affection for the man.

By the time a mother is becoming genuinely interested in a man and has begun to think of the possibility of remarriage, it is sensible from several points of view to have the man and the children become acquainted—gradually.

Ideally the child's affection for the man increases as the mother's does. Or perhaps the occasions when child and man are together show the mother with increasing clarity that the man would not be a good father at all and this cools her interest.

Immediate dislikes are often caused by simple jealousy—jealousy on the part of a child toward a new person who may interfere with a very cozy one-to-one relationship; jealousy on the part of a man falling in love with a woman toward all the important people in her previous existence. In a majority of cases these immediate dislikes yield in time if the people involved are mature enough to make an effort to please each other.

The third possibility is that the man's character and attitude toward the child—let's say it's a boy—look better and better to the mother; but the child, instead of learning to appreciate him, becomes increasingly hostile, presumably because of jealousy, as he senses his mother's growing affection for the man. This does not mean that the mother has to drop the man. She can consult a family social agency or child-guidance clinic over a period of time to clarify the basis of her child's objections and if it is due to abnormal jealousy, to secure psychiatric treatment. It is no favor to a child to give in to his pathological possessiveness, which will only crop up later in another situation and which will make his mother resent him for his tyranny over her life.

On the other hand, the man who wants to marry the mother really may not be a very likeable or admirable person, which the child may realize. The mother may be overlooking his faults because she values too highly the supposed security of marriage. In this case the marriage won't work, and the child is right to be against it. This possibility would also be clarified in the course of counseling.

A mother who is hoping to get her children to like a man may explain to them the possibility of marriage. But I think it is better not to mention marriage until it is fairly certain. A child loses a certain amount of respect for a mother who keeps talking hopefully about marriage when no marriage results. And if a child asks, "Are you thinking of marrying him?" I'd suggest answering, "We haven't known each other long enough yet." That shows that she has a healthy respect for marriage.

I have used the example of children living with a divorced mother because that is the commonest custody arrangement, and I have discussed the possible dates and remarriage of the mother. But of course the dates and the possible remarriage of the father will be very much a matter of concern to the child or children, because they love him and have possessive feelings for him and also because they have feelings of loyalty toward their mother.

A father who wants to retain his children's love ought to tell them if he is falling seriously in love and to arrange somehow for them to become acquainted with the woman before any official decision about marriage is made. Children should feel that they have the chance at least to pass judgment before the decision is final. Better still, if the children can visit their father frequently, is for their friendship and love for the woman he loves to develop gradually but steadily, in the way that his own feeling for her is doing.

By this I don't mean that a father should have the children meet every woman he takes a fancy to. He should introduce his children only to women he's proud to know. This may sound like unnecessary advice, but I have known of several cases where a father had a casual woman friend whom he really didn't respect help him prepare a meal and entertain his children. Consciously such a man could say that he was only being hospitable to his children with the help of a woman friend whom he could count on to be cordial. Unconsciously, I suspect, he was trying to tease and torment his ex-wife, whom he considered too proper and fastidious.

This last example brings us back to the main purpose of this discussion: to help divorced parents look at things occasionally from their children's viewpoint at a time when they themselves are naturally preoccupied with their own anxieties, resentments, and hopes.

:: 31 ::

Can a Mother Substitute for a Father?

Can a mother be a father too? This is a question I've been asked in one way or another by many a woman who has been widowed or divorced. She has read or sensed what a crucial role the father plays—not just in the day-to-day management of children but also in the formation of their characters. So she doesn't see any obvious solution, except possibly remarriage—which isn't so easy to arrange and which in itself may cause other problems for the children.

Some of the mothers who bring up this problem think of

it primarily in relation to their sons, and only secondarily or
not at all in regard to their daughters. How, they ask, will
they know how to play with their sons when they are young
or answer their questions when they are adolescents? How
will they make their boys obey when they are too big to
paddle or too fast to catch? Actually a father is as important
to a daughter as to a son, though in somewhat different ways,
just as you can also say that a mother is crucial in the upbringing of her sons. A girl needs a father—or substitute father—
so that she can know at close range what males are made of
and how you get along with them. Otherwise they may seem
too mysterious or frightening or glamorous.

More specifically, a girl needs a fatherly man to admire
and love from the age of three until she gets married. She
needs a father who will be protective of her, deeply and
reliably devoted to her. She needs a father who will have a
slightly romantic attitude toward her, as if he recognizes the
fact that someday she will be an attractive woman. But he
must restrain himself from acting too cuddily or talking too
mushily to her, partly because most of his romantic devotion
should belong to his wife, partly because he senses that his
daughter's eventual good adjustment to marriage will depend, among other factors, on her not being too tied to him.

To keep things in balance, a girl needs a father who is also
a sensible disciplinarian, who doesn't hesitate to remind her
when he thinks she is out of line and who backs up his wife
when his wife is being firm. Otherwise a girl, especially in
adolescence, will decide that her father is an angel and her
mother a witch, which makes for painful family tensions.

All of this is not to say that a girl can't grow up to be a
well-balanced person without a father; only that it's of some
importance whether a substitute or several partial substitutes are available. And even more important is her mother's
attitude toward the male sex. We'll come around to that
later.

Now to get back to those mothers who are particularly worried about how they can be fathers to their fatherless boys. My answer would be that they can't, and furthermore that it isn't necessary. Part of what a boy may get from his father is practice tossing a ball, going to a hockey game, talking about the standing of the baseball clubs, going fishing, doing carpentry together. A few mothers are able to do these things well and enjoyably, but very few. If a woman doesn't do them well, her son won't particularly want to do them with her, and if she doesn't do them with enjoyment, she'll be miserable herself. But the main benefit in father and son getting into such activities is not the skill or knowledge transmitted but the companionship, the discovery that despite father-son tensions, they can experience a harmonious pleasure at such times. I would say that in ninety-nine cases out of one hundred there is no comparable value in a mother's trying to play such a role.

A child is so constituted—let's say it's a girl—that even if she can't remember ever seeing her father or mother or hearing much about them (as in the case of a child placed in an institution because of parental neglect), she vividly imagines what her parents are like and can describe them down to small details. She gives them qualities that she would like them to have, such as good looks, wealth, devotion to their children. She also constructs images of her parents on the basis of characteristics she has observed in actual men and women. You might say that she patches together her ideal parent out of bits and pieces of other people. And it is when these people are friendly to her or approving of her that they particularly inspire her. Those who are strongly disapproving or quite indifferent will not become a part of her ideal parent.

What this means is that the mother, in the case of a fatherless boy, will help him to continually construct an image of his father by making opportunities for him to be occasionally with fond grandfathers, uncles, cousins, other male friends of the family. Also a friendly school teacher, camp counselor, minister, scoutmaster, can serve the same purpose. Even men seen quite casually and infrequently—a television re-pairman or a landlord who likes the boy and takes the trouble to speak to him—may have considerable influence.

A mother can't badger a male relative or acquaintance to befriend her son beyond a certain point. If a man, out of a sense of obligation, did more than he enjoyed, the forced quality would cancel out the benefit. So a mother can only hint gently and infrequently. It must be the boy's obvious appreciation that motivates the man to repeat the contact.

Should a widow or divorcee encourage men to date her or should she think more seriously of remarriage just for her child's sake? No use at all. It's true that a young child, espe-cially one of preschool age, may beg the mother to find a new daddy. But unless the mother and a new father are very much in love, are thoroughly suited to each other and are marrying primarily for these reasons, the marriage will sour and the child will probably suffer more than the adults.

Now I want to get around to what I consider by far the most constructive thing a widow or divorcee can do to make it up to her sons and daughters for their not having a father in the home. This has to do with her attitude toward the male sex in general and toward her deceased or divorced husband in particular.

If a woman shows an appropriate amount of respect and liking for males generally, including her sons this disposes her children to feel the same way, and it helps her sons to respect themselves too. If she acts as though she despises men or thinks they are dispensable or unimportant, it is difficult for her children not to feel likewise, and for her sons not to feel belittled. If she approaches all men indiscrimi-nately with seductiveness of manner or speech, she teaches her children not that men are to be loved but that they are to be snared.

I've left unanswered so far two kinds of questions that lone mothers often ask. The first is, "How do you answer a boy's questions about sex and being a boy, especially in adolescence?" Boys rarely ask intimate questions of either parent. They ask or listen to older boys or they read books. Besides, a mother knows most of the answers anyway.

And "How can a woman make a big boy behave?" Ninety-nine percent of managing and disciplining is done not by catching a boy, physically overcoming him, and beating him. It's done by moral suasion—making it clear to him what the parent expects, reminding him again whenever it's necessary, showing firm moral disapproval, and making emphatic demands for improvement when he deliberately misbehaves. This is how the child's conscience is gradually built up. And the older a child becomes, the more he and his parents have to depend on his conscience, since he is out of sight of his parents and other authorities more and more of the time. The average mother has just as much moral authority over her son—even a boy in his late teens—as his father does.

Chapter X
Grandparents

:: 32 ::

Are They Necessary?

Parents and children can get along without grandparents if they have to. But good grandparents—along with aunts, uncles, and cousins—can contribute rich extra values to any family.

Young parents as they encounter the inevitable crises, great and small, of starting a family have dozens of questions every week. They used to get satisfying answers from the grandparents—answers to questions on child care, home care, budgetary problems, and on how to find the way out of strains in family and other human relations.

A person doesn't need just the specific answers. More important, for anybody in a quandary is the prompt emotional comfort that comes from talking with someone familiar who is understanding and basically sympathetic.

Everyone craves this kind of relief.—The advantage of being able to turn to a reliable relative rather than to a friend is that one doesn't have to worry about losing the friend's esteem through exposing one's weaknesses.

Today in America a large proportion of young and middle-aged parents live hundreds or thousands of miles away from their parents. As a result they often have to turn to family social agencies, pediatricians, general practitioners, public-health nurses, clergymen, and marriage counselors for even relatively minor problems.

I'm not against using these professionals. I'm one myself. And I've often consulted internists, pediatricians, and psychiatrists about my own small, as well as large, family difficulties. But it is much easier for most people when they have a problem not to have to make an entirely new professional contact, or to start from scratch in explaining a situation and its entire background.

In America we are apt to forget about the comfort grandparents can be to parents because we have a tradition that emphasizes the opposite—the value to married people of being geographically and emotionally independent from their parents. In fact, we are apt to feel sorry for any couple if they have to have members of the older generation living close to them: "The poor Harrisons have his mother living with them," or, "Her mother lives just around the corner and she has to see her every day."

There are certainly disadvantages to living close to grandparents if, for instance, they are too bossy, too nosy, or too hostile to their son's or daughter's spouse. Also better not to live nearby if the grandparents are made nervous by the children's noisiness or are always full of complaints about their aches and pains or about not receiving enough consideration. On the other hand, in a majority of families the three generations could live close together quite compatibly, and ordinary sources of friction could be quite easily disposed of by frank discussion.

In America we put the highest value on independence. In many other parts of the world people take for granted the advantages of dependence. But both attitudes are an integral part of the relationship between the generations—in adult-hood as well as in childhood.

Babies start out totally dependent, but are beginning to feel and assert their separateness by one year of age. Six to twelve year olds try to stop copying their parents in appearance and manners and try to model themselves after their contemporaries instead. Youths strive to cut their residual deep ties of dependence and sometimes have to lash out in all directions to do so.

When emotional adulthood is finally reached in other parts of the world, whether at twenty or thirty, young people outgrow most of their rebelliousness and their fear of being controlled by their parents by making an almost complete emotional identification with them. They suppress the remainder of their rebelliousness. They typically say, "Now I understand what my parents were trying to accomplish in raising me. I think they did a good job and I'm going to raise my children the same way." They tend not to object openly to living close to grandparents or to accepting their superior authority and experience in child rearing and other matters.

In America, however, the young adults' identification with their parents is less complete. Many of us continue, as young parents, to be touchy about interference from the grandparents. We are apt to speak critically of how old-fashioned their child-rearing ideas are; we explain how differently we are going to manage our own children. To put it in other words, we retain more of our adolescent rebelliousness and insecurity.

This fear of interference from the grandparents explains the readiness American parents have always shown to listen to new professional doctrines, such as those of Freud and American educator John Dewey, whose ideas have had a much more profound impact on child rearing here than in Europe. The main reason, I suppose, is that our forefathers who came to this continent were the rebellious kind who were impatient with all the traditions of the old country. They were prejudiced in favor of new methods—in industry and in government as well as in raising children.

This impatience with customary methods, this readiness to experiment, has played a large part in our rapid material and scientific progress. But I think it has made child rearing a somewhat more difficult job. For the natural and easy way to raise children is the same way you were raised yourself; then you don't have to stop and think about what is right and best.

But if, in each of the hundred issues that come up every day with every child, you have to hesitate and ask yourself, "How differently do I want to handle this issue from the way my parents used to handle it?" it will take twice as long and use up four times as much emotional energy.

In making all these points, I'm not trying to dissuade any parents who definitely prefer almost total independence from the grandparents or who want to use quite different methods. I am just calling attention to the great aid and comfort that hundreds of millions of young parents around the world get from the grandparents, so that you can take this possibility into account in making your life plans instead of jumping automatically to the conclusion that closeness to grandparents or conformity with their methods is always disadvantageous.

For children there are real emotional advantages in having grandparents (as well as aunts and uncles and cousins) who live nearby and visit often.

Young children get most of their security from their relationships with parents and other close relatives. The tie to the mother is by far the most vital, of course. Next in importance come the ties to father, brothers, sisters. But ties to other relatives whom children see on a regular basis are also highly important.

Between visits small children talk fondly about their

grandparents. They ask when they are coming again. They get excited as the time draws near. They sometimes act embarrassed when a grandparent appears if there has been an interval of a couple of months between visits. The embarrassment comes partly, I think, because the emotional tie is so intense (the kind of embarrassment a teen-ager might feel if confronted with a worshiped movie actor); and it comes partly because the relative doesn't quite correspond to what a very young child remembers because the child has changed so much in those months.

Children in the six-to-twelve-year-old period like to make even spiritual matters very concrete and to count their blessings. My grandchildren boast, "I have one grandfather and two grandmothers and three uncles and two aunts and three cousins." All these devoted relatives seem to the child like so much money in the bank, from an emotional point of view.

Children of such ages usually have not thought out specifically the succession of people who might take care of them if both their parents died, since this is too worrisome an idea. But they are unconsciously aware of this important value of relatives as parent substitutes.

Grandparents can offer a strong relationship to their grandchildren. Their love and devotion are often as intense as the love and devotion parents give. And because grandparents don't have to feel the responsibility for shaping their grandchildren's characters every minute of the day as parents do, I think they are able to enjoy their grandchildren more. In turn the children are able to enjoy their grandparents. Grandparents usually have more leisure too, so they can translate their devotion into such time-consuming activities as reading aloud, playing house, and making excursions to zoos, museums, and the beach.

From both theoretical and practical points of view, good grandparents have considerably more to offer than babysitters with equally sound characters. Grandparents' love has that glowing, doting, and possessive flavor that is exactly what gives children their special confidence in and love for them. (If the doting is excessive, it may, of course, lead to spoiling the child.)

Children sense that grandparents will come to visit them if they possibly can, even at considerable inconvenience. (Aunts and uncles usually can't be quite that available because of their own children.) Even the most devoted of sitters whom children come to love and depend on are likely to be unavailable sometimes because of prior commitments. Or they may become permanently unavailable because they go away to college or get married or take jobs in other cities.

In listing these advantages I'm not merely trying to be practical. I'm encouraging young parents who are somewhat hesitant about becoming regularly involved with grandparents, for fear that the grandparents may be critical of the parents' child-rearing methods or that they may try to influence the parents' management, to weigh the positives and give the grandparents a try. Of course, I may be influenced by the fact that I'm a doting grandfather.

:: 33 ::

How To Get Along with Them

You begin to learn how to be a grandparent by first being a grandchild and appreciating what your own grandparents mean to you. You learn also while you're an active parent and you can see the interplay between the generations above and below you. You still can learn as a grandparent—from your small successes and failures. I've had the extra advantage as a physician of hearing from hundreds of grandparents and parents about their experiences with each other. Perhaps this discussion will be of some help to both parents and grandparents in understanding one another better and understanding the children's reactions too.

When, as a grandparent, you come to the young parents' front door for a visit, the grandchildren want to know immediately if you've brought them a present. Preschool children are usually frank enough to ask the question in just these words. My three-year-old granddaughter, who has already learned to be tactful, asks coyly, "What have you got in your suitcase?"

It's a bit disillusioning to realize that an important part of your welcome has a materialistic basis, but this is a fact of life. Children covet things. But also they sense that the parental and grandparental kind of love is the horn of plenty from which all the essential things of life pour—food, clothes, and allowances, as well as playthings.

So the craving for presents from grandparents is an expression of closeness and confidence as much as it is greediness. It's up to the grandparents not to let the presents constitute the main tie, not to go in for more and more elaborate gifts in an attempt to buy more popularity and love, but to show the children that the other aspects of the relationship are more important and more fun.

When I speak of buying love with extravagant presents, I mean that when we human beings unconsciously doubt that we have enough love to offer, or doubt that the other person will appreciate our personal qualities sufficiently, we have an impulse to try to make up for the gap with an expensive gift. But it has been learned from child-guidance-clinic experience that a boy whose father, for instance, doesn't love him much, but showers him with possessions instead, scorns both the gifts and the giver. This is sometimes the reason a child neglects or abuses certain playthings.

I don't mean that grandparents shouldn't ever, if they can afford to, buy expensive presents. In many families it is the grandparents who are in a better position than the parents to give the bicycle or the electric trains or the jungle gym. But these gifts should be for a grand occasion, like a birthday, and the fine present should be something that the child has been craving for a long time.

The present the grandparent brings on a visit can be quite simple and inexpensive as long as it shows thoughtfulness—a spinning top, a doll's brush-and-comb set, a coloring book, a kite.

Children's eagerness to experience and learn makes it particularly rewarding to take them to special places and events: zoos, museums, factories that accept visitors, sports events, theater, ballet, concerts, forts, skyscrapers, amusement parks, train rides, boat rides.

The best way to solve the problem of the children's constant demands for drinks, popcorn, ice-cream cones, and souvenirs, in my experience, is to present each child with $.25, $2, or whatever seems sensible to you, at the start of the excursion. Explain that this is the limit, and leave it to him to argue with himself about each temptation instead of arguing with you.

I think it's a mistake, though, to regularly provide outside entertainment, for then the child comes to think of you as just a ticket buyer and to demand a treat on every occasion. In fact, if the grandparents dislike excursions or get worn out easily, they shouldn't take the children on any. It isn't good for children to be able to make adults do what the adults don't want to do—and it isn't good for the relationship.

There are at-home activities that are even better for bringing grandparents and children pleasurably together, if the grandparents have the energy: reading stories, telling reminiscences, playing checkers or house, drawing or painting pictures, building with blocks, making models, doing carpentry, stringing beads. These can be carried out at the child's home or at the grandparents' home. It's wise for the grandparents to have playthings or hobby materials in their home that the children can count on finding there.

By listing so many activities I don't mean that grandparents must play with their grandchildren in order to show their interest and love. When I was a child neither of my grandmothers would have dreamed of participating in any childish activities; they wore black lace dresses with high collars held up by whalebone, and didn't lift a finger except to pour tea.

We grandchildren were not even permitted in the parlor until invited—to receive one cookie each. Then we were expected to say, "Thank you" and promptly go outdoors again. But my sisters and brother and I knew that we could count on our grandmothers' love.

What children, like people of all ages, enjoy most is someone who is interested in them, sympathetic to them. This means, quite simply, someone to keep them company and to listen to their accounts of their adventures and tribulations and to their fantasies.

This may sound easy, but most people are poor listeners. They haven't got the time; or they want to do all the talking themselves; or—especially in the case of parents' and other adults' conversing with children—they can't resist the urge to correct and scold, however gently. Or they ask stereotyped questions that sound to the child like a district attorney's interrogation: "What did you learn in school today?" Grandparents, more often than parents, have the time to be good listeners and are freer of the obligation to correct and scold.

I have also gained credit with my grandchildren by driving them on errands that they thought were urgent and by visiting their schools.

There is one caution about conversational intimacy when children are adolescent. They may want to complain—or hint at complaints—about their parents' strictness or stinginess or whatever. This may present quite a temptation to the grandparent to agree with the criticism, particularly if the grandparent happens to share the child's judgment. But if a grandparent (or any other relative or friend) encourages a child to complain about a parent, in the long run it increases resentments and leads away from solutions.

The grandparent doesn't have to scold the child or side with the parent. He can say something that shows he understands the child's feelings without taking sides with either child or parent. He can say, for instance, "I can see how this misunderstanding upsets you." And he can suggest that the child try again to discuss the problem with the parent.

Several times my wife Jane and I have taken care of our grandchildren in their home while their parents were away on a trip. On occasion, when we told the children to do something, they challenged us with the defiant statement, "Our parents don't make us do that!" Of course grandparents don't want to change the parents' rules or be thought mean. Even basically honest children, however, will shade the rules a bit in their favor, or quote an actual rule but misapply it.

In some cases the issue is not of sufficient importance to argue about, and the grandparents would do well to give in; in other cases the decision can be postponed until the parents return. But if the grandparents consider the issue to be important for health or safety, they should insist on their decision; and the parents should back them up, even if it turns out later that the children's interpretation of the rules was correct. In other words, it should always be understood that when the parents are away, the sitter has the final say.

The recollection of our grandchildren's rebelling against our rules, and of how threatened in our discipline my wife and I felt, prompts me to advise grandparents to be as firm as they feel is necessary but to try to avoid anger, for anger is somewhat disturbing to children, especially if the parents are away. But of course it is just when you feel uncertain in your discipline that you are most apt to become angry.

Children can be understanding about your anger if it is justified. Once I scolded my three-year-old granddaughter rather sternly for rudeness, and she glared back at me. But half an hour later at the dinner table she reached over and murmured, "Hold my hand." At least she knows how to get around a grandfather.

How much control or discipline should grandparents exert when the parents are present? And should grandparents and parents feel free to criticize each other's management of the children? These are touchy matters that stir up any tensions between grandparents and parents that have been left over from the parents' childhood and adolescence. For instance, if the young parents are still quite rebellious, they may unconsciously encourage their children to be uppity with the grandparents, fail to correct the children and show resentment if the grandparents then try to reprimand the children.

I'd say—and others may not agree—that when the parents are present it should be their job to see that the children behave, in the sense of politeness, cooperativeness, respect for property. If the parents are present but are not exerting the control the grandparents consider necessary, the grandparents' attitude should depend on where the visit is taking place.

If it is in the parents' home, the grandparents are certainly entitled to ask for politeness to themselves but shouldn't interfere otherwise with the parents' way of doing things. In the grandparents' own house, however, the grandparents should feel free to ask for cooperation and for respect for property and for themselves whether or not the parents are there.

Sometimes when the grandparents are taking care of the children, without quite realizing what they are doing they may set out to tease the parents by letting the children do things that the parents would never let them do. I can still remember from my early childhood, when my mother was extremely particular about what I could and could not eat, that my paternal grandmother and aunt took me and my cousin on a trolley-car ride to Savin Rock, an amusement park outside New Haven, Connecticut. They fed us, among other things, Cracker Jacks.

From my mother's strict point of view this might just as well have been whisky, she considered it so unhealthy. She spoke indignantly of this episode for years afterward.

As a pediatrician I recall a number of cases in which the grandparents deliberately gave the children what they knew the parents disapproved of. The first couple of times, I was shocked to hear of this kind of uncooperativeness. Then I concluded that it must express some hidden impulse on the part of the grandparents. Perhaps it expresses the irritation of the grandparents, who, after all, brought up their children healthily enough, at being told in effect that they don't know what is good for the young.

In addition, I suspect that having finally reached the stage when they no longer have to be responsible for making their own child eat right and behave right, the grandparents now feel entitled to kick over the traces. At the same time they can get an unconscious revenge for all the unnecessary worry their own child caused them by feeding his or her children disapproved foods.

Of course grandparents should not deliberately disobey the parents. This not only creates mistrust in the parents; it creates what the child psychiatrists call conflict of loyalty in the children, which is distressing for all concerned.

Many grandparents are accused of spoiling their grand-children, and of course this is true. But I don't think there is too much harm in this as long as the grandparents keep the children's respect. Perhaps it would be desirable for every one of us—old as well as young—to be spoiled by at least one person as a salve for all the bruises and demands of life. Just because you are spoiled by one individual doesn't mean that you become a corrupted character; you know that you can't get away with spoiled behavior with the rest of your relatives and the world.

What if the parents ask the grandparents to do things in managing the children that the grandparents disapprove of —for example, being too severe with a sensitive child? It would be best if they could discuss the issues with the parents beforehand and come to a solution or compromise. If they can't, the parents should not ask the grandparents to take care of the children—or, if they do, the grandparents on their part may well prefer to decline.

Sometimes the disputes between the parents and the grandparents, which both sides take with great seriousness, don't really amount to a small pile of beans. What is going on in these cases is just an old-fashioned family quarrel, based on the rivalry between the generations, using an issue of child care as the ammunition. All that is needed here is a little sense of humor.

I've been concentrating on rules in the relations and disagreements between grandparents and parents in order to make certain points clear. But ultimately these matters can't be as well settled by arbitrary rules as they can by discussion and mutual understanding.

When Jane and I first became grandparents, we assumed that we should never interfere in the slightest degree with the rearing of our grandchildren. That was the way we had been treated by our parents when we were young parents, and we took it for granted that this was the right way. (My mother, who devoted her life completely to rearing her six children and who controlled us with a short rein and a very firm hand, promised that she would keep hands off from the day each of us married. And she kept her word.)

Jane and I thought it was particularly important that a

grandfather who had written a book and dozens of magazine articles on child care should lean over backward to avoid exerting any influence or showing any disapproval. We certainly tried hard. The parents of our grandchildren on a few occasions invited our comments, but we were too inhibited to be able to take them up on their offer.

They actually did a wonderful job of raising their children —partly by using the same principles on which they themselves had been brought up, partly on quite different principles of their own choosing. But as the years passed it gradually became clear that our grandparental efforts to avoid interfering by even raising an eyebrow were not noninterference after all.

Young parents can't help but be sensitive to any critical feelings on the part of the older generation, no matter how carefully these are concealed. So the only effect of the attempted concealment is to keep any differences of opinion from being discussed, clarified, and perhaps resolved. In fact, misunderstandings can become greater than they need be, for the young parents may interpret a slight look of tension on the part of the grandparents as disapproval of a certain aspect of their child care when it really reflects something quite different. Our unlucky children even had to wonder whether my magazine articles were actually delicate hints to them to do differently.

The most workable and comfortable relationship between grandparents and parents (as between other close relatives, friends, and associates) is one in which there is freedom to express feelings on both sides. This doesn't mean that grandparents have the right to be rude or bossy or tactless, or to make the final decision; the final decision is always the parents'.

But the parents can make the grandparents feel that it is all right to make comments and suggestions on the basis of their love for the children and of their experience. Then, ideally, there can be open discussion, not in the spirit of criticism, but in the spirit of concern for the children's well-being. This is what we have come to in our family with comfortable results.

Discussion does not always result in agreement—this is not necessary. But it should lead to a clearing of the air and to a greater understanding of the others' point of view.

:: 34 ::

The Domineering Grandmother

There are often strains—of small degree, at least—between mothers and grandmothers. Some come primarily from the sensitivity of young mothers about their lack of experience and competence—intensified, of course, by their underlying rivalry with their mothers. Other conflicts can be ascribed mainly to the bossiness of certain grandmothers and their natural rivalry with their daughters.

The need to prove to ourselves and to others that we are competent is a drive that in one form or another gnaws at us all our lives. You can see it in one year olds when they take the spoon away from their mother in order to try to feed themselves, in six year olds who burst into tears if their teacher corrects them; in the teenagers who say, "Yes, I know all about that,"even if they don't, whenever you try to tell them something.

Some individuals may be more easily embarrassed by their inexpertness than others, sometimes because they have greater inadequacies to admit to (the person who is naturally clumsy, for instance, or who has a visible handicap), but more often because they have been made sensitive by critical parents.

The rivalry between the generations begins early in childhood and persists at least to full adulthood, sometimes through middle age. A parent is always bigger, smarter, more privileged, and able to take out his bossiness on his offspring. (If you boss friends or employees too much, they just leave.) Finding a job, getting married, and having children represent in one sense the achievement of equality; yet this equality is somehow incomplete as long as a young person feels like a beginner. So the sense of rivalry may persist until he or she has proved to be a great success. (In a highly ambitious man this stage of relaxation may not come until he achieves the presidency of his firm in his sixties.)

Conventionally we don't think so much about the competitiveness of parents with their child. If it exists, it is likely to come to the surface in the child's adolescence and youth. For then it is the young person's turn to have the visibly active romantic life and to plan for a great career. The parents then must anticipate taking a back seat. A mother has to relinquish her pre-eminence more obviously than a father. While her daughter blooms, she gets the wrinkles; and though consciously she may not want any more babies, symbolically they are still very important, and it is her daughter who will be having them now.

If children grow up with a parent who is more competitive than average, particularly if the parent's rivalry takes the form of being critical of the children and of minimizing their achievements, the children are more apt to be insecure about their capabilities, to dread being belittled and to be on the lookout—consciously or unconsciously—for ways to prove their parent wrong.

In some rivalry conflicts it is not the maternal but the paternal grandmother with whom the young mother is battling. Here, of course, the rivalry is not so much over the child as over the young husband. His mother may think that his wife is an adventuress who has taken advantage of his innocence. His wife may see his mother as a possessive witch who is determined to break up the marriage.

A common type of mother-grandmother conflict occurs when a mother continually emphasizes the newness and the scientific correctness of the child-rearing methods she is using or when she carries them to extremes. I occasionally get letters from grandmothers complaining of the wild methods their daughters or daughters-in-law are using.

One grandmother will say that her daughter is so determined not to overdress her small son that she sends him out to play in winter with only a cotton jacket on and that his lips are often blue with cold. The grandmother is so distressed that she asks me to write to her daughter—who, she says, has great confidence in me—telling her to put more clothes on the child. (I smile to think of the amazement of her daughter if she were to receive such a letter from me.)

Another woman will write that her daughter is feeding her two-month-old baby three adult meals a day, including frankfurters and fried potatoes.

Another complains that the toilet training of her three-year-old grandson has not even been started yet and that the child's mother says there is no hurry.

In such cases the young mother has got hold of an idea that may have some validity but is pushing it to extremes. This is done partly to show the grandmother how out-of-date her child-care concepts are, partly to keep her slightly miserable in her anxiety about the child's welfare. The mother doesn't feel too guilty about the agitation she's causing the grandmother because she feels that any interference from her is against the rules of civilized society and she considers her specific complaint to be completely unjustified.

So much for the rebellious mother who's teasing the grandmother. Now for the bossy grandmother.

As a practicing pediatrician I've often heard complaints, in the office and also by letter, about the interfering or domineering grandmother. At least that is the problem as the young mother sees it.

In a simple case, a grandmother visits often and makes many suggestions—admittedly in a polite manner—about how the baby might be fed or clothed or managed differently. But a more aggressive grandmother may not hesitate, if her recommendations are not followed, to become overbearing or even insulting.

I know of women who've accused their daughters face to face of gross incompetence and of jeopardizing the life of the child. And a few paternal grandmothers even have tried to persuade their sons to divorce their wives for such reasons.

I remember a young mother who dreaded and resented her mother's frequent, interfering visits but never could find the inner authority with which to stop her. This grandmother showed the nominal courtesy of calling up before appearing. She would ask, "What are you having for dinner tonight?" And whatever her daughter listed, she'd say, "That sounds good to me," and invite herself for the meal and the evening.

Why is it so easy for mothers to dominate their grown daughters? Usually the pattern has existed through the daughter's lifetime; that is the external explanation. But if we let it go at that, there is no solution, no hope, since the grandmother is unlikely to change all by herself. The more important question is why the young mother, a grown person now, feels powerless still to stand up for her rights. If she can understand why, she may be able to change the situation.

Anyone who's being dominated can't help but resent it. She or he develops a counterhostility, though this may be deeply repressed in the unconscious. But if the dominating parent has been at the same time a loving parent (perhaps not an ideally loving parent, but still loving), the child's hostility is bound to make the child feel guilty.

It may not seem logical or fair by adult reasoning that victims should have to feel guilty about their inevitable resentment, but this is basic human nature in regard to children's feelings about their parent. This guilt is what makes it difficult for the child—at any age—to dare to fight back. (I am discussing here the parent who effectively dominates, who manages to squelch any rebelliousness. Commoner today is the parent who is somewhat aggressive, who has the impulse to be overbearing but who is easily stopped and made to feel guilty by a child who flares up. In such a case, though the child is likely to grow up a cantankerous person, he or she is not likely to be consistently submissive.)

Is it possible for the young mother who always has been dominated, and who still is locked into submissiveness by her feelings of guilt, to free herself? It can be done gradually, in most cases, preferably with the help of a psychiatrist or of a family social agency.

The essence of the cure is for the young mother over a period of months to come to realize, by analyzing each clash, that the grandmother does not have any actual power to control her or demolish her, that it is only her own guilt and submissiveness that trap her.

There is no point in the mother's working up her indignation each day over how wrong and mean the grandmother is. This is an exercise in self-pity that intensifies the masochistic element in the mother's personality and deflects her from finding an escape.

The mother must keep practicing the skill of standing up to the grandmother. When the grandmother says, "Charlotte, don't you think you ought to put warmer clothes on the baby?" the mother has to learn how to say, "No. I think her clothing is just about right for a day like this." Or, about the amount of kinds of food offered: "Well, I'm following Dr. Jenkins's directions to the letter."

If the grandmother is inviting herself over too often, the mother can make repeated excuses about why this is not convenient. The message will get through eventually to all but the most insensitive relatives.

After a while the mother may acquire the courage to discuss her feelings more frankly with the grandmother: how sensitive she is to criticism; how she herself, at this early stage of motherhood, needs to gain confidence by seeing that she can care for the baby all by herself; how visits from the grandmother more often than once a week undermine her own limited sense of adequacy.

In such statements the mother may seem to take the blame, apologize for her own lack of confidence or ask for the grandmother's understanding and patience, rather than accuse the grandmother of trying to take over. This is not because the problem is really all the mother's fault but simply because a mother who finds it difficult to claim her right to care for her own child will find it even more difficult to criticize face to face the aggressive woman who is interfering.

After a mother has gained some confidence in asking for the grandmother's understanding she may be able gradually to become more candid in pointing out the grandmother's faults, if that is necessary. In some cases the mother may come to see that the grandmother is not really as aggressive as the mother's timidity had led her to believe in the beginning.

A young mother who is being bossed around by her mother or mother-in-law can't help but accumulate considerable anger, no matter how she conceals it or inhibits its expression. And it may be that the only time she can stand up to the older woman is when, after long suffering, she loses her temper. But in general the mother should try to speak up—if only to apologize for her own inability to accept suggestions—just as soon as the grandmother begins to interfere, long before the mother feels ready to explode.

This is because a really overbearing person knows when she is making a victim squirm and unconsciously enjoys it. And though an angry outburst on the part of the mother is in one sense a revolt, it's a delayed revolt that comes only after considerable helpless suffering; it is really composed of a thin surface of last-minute rebellion that surrounds a more solid core of submission. In the unconscious mind of the dominating person the outburst is basically an evidence of successful bullying, even if the oppressor did go a bit too far this time.

To make my points I've called certain mothers mean teases. I've described some grandmothers as almost fiendish in their overbearing ways, and I've called their victims masochistic. Of course there are very, very few individuals of either generation who carry things this far. But there is a trace of these tendencies in most mother-grandmother conflicts. I think that analyzing the extreme cases throws light on the meaning of the subtle cases.

There has been no mention of fathers and grandfathers in this discussion. Aren't they involved? Certainly the father has an important part in both types of conflict that I've described.

Even if he suspects that he and his wife are going a bit too far in disturbing the grandparents with their newfangled or exaggerated methods, he still may spur her on because of his own continuing rivalry with his parents. This united front of mother and father may make it harder in the end to find a compromise.

It would be more useful, if the father thinks his wife is sometimes going too far, for him to point this out to her—in a sympathetic spirit, of course. But he should not side with his or her parents in their presence against his wife. One of the most crucial functions of a husband is that he show his understanding of his wife's feelings and prove his basic loyalty to her whenever there are disputes with relatives.

In the case of the bossy grandmother and the submissive but resentful mother, the young father can make a great contribution, especially if it is his mother who is the offender. He can show his loyalty to his wife by encouraging her to stand up for her rights and by giving her examples of how to carry this out.

And he is the right person to reason with his mother or put her in her place; he should know from his own experience what is going on between his mother and his wife. If his mother is interfering—partly, perhaps, because of her possessiveness of him—he has the responsibility of showing that her effort to separate him from his wife is having the opposite effect.

From my professional experience I'd say that a majority of grandfathers tend to avoid involvement in the kinds of disputes I'm discussing. Partly this is due to the common but mistaken American tradition that child-care issues should be left to the women. Partly it is the grandfather's fear that he may get himself into an unpleasant relationship with one or the other woman at an age when he no longer is interested in solving problems, but in peace.

The grandfather's main usefulness, when his wife becomes upset about the care the grandchildren are receiving, is to remind her not only that the grandchildren belong to their parents, for better or worse, but that her agitation will only make the mother more determined to stick to her extreme methods.

In the case of the truly dominating grandmother, her husband may have little influence on her at this late stage of their marriage. Perhaps then the best he can do is give his daughter or daughter-in-law a disloyal wink when she is trying to stand up for herself, to show his sympathy and to give her encouragement.

Chapter XI

The Changing Family

:: 35 ::

The Needs of Young Children

Women are demanding the equality and justice that have never been granted them in our society—in employment, in the universities that hold the keys to entrance into the professions, in the courts, in the family.

Women see that they will not be able to compete on an equal footing for the better jobs if they are expected also to do all the child care and the housework. Of course many of them happen to like these home jobs. Others despise them as slutwork, unappreciated by family or society, therefore unpaid.

There is also, today, widespread criticism of marriage and the family by young people, on more general principles. They point to the high divorce rate and the frequency of family tensions. They blame particularly the ingrown structure of the nuclear family (see Chapter I).

For whatever reasons—desire for a career, need for money, enjoyment of company—more and more women are taking jobs and I assume that this trend will continue.

But if more and more women want to have uninterrupted careers, and if they and their husbands want to have children, too, how will the children be cared for? Young couples —and also unmarried young people who are thinking ahead —give various answers. They say, on general principles (and I agree) that when mothers work outside, fathers should shoulder 50 percent of the housework and child care. And if careers have to be limited temporarily to provide parental care for young children, equal consideration should be given to limiting the careers of both father and mother. They ask for day-care centers provided by the state for the all-day care of children from birth until they can attend school at six years of age; staggered work hours for the father and mother so that there always can be a parent at home; a number of families living together in a commune where domestic work and child care are shared sociably or where the women who prefer to stay at home can care for the children while others may go out to work. They suggest that in some families the father might stay home permanently while the mother works.

In a society changing as rapidly as ours is now it is inevitable that the roles of both sexes, the relationships between them and also child-rearing patterns will shift. I consider it a good sign that young people want to think realistically and idealistically about such matters.

But babies and children have very specific emotional needs. These have been studied intensively in the past seventy-five years, and they have to be taken into account when new patterns for family living are being discussed.

I've talked with some parents who assume that the time it's most important for them to stay at home is when their children are of school age, because, they say, children are more likely to get into real trouble then. (These are generally parents who live in neighborhoods with high delinquency rates.) Other parents think they should try hardest to be at home when their children are two, three, four years old, because they cling a great deal, act worried when the parents leave them and need a lot of watching and comforting.

Quite a few parents assume that during the first couple of years an infant's needs are so simply met that parents can go to work with relative impunity at this time. But studies of children who were brought up in orphanages from birth, and insights gained from numerous other psychological and psychoanalytic investigations, all agree that the first two or three years are the most crucial ones. The personality is more pliable then. During those years children are constantly being molded by the parents or by the substitute who spends the greatest amount of time with them. Will they become predominantly trusting or suspicious people? This will be determined by whether the parent or substitute is responsive in meeting their needs or is disturbingly unpredictable. Will they become loving or cool? To a great degree they will mirror, for the rest of their lives the lovingness or coolness of the parents or substitute.

One person acts toward children as if they are basically bad, always doubting them, scolding them. Another trustingly assumes that they are good except when proved otherwise. Children respond by being what they are expected to be. A parent or substitute with more-than-average hostility finds a dozen excuses every hour of the day for venting it— openly or subtly—on children, and the children's character acquires a corresponding hostility. There are lots of people who have the itch to dominate children. Others always want to make them feel guilty. Unfortunately, they can succeed at either effort if they are consistent about it.

A good parent or substitute doesn't merely meet a baby's physical needs for food, warmth, and cleanliness. Let's take the example of a father and his infant daughter. He takes a great and special delight in her. He tells her she's the cutest, brightest baby in the world (no matter what another person might say), and she shows she appreciates his infatuation even though she doesn't understand the words.

A good father (or mother) has a drive to foster his baby's intellectual, social, and emotional development. He tries instinctively to get a smile out of her, and when she responds he encourages her with noisy delight to do it again. He uses baby talk to teach her the names of her family and her foods and a few favorite articles. And when she makes sounds that are slight approximations of the names of persons or things, he shows his pleased understanding and keeps repeating the correct sound, as if she had said it right. He teaches her pat-a-cake and peekaboo. He plays her favorite records and points out the pictures in her books. These aren't just intellectual teaching exercises. They are instinctive expressions of an intense emotional relationship, and that is why they succeed and that is why a loved baby keeps surging ahead intellectually, socially, emotionally, while an unappreciated baby changes so slowly.

During the first year, when a baby is helpless about getting inanimate objects or human attention for herself, she must depend on a great indulgence, a dotingness in her parents or in a substitute. Sensitive psychological observations have shown that the baby who can't make her parents serve her within reasonable limits—because they are unloving or insensitive or depressed—will become somewhat apathetic and depressed herself. So we can see that parents and grandparents are meant to talk baby talk and lavish ridiculous compliments on infants and act like happy slaves to them— as long as their wants are reasonable. A substitute should have this kind of enthusiasm too.

After about a year the child learns to walk and becomes increasingly capable and independent. This just naturally diminishes the inclination of adults to dote and pamper. Furthermore, the child becomes quite particular about what she wants, demanding about getting it, balky about giving in to guidance, and explosive to a degree in throwing tantrums when thwarted. So now she particularly needs people in charge who have a neat balance in leadership qualities— friendliness, definiteness, tact, ingenuity. The adult who is too timid to lead is in for a lot of frustration. The one who tries to meet every small issue by a head-on collision may be in for even worse trouble.

Good parents change somewhat the aspect of themselves that they present to their children at various ages, because they sense children are different kinds of people at different stages, with differing needs. Parents don't have to consult a book or even think about how to do this. It comes to them naturally through instinct, tact, and through having been children themselves.

Children who grow up to become adults who have the extra motivation and capability to go to college and to carry out an occupation that is above the average level are those who have lived with, felt cherished by, and wanted to be like parents who had such aspirations for them. And we have learned from psychoanalytic studies that the influence that makes a very few individuals become extraordinarily pro- ductive or creative in their fields is, most often, the inspira- tion they received from a particularly strong relationship with a mother who had especially high aspirations for her children.

All through the early years a child has a very special need of which some parents are unaware—the need to have the same person or persons taking care of her. The reason that continuity of a parent substitute is important is that a young child by her very nature is meant to be deeply, intimately dependent on her parent. She acquires security and charac- ter through the emotional roots she normally has in her par- ents—the mother, more often, in the early years. If her mother disappears completely, she will be depressed and anxious for a long period. If her mother goes to work full time or for a large part of the week, the infant or young child will grow part of her roots into the substitute. Then if the substitute suddenly disappears, the child will be depressed and anxious. We believe that in some cases where a child's dependence has been repeatedly established and then broken, with a number of substitutes who have taken over a large part of her care, she may react eventually by refusing to develop love or trust in any more people. This can mean an emotionally cold and lonely life.

:: 36 ::
The Daytime Care of Young Children

In the light of this description of infants' and small children's emotional and intellectual needs, let's look at several of the alternatives for their care. We'll start with nurseries or day-care centers for children from birth to three years old. (I'm not discussing here the care of those over three years.)

First some definitions. The term *nursery school* has usually meant school for children three to five years old, conducted by professionally trained teachers, from 9:00 A.M. to noon or to 3:00 P.M. most commonly supported by parents' fees. The term *day-care center* is more recent; it means all-day facilities for the care of children of working parents, conducted cooperatively by trained teachers and untrained people from the community, supported mainly by government funds. The age range is commonly two or three to six years; a few centers may take children under two years, and also children over six years, from the hour when elementary school lets out until parents can pick them up after work. The term *nursery* or *day nursery* is over a hundred years old and has usually meant untrained care of children of working mothers from birth to elementary school age.

Most day nurseries that have existed in the last one hun-dred years in the United States have cared for the babies and small children of mothers who were compelled to work (usu-ally, before the days of welfare payments, because they had been widowed or deserted). These nurseries suffered from multiple handicaps. Staff was inadequate in number, in train-ing, and in maternal temperament, and the babies frequently lay isolated and deserted in their cribs. Children over the age of one had few constructive playthings or activities and re-ceived too little attention and affection. Some mothers who took them home at night were so demoralized by their own bitter life experiences that they could not provide much visible affection or even attention. Many of these deprived children made poor records in school and in life. And nurser-ies got a bad reputation with child-care professionals.

In recent years, some of the more responsible of the old day nurseries have upgraded their staffs and programs and taken only children of three years or older. A limited number of new, conscientious day-care centers taking children under as well as over three years have been established with gov-ernment funds, for the benefit of working mothers, but their long-term values and liabilities have not been carefully eval-uated. Old-fashioned, custodial day nurseries are still li-censed in many cities. In addition there are numberless unlicensed, unsupervised baby farms, run for profit by "a woman down the street" to which working mothers bring their children and which are not detected unless a city has a vigilant inspection system.

Haven't nurseries proved satisfactory for children of working mothers in the Soviet Union, and in Israel's *kibbut-zim?** In a general way they have satisfied the authorities in

*The kibbutzim (plural of kibbutz) are agricultural collective communi-ties in which both parents work and the children are cared for in nurseries,

both countries. They have been amply staffed with selected, trained attendants. But the results of group care in the crucial first three years have not yet been proved excellent enough to overcome the skepticism of professional people like myself who have high aspirations for our children and who have anti-group-care prejudices left over from the past. And the situation regarding the recruitment of nursery attendants in the United States is not nearly as satisfactory as it is in Israel and the Soviet Union.

The group upbringing in the kibbutz has produced a noticeably different personality type. The older intellectual settlers from Europe was most commonly philosophical, imaginative, sociable people with a worldly, self-deprecating sense of humor and strong possessive and dependent ties to relatives. Their kibbutz-raised child or grandchild is more apt to be a matter-of-fact, highly practical, cooperative, and dutybound citizen, often hard to get to know, in some cases even curt to strangers.

School achievement test results of children raised in the kibbutzim tend to be concentrated in the middle zone of the range for Israel. Of the Israeli children raised in their own homes, a greater proportion are either in the high or low zones, depending on the quality of the home atmosphere. In my opinion, the close emotional ties of an all-round good family provide the strongest stimulus to mental and emotional development.

I don't have such specific data from the Soviet Union, but I do know that Soviet educational and psychological authorities in the past expressed great pride in their day nurseries and boarding institutions for infants and young children. I think it is significant that they now are emphasizing the contribution of family relationships in the development of sound

---

in kindergartens, and in schools in which they stay except for visits to the parents in the evenings and on the Sabbath.

personalities and admitting that those children raised in boarding institutions run the risk of "deprivation of psychological stimulation" and of "one-sided or retarded development."

Soviet authorities also are discussing the need to go beyond, or even to reverse, their educational system's previous primary emphasis on creating the duty-oriented citizen. They stress instead the need to foster the unique potentialities of the individual so that he may be able to make "original or even revolutionary contributions" to the society. I, with my beliefs, interpret these statements to mean that the Soviet authorities realize that they have been producing drones with their group care in the early years.

In Israel and the Soviet Union the nursery care of babies and young children so that both parents can work is considered patriotic and dignified work by young women. In the United States such nonprofessional care carries no prestige. As a result it is difficult to recruit suitable people here.

So I am saying that the proposals to place babies and children under three years of age in all-day nurseries in the United States raise serious questions in the minds of people like myself. If we could set up high-quality programs and recruit adequate attendants who would serve for years, providing children with real substitute mothers, we might produce average children. But I doubt that most of the young idealists who propose nurseries would really be satisfied with average children.

If in the first three years children need a parental kind of care—devoted, responsive, and individual—then how are young working parents to plan?

A career primarily in the home (perhaps combined with community activities and absorbing participation in arts or crafts) may be just as productive for society and as fulfilling for many individuals as designing advertisements or being an officer in a bank—at least until the youngest child is six, seven, or eight years of age. I hope that soon the social climate will make it possible for men to share or even take the larger part of the home-making responsibility.

When both parents want continuous careers and they also want children, what are the possible arrangements? I don't see an ideal solution at present that has wide application. There are currently compromises available which are fairly satisfactory for many couples. I'll mention some eventual solutions that would be a lot better.

Fortunate is the family that can turn for a substitute to a willing and reliable grandparent of whose child-rearing methods the mother and father approve. These conditions are more often met nowadays in certain groups in the population that still have old-fashioned traditions about relatives' living close together, making a great effort to get along together, and helping one another out. In such groups the methods of rearing children are not as likely to keep changing in accord with new scientific doctrines, so the parents know just how a grandmother will be caring for the child and approve of her. In fact, the grandmother is apt to be considered a great expert by the young parents in such groups. A grandmother can be counted on to cherish her grandchild as much as she cherished her own child. If appreciated, she is much more likely to stick to the job than a hired person. Sometimes, in close-knit families, an aunt can take over a child's care.

However, the commoner pattern in America—especially in college-educated families—is quite different. The father expects to go anywhere for the right job, and this usually takes his family far from where his and his wife's families live. Even when the young couple live in the old home town, they often do not have confidence that the grandmother's methods are up to date; also the grandmother is less often willing to settle down to another decade of child rearing. Certainly when a grandmother is available and willing, working parents should consider her first of all and make every effort to be tolerant of her methods.

The most usual compromise is when father, mother—perhaps in conjunction with a parent substitute—dovetail their schedules so that the parents between them can care for the child for a good part of the child's waking hours. (The child's waking hours increase with age; but even a three or four year old will nap for an hour or two after lunch if encouraged.) For example, the mother is a schoolteacher who can get off at 3:30 P.M., the father is a salesman who can postpone going to work until mid-morning, and a sitter or sitter-housekeeper fills in between. Or the mother is a nurse with three possible shifts to choose from and the father is a student who has considerable freedom in arranging his classes. In some occupations—medicine, nursing, social work, psychology—which have been chronically shorthanded and in which employers therefore have a strong motive to accommodate workers, mothers and fathers have been able to arrange to work certain days or half-days of the week and to take other days or half-days off. Parents, by organized effort, should be able to pressure other employers into providing flexible part-time work patterns; or to pressure legislatures to pass laws requiring employers to offer jobs on a less than eight-hour-day, forty-hour-per-week basis, for those who need them, with correspondingly reduced salaries and seniority.

We shouldn't assume that the eight-hour workday will continue forever. It's said that automation, aided by the demands of labor, will progressively shorten the workday—to six hours and later to four hours. Then it would be a lot easier for father and mother to dovetail their work and their child care.

I myself believe that the government should pay a salary to parents to the extent that they stay at home to care for their preschool children, for children should not be deprived of the parental attention which creates security and sound character just because of the family's financial needs. More specifically, it would be worth the cost to a nation to prevent the serious neglect of some children which is the main cause of the character defects that result in poor application in school, truancy, delinquency, and, in adulthood, irresponsibility and petty criminality.

And parents should not be put in conflict between child care and the earning of essential income.

As for the parent substitute or sitter, the problem, of course, is to find a satisfactory person. The isolation involved in child care and domestic work doesn't appeal to many people when it's not their own child or home—at least not in America. There's no prestige involved in the care of normal children here (except in the case of teachers) as there is, for instance, in Israel or the Soviet Union, where it's thought of as an important service to the country and to childhood. Furthermore, the woman who loves children is apt to soon get married and have a child of her own.

In engaging a person who will be at home with the child all day, it is of the utmost importance that the substitute be a person of whose character and approach the parents thoroughly approve and one who is likely to stay. These crucial questions can't be answered in a hurry and parents should not rush off to work—whatever the excuse about the job's not waiting—until they are convinced.

During the first interview the parents can see how the other woman approaches the child and how the child responds. If the parents engage her, it should be for a trial period of a week or two. The father or mother should stay at home during this period and watch the mutual reactions of the two as the substitute gradually takes over. In this way too the parent maintains the child's security until the child develops enough familiarity and trust in the substitute.

Before I go any further I should interject that of course I don't mean that parents have to worry about the perfection of character of everyone who has regular contact with a small child. If the parents take a good portion of the care of their child, they will be the main influence on character. It is good for children's personalities to become acquainted with a variety of people—relatives, neighbors of all ages, storekeepers. They will enrich children's personalities.

I would call it unimportant if a potential sitter has an accent or uses ungrammatical English or is somewhat messy, lazy, or forgetful. The important questions are whether a sitter likes children and can control them easily. I wouldn't touch a sitter who seemed at all mean, threatening, dominating, or teasing.

Foster day care is an alternative to engaging a sitter. It is usually easier to find another couple in the community who will take a child into their home during the day, than to find someone to care for the child in his own home. Next in importance to the satisfactory personalities of such a couple would be that they have not more than one other child under the age of four years to care for, because infants and very young children don't do well on a skimpy amount of attention even when the foster parents are kindly.

Much the safest way in a city to find a couple who will take a small child into their home is through a children's or family-and-children's social agency that, as part of its professional services, recruits, selects, and supervises homes for foster day care of this type. If there is no such agency in a smaller town, parents should, of course, make careful inquiries and then observe for themselves. Their child should be introduced gradually to the foster home, and they themselves should spend several days visiting it with their child to bridge the transition. This should give the parents the opportunity to learn whether they and the foster mother see eye to eye.

A few young people are experimenting with, or talking about, living together in communes. In these collective settlements—usually rural but sometimes urban—people share their money, labor, and talents and set up their own rules for running the community. They are seeking in one another—and in the land, if the commune is rural—mutual love, spiritual rebirth, and work that is meaningful and fulfilling to the individual and to the community.

Communes vary widely in structure and membership, but the most successful and long-lasting ones retain such constraints as orderly work routines and community-health regulations. They carefully select as members those people who will be steady, (nontransient) contributors to the community. Success does not come easily.

Communes tend to function as extended families. By interdependence and sharing, the members within such a settlement seek to avoid the isolation, rigidities, and tensions inherent in the conventional small, two-generation, nuclear family of today's society. The goal is to provide a wide range of companionship—both deep and casual—for children as well as for adults, a more enjoyable sharing of domestic chores and a more efficient and satisfying division of other labor.

Parents in this type of commune need not be isolated with their children all day long, for they can have plenty of adult company as they care for them and as they go about their work and other activities. They are also likely to have fewer practical child-care problems than most parents because in a commune all children are to some extent looked out for by all adults.

Members of this extended family sometimes relieve the parents in the care of their children when it is helpful, so that parents don't have to cook, feed the baby, and watch the toddler all at the same time; or, when it is necessary, so that the parents can do certain chores, or work. Still, unless parents take an outside job—which is more likely in an urban than in a rural commune—they probably will spend the greater share of each day with their infants and small children.

I believe that a baby or small child should be cared for

mainly by one or two people, even though others may help out at times. If a child's parents go to work, for example, only one other person should serve as the principal substitute parent. The child then would not have to shift dependence from one substitute to another. Therefore, I'd say that parents who join a commune and plan to do outside work should not turn children over to a substitute until the children become accustomed to their surroundings, until the parents know the substitute well enough to trust her or him implicitly in shaping their children the way they want them shaped, and until it is fairly certain that the substitute is committed to living in the commune for a prolonged period. Of course, it's even more important that a young couple who want to live in a commune take the time to select a stable one that will serve their children as well as it will serve them.

From the age of three onward most children are independent enough to be able to be in a group for half a day without becoming distressed. They are sociable and cooperative enough to enjoy and profit by playing regularly with other children.

A good nursery school or day-care center makes a satisfactory solution for the care of a child for three to five hours a day, just as long as the child does not fall ill and as long as it is not vacation time. But parents must remember that colds, coughs, sore throats, ear infections, and influenza, often with high fever, are at their most frequent at this age, and that careful nursery schools don't want sick children around, exposing the others. So this solution will be satisfactory only if one parent has a job from which it is possible to take time off without upsetting the boss and fellow workers or if there is someone else who will gladly care for the child who is sick.

If a first-rate nursery school is not available, the child of parents who work should be in good foster day care or in the care of a person whom the parents engage to come to the home.

Children between three and six years are still sensitive and dependent enough so that a parent should try to be with them from midafternoon onward, I'd say.

By the age of six children will probably be in school two-thirds of the day and will have even more independence of spirit than before. However, there is still a very definite need for them to feel that they belong to someone when they come home from school, either a parent or a neighbor who has officially and fully taken the responsibility of being there and welcoming them. And there will still be the times when they will be ill, even though the frequency and duration of illness goes down rapidly from five years onward.

There should be and could be after-school recreational, hobby, and special-study programs in school buildings from 3:00 until 5:00 P.M. if parents persisted in demanding them, not only through PTA channels but also by lobbying in city councils and by electioneering for sympathetic councilmen.

:: 37 ::

A Father's Role

"I wish you would write something directed to fathers. I know my husband wants to do the right things for our boys, but because of all the troubles in the family in which he grew up, I don't think he really knows how to be a good father. He loves our boys and is kind and fair with them, but when I ask him to take them places, he won't. When they were young I played with them, but now I feel they should be developing a closer relationship with their father. The boys need him and need to have fun with him, and he is missing so much fun with them. I don't think it's healthy for me to do so much alone with them—I feel as if I'm becoming their father too.

I'm sure my problem is not unique, so perhaps a good strong article directed to fathers on how to be fathers would be a great help to others as well as to us."

This letter raises a number of subjects that I'd like to discuss.

You can see that this mother wants me to write that a father ought to play with his sons; then she'd show him the article and he'd have to do it. But if I wrote the piece that way and if he obeyed it, he probably wouldn't do the boys much good. A father who doesn't ever feel like playing with his sons but does so because he feels he ought to will be a sorry playmate—he'll be embarrassed or irritable. Better the boys find other children to play with.

The father—any father—should be sharing with the mother the day-to-day care of their child from birth onward, I believe. This is the natural (unforced) way for the father to start the relationship, just as it is for the mother. Then no distance need exist, at any age, between father and child. As the baby grows into small child and gets into more trouble and makes more trouble, the father, if he is part-time supervisor of meal time, bath time, bed time, getting-dressed time, shopping time, will inevitably become involved in explaining, directing, rescuing, comforting, correcting. These are the very essence of any parent-child relationship. Then if, in addition, there is the energy and the inclination—in father or mother—for a recreational companionship with the children, so much the better.

I feel that a father during the hours when he is at home, in the morning, in the evening and on week ends, should put in as much time as the mother on child care, whether or not the mother has an outside job too. She is either tired as a result of her job or she is tired of taking care of the children.

The father should, I believe, take on a fair chunk of the house chores too in the evening, on weekends, and on vacations. American fathers have traditionally tended lawns, washed cars, cleaned basements, put up and taken down storm windows and screens, and that's good. In some families they've helped with dish washing. But only recently have increasing numbers of them taken their turns at shopping, cooking, cleaning, tending the clothes washer and dryer, if their wives held outside jobs.

A father's participation in child care and home care isn't simply a matter of fairness to a mother—especially to a working mother. More importantly, it shows her that he considers these jobs just as vital, just as worthy, just as challenging as his work in the shop or office. I say "more importantly" because what takes the enthusiasm out of women—and makes plenty of them mad—is the implication given by so many men that their work is the real work, the demanding work, and that children and home work are only necessary chores that anyone can perform.

Besides, women—or at least many women—would like the companionship of their husbands in the house jobs. Some women would also like to share companionably in lawn, cellar, and car chores.

We have to face the fact, however, that there are still millions of fathers today who have not participated much in the care of their children. And there are thousands of them who can't be comfortably companionable with their children, particularly their sons. The first question is whether the children will suffer as a consequence of this lack of relationship. Not necessarily. A child can admire and gain inspiration from a father who is so dignified or so unhandy at making things or so uninterested in sports and nature that he can't enjoyably do any of these things, if father and child are reasonably comfortable with each other and can chat spontaneously at the dinner table from time to time. This amount of contact is enough to enable most girls and boys to develop quite normally in Europe and Latin America, for example.

In America we take it for granted that all fathers and

mothers play, or should play, with their children and that this is always good for them. Children do usually profit from having parents who enjoy being with them, provided the parents are acting the role of parents at the same time. But there are many fathers and mothers—even in American and even quite normal ones—who don't play with their children because they don't feel comfortable doing it.

In simpler societies where people live by hunting or fishing or primitive agriculture, a father will begin initiating his sons into the techniques and mysteries of his occupation at whatever age is considered suitable. And a girl is allowed to begin helping her mother, perhaps by carrying a real baby on her hip from the age of four or five. In a way this is the most natural kind of playing, because when children are playing they usually are trying to practice and master adult occupations.

So it is theoretically more appropriate for the child to be striving for an adult level of interest and performance—and for the parent to be helping him to reach it—than for the parent to be trying to be a child. But in our urban and industrial civilization this system wouldn't work too well. A boy child can't join a father on the assembly line or in a law office. So there's more justification in our society for a father to set aside a little time for doing carpentry or for tossing a football with his child.

There are opportunities for companionable activities that don't have to be invented, in lawn work or car washing or cellar cleaning. They aren't utilized as often as they could be. Fathers tend to do these chores until their children get to be twelve or fourteen, depending on how responsible they are, and then turn the jobs over to them. Of course, children younger than this aren't usually much help; in fact, they are more likely to slow the job down. But I still think it is worthwhile for eight and ten year olds to go through with it for the sake of the companionship and the learning of good work attitudes. Moreover, I wouldn't let a small child who was trying or pretending to help become a nuisance by scattering the leaf piles or splashing the car after it had been wiped dry. You can't expect young children to work for long, but I'd teach them to work seriously for half an hour and then excuse them.

I think that solid, enjoyable conversations, in contrast to conventional remarks, flow most easily when people are working side by side. When they temporarily run out of talk and prefer to think, the work fills the gaps.

There are two reasons why a father might keep on working at chores with his children after they are old enough to carry on by themselves. It may be the easiest and most natural way of maintaining a casual companionship, especially when adolescence begins to introduce strains. It may also be the least painful method to keep children at their chores. Lots of youths in their teens covet the money to be earned at chores and fully intend to work several hours every weekend. They work like beavers the first time, finger the pay like misers, dream dreams of affluence or motorcycles. But a couple of weekends later they accept an invitation from a friend without thinking, or put off setting to work while they watch a few television programs. (Adolescence, like spring fever, brings shifting moods—absorbing daydreams, sudden enthusiasms, spells of listlessness.) Soon a parent can see that the work won't get done before some other obligation comes due. So there has to be first a reminder and then a little nagging, which tends to get worse each weekend. But if the father is working nearby on the same time schedule and makes a point of expecting his child to stick with it, he may be the stabilizing influence that's needed. Children often prefer to have a clear-cut separation of their jobs from their parents' jobs even though they work close enough to converse.

Excursions, picnics, athletic events, fishing, and camping

trips are fine with two important provisos. The parents must be able to enjoy them: If they can't, the child won't either, and it will have been better to save the time and money. And the child must be able to participate in a way that doesn't bother the parents too much. Boys, even more than girls, have a drive to invent restless projects that have nothing to do with the official purpose of the trip—playing hide-and-seek in museums (not that this kind of nuisance should be tolerated); throwing good food in large quantities to squirrels during picnics; playing alphabet games with advertising signs at sports events instead of watching the game, and wanting to buy food and drink from every vendor; building dams on fishing streams. How much trouble these side projects will make will depend on the maturity of the child and the control and the patience of the parents. Anyway, the parents ought not to invest time and money in ambitious trips until they have tried small ones. Sometimes it works better when two couples have each other's company on excursions and let their children be semi-independent on the same trip.

Often the easiest method for parent and child to be companionable is reading aloud. I found as a parent that though there were some children's books that irritated me, there were plenty that I liked well enough or even a lot.

However, there are some fathers who have grown up with such an uncomfortable relationship with their fathers that they can't be at ease with their sons—fathers who always seem to be hidden behind the paper when their sons appear, who manage not to seem to notice them at meals and who leave all the disciplining to the mother. This is likely in turn to impair these boys' relationships with other boys, with men when they grow up, and with their own future sons. Certainly it would be worthwhile for such an uncomfortable father to get some kind of counseling or psychiatric help, not only for his son's sake but also for his own, because he proba-

bly feels a lot of tension in his occupational and social relationships with other men. If he declines counseling, as such
a father may do, the mother can discuss the child's problem
in a child-guidance clinic or family social agency to determine how much tension or deprivation the boy is experienc-
ing and whether treatment for the boy would be valuable.

This kind of father who is distinctly uncomfortable with
his son and doesn't want to discipline him is a relatively rare
problem. Much more common in America today is the father
who is a great pal to his son and still leaves all the disciplining
to the mother. He may say that he doesn't want his son to
resent him the way he sometimes resented his own father.
You get a sense in some such families that the father feels like
one of the children. He cheerfully ignores the little crises
that arise all the time in any family. And when his wife
realizes what's going on and begs him to take over some of
the control when he's at home, or at least to back her up
firmly, he does it too halfheartedly to have much effect or he
gives some excuse—he's too tired from working all day or he
doesn't want to come home at the end of the day and be the
ogre. In some of these families the father, without realizing
it, is in league with the children and is subtly working against
the mother's authority—not with conscious animosity but in
a teasing or absent-minded manner.

This reluctance of the father to be a disciplinarian is just
as important a problem as that of the father who never plays
with his children. It doesn't bother his children; they think
it's fine. It bothers the mother. It may be passed on to the sons
and it will bother the sons' wives. It is part of a broader
problem—the tendency in a fair proportion of American
families for the husband to act somewhat like a son to his wife
and for the wife to act like a mother to her husband. Both
attitudes are aspects of the same disturbance, which is being
transmitted through daughters as well as sons.

One difficulty that often turns up when a mother complains that the father is not doing his share of the management is that she expects him to carry through on every disciplinary issue she starts, whether he agrees that it was a wise move on her part or not. Or when he tries to reform himself and take more of the initiative in controlling the children she, from long habit of being the authority, may interrupt or disagree or countermand his directions. If she wants him to be more masterful, she has to let him decide when and how. That's what masterfulness means.

I include the problem of the palsy but nondisciplinarian father because it is such an important part of the larger topic —what do sons need from their fathers? It isn't enough for a father to be a pal. A boy should be able to find many pals, but he has only one father. He needs to feel the strength of his father and to have a respect for his father as an older, more authoritative person. He is even expected in nature's scheme of things, I think, to feel at least a little awe for his father. When a father denies his son these aspects of himself because he is afraid to be anything but a pal, it gets the boy's deeper instincts somewhat tangled up inside. He may grow up to be a very agreeable person and a good citizen, but he will fail to give his wife the support she needs and he will set a weak pattern for his sons to follow.

When I say that a boy needs a father who assumes his share of the disciplining, I don't necessarily mean spanking or isolation or deprivation. Any of these punishments should be necessary only rarely. I just mean that the father should be the one—at least half the time when he is at home, more of the time as the boy grows older—to ask his son to pick up his things, to come in for meals, to stop horsing around in the living room, to go take his bath, to be quiet after he gets into bed. Before I leave the topic of the father's role, I want to mention a couple of ways in which some fathers get carried away by their enthusiasm. The first is stirring up excitement. Many fathers enjoy tossing their chortling infants in the air or pretending to be bears and lions for their small children who ask to be scared, or engaging in nightly wild pillow fights. Child psychiatrists have learned from their cases that this amount of excitement often is unwholesome for children, evoking strong emotions that the personality is not mature enough to cope with. But when they point this out, some of these fathers don't want to hear it and won't really believe it. They protest that their children beg for more, which is true enough but it doesn't answer the objections.

Since the mother who inspired this discussion asked about fathers' relations with their sons, I have focused more on them. But I want to be sure that parents in general and fathers in particular know that fathers' relationships with their daughters are just as crucial. Girls learn how to be women primarily from their mothers. But there's the other half of the human race that girls and women have to learn to get along with and even marry. This they learn first of all from living with and loving their fathers. So fathers have to be suitably livable and lovable. Here are some extremes that may work out badly. If a father pays attention only to his son, his daughter may grow up feeling somehow unworthy of a man's love. If he has no son and enjoys his daughter only when she acts the tomboy, this may tug her personality very strongly in a masculine direction. At the other extreme, if he is much more companionable and affectionate with his daughter than he is with his wife, he may make his daughter too rivalrous or too guilty toward her mother; or his daughter may find him so mature, considerate, and fascinating that no youth her own age will ever appeal to her.

The listing of all these extremes may make it sound as if a father's companionship with his daughter is as difficult as walking a tightrope. Not at all. A father needs only to show his daughter attitudes that come quite spontaneously in most cases—his affection and his appreciation of her capabilities and her individuality.

:: 38 ::

Should Girls Be Raised Like Boys?

Women working for equality for their sex have come to realize that prejudice against them begins to be built up—in girls as well as boys—in early childhood.

In most children's storybooks it is boys who carry out the exciting and imaginative activities and the girls who watch or engage in gentle games or domestic play. Fathers go out to dramatic jobs while women keep house. Boys, already prejudiced at a young age, tell girls that they can't join in ball games because they are no good at them, though they have no evidence. Some old-fashioned parents still warn little girls not to try to climb trees even though their brothers do. They still give teen-aged girls the idea that they're fragile and vulnerable during their menstrual periods.

Leaders of Women's Liberation groups have focused criticism and indignation on me because in my book *Baby and Child Care* and in articles I have encouraged parents to think of their boys and girls as quite different in makeup and to treat them differently.

In an article in 1964, "Are We Minimizing the Differences between Boys and Girls?" I was very specific about the importance, for reasons of mental health, of a boy's being brought up with a strong sense of his masculinity and a girl of her femininity. I deplored similar clothes for young boys and girls. (In 1964 teen-agers had not yet come to identical blue jeans, beads and long hair.) I suggested that boys' chores be predominantly those of the yard, garage, and cellar in contrast to girls' jobs in the house—though I fortunately added that it still would be appropriate for boys to tend to their own rooms and do some of the dishes. I even suggested that if a little girl asked for a pistol, she might be gently dissuaded.

I've been pounced on for having said in *Baby and Child Care,* concerning a father's attitude toward his daughter, "I'm thinking of little things he can do like complimenting her on her dress, or hairdo, or the cookies she's made." (The critics don't quote my next sentence: "When she's older, he can show that he's interested in her opinions and let her in on some of his.")

Freud taught—and I still believe—that girls acquire in early childhood an unconscious sense of bodily inferiority, to one degree or other, from a misunderstanding of the physical sexual differences. Of course, feminists consider that Freud was so biased against women as to be almost totally unreliable. I admit he had the usual male prejudices, but I don't think that this discredits his basic, verifiable discoveries.

Young boys too get definite feelings of inferiority when they finally have to admit that they can't grow babies the way girls can. And some males are made so anxious by their misunderstanding of the sex differences that they yearn to be women all their lives.

I believe now that to help women find justice and fulfillment we must do everything possible—especially in bringing up our children—to counteract prejudice.

One approach that appeals to many idealistic young people today is reducing the distinctions between the rearing of boys and girls to the absolute minimum. In buying clothes parents could select more or less the same things for their young sons and daughters, for clothes suggest what a person wants to be and how he wants to be thought of.

Feminists have at least half a point when they say that frilly dresses, patent-leather slippers, and permanent waves on a little girl, when boys are got up quite differently, encourage her to think of herself to some degree as a passive object for admiration, rather than as a doer. She learns to see herself as someone who can get deviously what she wants out of life from other people by seducing them (figuratively speaking) with her appearance.

I agree that neither girls nor boys should be made self-conscious, narcissistic, or passive by being made the focus of attention too much of the time—whether by being fancily dressed or by being made to perform or simply by being the center of conversation. But I don't think that parents should be scared out of dressing up their children on occasion or when the children want to dress up for dramatic play. It's a matter of degree.

Feminists and many young people suggest that when little boys ask for dolls—and almost all little boys do ask for them—they should be given them without reproach or question. Little girls should be permitted to have baseball mitts and trucks without being teased. Boys should be expected to make as many beds and wash as many dishes as their sisters of comparable age, and girls should mow lawns, rake leaves, and wash cars just as their brothers do.

Now I'll raise an important theoretical question: If some families rear their sons and daughters with minimal sex distinction, will their children have an insufficient sexual identification? Will they feel, in effect, that they belong to one common sex? And would that be psychologically harmful?

It is hard for us to imagine what would be left of the male and female identities if boys and girls were brought up with the idea that the only real differences between them (aside from individual differences) were in their anatomies and in their generative functions.

Other societies assign roles to men and women that are quite unlike ours. But no country I know of has tried to bring them up to think of themselves as similar. Such an attempt would be the most unprecedented social experiment in the history of our species.

Most psychiatrists have assumed in the past that a definite

sexual identity—knowing clearly that you are male or female —is a vital element in mental health. Psychiatrists came to this belief from working with patients who had a disturbance of identity, such as men who, because of atypical relationships in childhood, ended up feeling and acting like women; or women who feel and act like men; or other men and women who were conflicted or confused about their roles. So a psychiatrist (or a pediatrician with psychiatric training, like myself) naturally will be uneasy and uncertain at first about the idea of bringing up children with a minimal sense of sex distinction. That's just why, several years ago, I wrote that article recommending the opposite.

But now, after further soul-searching, though I still believe a definite sex identity is important, I don't think it needs to be built through an emphasis on differences in clothes or playthings, or on parental reminders of what little boys are meant to do and what little girls are meant to do.

Sexual identity comes in part from glandular influences, especially from puberty onward, partly from a recognition of anatomical differences in early childhood and the psychological reactions to that recognition; but most of all sexual identity comes from a good identification with the parent of the same sex. I stress this last factor because it is clear in cases of effeminate men and masculine women that these are partly traceable to off-kilter relationships with parents, despite normal glands.

What makes a boy feel securely masculine is loving, being loved by, and patterning himself after a father who enjoys being a man and feels adequate in his competitive and cooperative relationships with other men—according to the customs of his particular society.

A good sexual identity in a growing boy doesn't depend on whether the men of the community, including his father, hunt lions or carve statues or work on the assembly line; or, in a particular family, on whether the father cooks all the meals and changes all the diapers or has nothing to do with these things—as long as the father feels psychologically comfortable as a man and has a good relationship with his son.

To make this point clearer you can say that a father who has always felt insecure about his masculinity will keep revealing his uneasiness to his son—in a variety of subtle ways, always inadvertently. This will interfere to some degree with the boy's acquisition of an ideal, comfortable male identity.

The father's rejection of any domestic chore as womanly is one of the ways in which he indicates his uneasiness to his son—and the boy senses this and unconsciously takes on some of the same uneasiness. If such a father, out of his own anxiety, scolds his small son for wanting a doll, the boy learns not manliness but the fear of being considered unmanly.

A girl grows up wanting to be a woman, and prepared to be a successful one, by being loved and approved of by a mother who enjoys a woman's role, whatever that may be in her society or community—whether the mother is a peasant farmer in China or a busy, fulltime mother or a physician in America.

Psychiatrists have long believed that though a boy gains his predominant identification from his admiring relationship with his father, he also identifies to a lesser degree with his mother. Girls acquire the same mixture of identifications, primarily with mother, secondarily with father. If males and females could not identify somewhat with each other, it is said, they probably couldn't understand each other well enough to be able to live together.

What I've been saying is that if we could quit making an issue over just how different boys and girls are supposed to be in terms of clothes, playthings, behavior, and life expectations, I don't think they would become less sure of their basic, predominant identifications. In fact, I imagine they would feel more comfortable about whatever personalities and attitudes they had acquired through their mixed identification with two parents.

Boys would be less afraid of being called sissies. Men could more freely get into occupations that really appealed to them but that are sometimes considered feminine—ballet dancing or interior decorating, for example. (In the Soviet Union there is no prejudice against men ballet dancers, and it is plain from their gestures that most of them are as masculine in feeling as our football players.) Women in larger numbers could consider engineering, manufacturing, airline piloting, and the ministry.

Similarity in the rearing of boys and girls should increase boys' enthusiasm for becoming fathers and for doing their full share in caring for their future children because it would diminish the teasing of boys when they show interest in these activities.

I have added together these reasons why children of either sex should be freely allowed to play with—and own—toys that traditionally have been thought of as belonging to the opposite sex. There is no psychological reason to believe that this will push them toward the opposite identification. It can only help them work through and digest the partial identification with the other sex that is an aspect of every human being. And the fact that parents and children are tolerant of such play will help children as they grow to find their individual, mixed, adult identities without anxiety and shame.

On the other hand, I myself do not think it is necessary or important to try to make the upbringing of girls and boys exactly identical (I leave it to parents to come to their own conclusions) provided it is always freely acknowledged—and acted out in the home—that there is no superiority in maleness, that women should have as free a choice of occupation as men, that child care and home care are potentially as dignified, productive, and creative as any outside job—and that men have equal obligations in these home activities, especially if their wives work outside too.

:: 39 ::

Should All Girls Be Prepared
for Careers?

Should girls be brought up expecting to get an education that will prepare them for a career, and expecting—as boys do—to have a career?

This is a straightforward question for parents. But the answer, to my mind, involves a variety of complex considerations: the problem of the prejudice against women in employment (a prejudice women themselves often share); the casual attitude toward education and a career on the part of many girls and young women until too late; the question of whether dedication to a career will suppress a mother's interest in family, as it often does with fathers; the part that fathers should play in the home; and—the most complex consideration of all—the kinds of work, for women and men, that will be most favorable to family life and to solving the nation's grave problems.

A potent reason why some girls and young women shy away from a commitment to a career is that they've been persuaded they don't have what it takes.

The women in the liberation movement who are trying to end the pervasive discrimination against their sex have come to realize (as psychologists have discovered in studies) that a serious stumbling block is the prejudice women have acquired against themselves. Most girls have been conditioned from early childhood to believe that they are inferior to boys in various respects. It starts with differences of anatomy. It goes on to supposed differences in physical skill and strength.

Then, though girls do better in most subjects in school and

256

college, they hear that they have low aptitude for mathematics and sciences and other abstract fields. And it's said that because they are more emotional, they don't often make good executives. There is no scientific basis for most of these claims; but in the high-school and college years many girls are afraid to express an interest in such fields as chemistry, physics, medicine, law, engineering, and manufacturing. They also give up aspirations for the higher-level jobs in business and in the university.

In adulthood the teaching of prejudice against women continues and discrimination becomes even more real. Whatever their level of educational achievement, women often are offered the humbler jobs, paid less than men for the same work, denied equal consideration for advancement.

Women are referred to—by men and by themselves—as girls, though men aren't called boys. On magazine covers, in girlie magazines, and in men's jokes women often are presented as merely appetizing objects for men's delight.

Just as harmful to women as the denial of their just rewards is the lack of self-confidence, the impaired self-esteem that their prejudice against themselves produces. It will interfere with their performance, at least at times, and will surely exact a heavy emotional toll.

Prejudice against women corrupts the attitudes and the characters of men too, (just as racial prejudice corrupts the dominant white group). It encourages men to gain their sense of importance by thinking of how superior they are to women. More specifically, individual men are tempted to take out their defeats and frustrations in dealing with other men by finding things to carp at in their wives.

I've been reproached for contributing to the prejudice. A number of years ago, before there was a Women's Liberation Movement, I wrote that girls should be brought up to think of child rearing as exciting and creative work. "Brainwashing!" said the feminists. Of course I should have said—as I honestly believe—"Girls and boys should be brought up to think of child rearing as exciting and creative work."

I've admitted that I showed the usual male discrimination in my earlier assumptions that, if either parent has to cut down on work outside the home in order to ensure that a young child will get good, loving care, it should be the mother, not the father, and not both parents equally.*

If girls are to grow up without a sense of being significantly different from boys in capabilities and if women who want good jobs are to have an equal chance to get them, then parents from the beginning must be quick to contradict the belittling aspersions that their young daughters report. More positively and more importantly, parents should prepare girls for careers throughout their childhood—psychologically and educationally—as they prepare their sons.

Take, for example, the kind of parents who themselves have been to college and who take it for granted in talking with their sons that of course the sons will get university degrees, find challenging careers in the professions or industry, and win advancement or distinction. Such parents, if they are to show no discrimination, should take an identical line with their daughters.

For if they accept casually the idea that their daughters may or may not seek a degree, may choose marriage instead of (rather than in addition to) a career, or may work only at a stopgap job until marriage, there is the implication that girls are quite different from boys, at least in the occupations the world expects of them. And some of these daughters will feel quite free to terminate their education when they are only sixteen, seventeen, or eighteen years old, before they have acquired sufficient maturity of judgment.

---

*In my defense I'll add that I've always believed women could do well at any job that they had a real drive to tackle, if given the opportunity. In three of my most important jobs I served under women.

Once a young woman (or man, for that matter) has quit school early, especially if she has then married and had children, it will take unusual determination on her part to get back to college at an older age. (I'm leaving out of this discussion the young women and men who today deliberately turn their backs on traditional education and traditional careers in protest against all the institutions and beliefs of our society that they consider thoroughly corrupt.)

But if we should bring up all girls assuming that they will have careers like their brothers, will they have a decreased enthusiasm for bearing and rearing children of their own?

And will we be instilling in them the same compulsive drive for success that creates ulcers and coronaries in men and that keeps so many fathers from giving enough time and attention to their families?

These are not imaginary concerns. Some sociologists believe that family life in America already is being progressively impoverished by parents' work schedules, by children's absence from home not only for school but for other activities, by children's absorption in television when they are at home. Other factors lessening the sense of security the family traditionally has given are the average family's frequent moves, its resulting lack of roots in the community, its distance from other relatives, and the frequency of divorce.

A person's enthusiasm for having children comes primarily from having been abundantly loved from earliest childhood. I don't think that if it was strong to start with, this enthusiasm would be easily blotted out, though it might be somewhat decreased by later aspirations for a specific career.

Both women and men who have no great enthusiasm for children will be less and less inclined to have them in the future, I think, because of the recognition of the world's overpopulation and because fewer couples nowadays feel an obligation to conform to the conventional patterns of the past.

:: 40 ::

A Changing Society

I believe that a major reason we are in such trouble in this country—with our extremely high rates of divorce and marital tension, brutality to children, crime, delinquency, drug addiction and alcoholism, worsening racial hatred, an often ruthless and dangerous foreign policy—is that we have greatly overemphasized certain aspects of the American credo: competition, materialism, each man out for himself, and success measured in dollars and power.

I'm convinced that if we are to survive, men and women in much greater numbers, in whatever field we work, will have to be inspired by a quite different ideal—that of loving service to our fellow beings, whether the work we do is in a big industry or in a small shop or office, whether it is paid or volunteer, whether it is outside or inside the home. All these sorts of work can be fulfilling and creative and generous in spirit. Or they can be the opposite.

The emphasis should be on personal helpfulness in as direct and informal and friendly a manner as possible. Service in this spirit is more usable and gratifying to the recipient. It is less likely to turn the worker into a routinized, depersonalized, self-promoting, authoritarian cog—like so many of the people we have to deal with today in businesses, the professions, and government bureaus.

Big hospital clinics, for example, could be divided and dispersed into small, friendly, neighborhood clinics. Social work—whether counseling for the individual or group work or community organizing—could be carried out by small groups or by individuals in each locality.

Teaching should be progressively removed from the

huge, rigid metropolitan school systems and the giant, impersonal universities. In small schools and colleges there could be more meaningful relationships and, therefore, a more inspiring atmosphere for each student. Experimentation and change could take place more readily.

Nowadays most people get their diplomas and degrees in their youth and then consider their education done. It would be better if they could think of education as a continuing process. They could return to school again and again as their needs and the needs of society changed. This philosophy would be particularly helpful to mothers and fathers who had taken time off to care for their young children and were now ready for additional education, perhaps for a revised career.

Another ideal that has been neglected, or squeezed out, by our industrialized society is creativity. Formerly individual craftsmen designed and made the fabrics, the clothes, the jewelry, the furniture, the pictures, the cooking and eating utensils, the vehicles.

But today the overwhelming majority of those who work in manufacturing have no part at all in designing. What's more, they usually don't have the satisfaction of making a whole object or even a major part of it. They monotonously repeat a small step, such as tightening a nut, only one of perhaps a thousand steps in making the product. So the job is deprived of meaning and gratification.

A greater emphasis on creativity for everyone would mean, for instance, that more articles of adornment, furniture, and furnishings would be made at home, as some young people are already doing; that more drama, music, and dance programs would be produced by neighborhood groups; that community-improvement projects would be planned and carried out by the residents. Such activities make the participants glow with pride. They strengthen family and community ties. They break down rigid concepts of what work is.

In our highly industrialized country it is just a few huge

corporations that make most of the products, provide the largest number of jobs and truly make the decisions about how our lives are to be lived. The products and the jobs are not designed primarily to make life good for us. They are designed to enable these industries to make the highest profits. Then advertising is used to whet our appetites for clothing and adornment of the latest style, for more elaborate home furnishings and equipment, for enormous cars. All these give pride of ownership when first bought but they don't make life more meaningful.

It is because the assembly line is more efficient and profitable that work has been made increasingly boring, meaningless, and dehumanizing. In place of the satisfactions of individual creativity, the industrial system has substituted and extolled other pleasures: the excitement of successful competition, pride in advancement over the heads of others, the joy in earning a lot of money and in having impressive possessions. The trouble with these rewards is that they pit each man against his fellows, and only a few can win. Groups that are discriminated against are sure to end up bitter. And women who tend children and home are made to feel menial and frustrated because they have no titles or salaries.

If we are really to solve the problems of the resentments of women, the rivalry between the sexes, the care of children (as well as the bitterness of the minorities and the poor), I believe we must no longer be motivated by the search for maximal profits but must instead put the highest priority on improving the quality of life for every individual—as consumer and as worker. The ingenuity and the kindliness of the American people—combined with our national resources, our high level of education, and our productive machinery —will ensure success if we can visualize our aims clearly.

The point I've been leading up to is that if we can shift the ideals of our whole society in the direction of helpfulness to each other and creativity, our children would not need to think in terms of a sharp, arbitrary choice between a traditional job in an organization or homebound parenthood or a somewhat difficult compromise between the two.

Instead we could be talking to our sons and daughters from time to time throughout their childhood along the following lines (my actual language here, of course, is too stuffy to use with children):

"There are many aspects to living and serving humanity. The most fundamental and gratifying one, we think, is to create a loving family. This is the responsibility equally of husband and wife.

"Couples should share all their responsibilities to the greatest possible extent.

"If and when a mother desires an outside career, her husband should be ready to make whatever adjustments are necessary to share equally in the home obligations.

"A father's participation in home care and child care gives him the satisfaction of fostering and watching his children's development. It also lets his wife see that he really does consider these jobs to be truly important, creative ones. Then she can gain a greater sense of fulfimment from them herself.

"Your future children, to become really productive people, will need all the companionship, affection, and inspiration that you, their fathers and mothers will be able to give them.

"There are many vital activities to work at aside from salaried jobs: child care, meals, and housework, making the home and garden beautiful. There are the volunteer jobs in the community. There are neighborhood groups that provide for active participation in the arts, drama, dance, crafts.

"Each kind of work can be soul-satisfying if you feel you are contributing and creating, and more so if your work is appreciated.

"Housing, clothing, food, and other essentials have to be

secured but they don't need to be expensive and ostentatious. The essentials can be bought, but they can also—in part —be created. So the income is not the most important consideration in choosing work.

"The outside jobs of either or both parents should be judged by their value to society and by the spiritual gratification they yield more than by the pay and prestige. Fathers as well as mothers, in choosing a job, should be sure it allows plenty of time to be with the family.

"It is important for girls just as much as for boys to prepare themselves for skilled service to society for several reasons. The world's needs are endless. At a period like the present, when couples marry and have their few children at a young age, they will have more years remaining when they are not necessarily needed at home. In the climate of today large numbers of women do not feel fulfilled by home care and child care alone.

"This does not mean that a woman should feel apologetic if, throughout her life, she never takes a paying job. She may be utilizing to the full all her capabilities and her education in being the central source of inspiration in her family. She may also, through the warmth of her relationships, be a powerful influence in making the so-called community in which she lives into a genuine community.

"The same philosophy should apply to a man. If his wife wants to work outside and earns enough to support the family, he might choose to make his greatest contribution not on a payroll but in the family and in the community. (It will probably take some time for men to feel comfortable about their wives' earning the family's entire income.)"

I want to emphasize my main point once more at the end: It is too much to ask women or men to make an ideal adjustment to some combination of family care and outside work as our society is now oriented. It's time for the society to become more adapted to human needs.

Index